SOCIAL SCIENCE RESOURCES IN THE ELECTRONIC AGE

SOCIAL SCIENCE RESOURCES IN THE ELECTRONIC AGE

Volume II
U.S. History

**Elizabeth H. Oakes and
Michael S. Mayer**

GREENWOOD PRESS
Westport, Connecticut • London

Library of Congress Cataloging-in-Publication Data

Oakes, Elizabeth H., 1964–
  Social science resources in the electronic age.
      p.   cm.
  Includes bibliographical references and indexes.
      Contents: v. I. World history / Elizabeth H. Oakes and Mehrdad Kia — v. II. U.S. history /
  Elizabeth H. Oakes and Michael S. Mayer — v. III. Government and civics / Elizabeth H.
  Oakes and Jeffrey D. Greene — v. IV. Economics / Elizabeth H. Oakes and Michael H.
  Kupilik — v. V. Geography / Elizabeth H. Oakes and Jeffrey A. Gritzner.
      ISBN 1–57356–589–X (set : alk. paper) — ISBN 1–57356–474–5 (v. I : alk. paper) —
  ISBN 1–57356–473–7 (v. II : alk. paper) — ISBN 1–57356–476–1 (v. III : alk. paper) —
  ISBN 1–57356–477–X (v. IV : alk. paper) — ISBN 1–57356–475–3 (v. V : alk. paper)
      1. Social sciences—Computer network resources. 2. Humanities—Computer network
  resources. I. Title.

  H61.95.O25   2004
  025.06′3—dc22   2003060400

British Library Cataloguing in Publication Data is available.

Library of Congress Catalog Card Number: 2003060400
ISBN: 1–57356–589–X (set)
        1–57356–474–5 (vol. I)
        1–57356–473–7 (vol. II)
        1–57356–476–1 (vol. III)
        1–57356–477–X (vol. IV)
        1–57356–475–3 (vol. V)

First published in 2004

Greenwood Press, 88 Post Road West, Westport, CT 06881
An imprint of Greenwood Publishing Group, Inc.
www.greenwood.com

Printed in the United States of America

The paper used in this book complies with the
Permanent Paper Standard issued by the National
Information Standards Organization (Z39.48–1984).

10 9 8 7 6 5 4 3 2 1

Contents

Introduction

Social Science Resources in the Electronic Age: U.S. History is designed as a one-stop resource for cutting through the chaos of the Internet to find authoritative, age-appropriate information. The book is divided into five chapters. In the first chapter, "Resources in U.S. History," you'll see how specific kinds of electronic services and print media can be mined for your research projects. We also point you to the Web's top-notch sites offering general information about economics.

The heart of the book is chapter 2, "Researching Individual U.S. History Topics on the Internet." It provides you with a treasure map to quality information on the Web that will save you hours of your own research time. Here, we point you to the Web's top-notch sites offering key information about U.S. history. These topics were chosen based on a review of national curriculum standards and were screened by an expert in the field.

For each topic, you'll find reviews of several Web sites, giving you all of the goodies you need to know: the name, URL, appropriate grade range, and a thorough discussion of how to use the site for research. When you log on to the Web to find a tidbit about the Stock Market Crash of 1929 or to gain a fuller understanding of the Harlem Renaissance, you'll now have four or five handpicked sites as opposed to the thousands that might turn up with a keyword search. In case you choose to conduct your own online search for a key topic, we let you know which search engine and keywords provide the best hits.

In chapter 3, "Materials and Resources for U.S. History Teachers," we review a number of excellent Web sites that offer materials and resources, such as free maps, government document reprints, lesson plans, and downloadable U.S. history software, U.S. history educators will find useful. Hands-on opportunities are covered as well.

The "Museums and Summer Programs for U.S. History Students" (chapter 4) surveys web sites that offer unique online museum exhibits, interpretive centers, summer programs, and other interactive opportunities for students of history.

The final chapter of the book, "Careers," turns attention to web sites that provide career information in the field of history. Here, we review sites for professional associations, academic groups, conferences, workshops, programs, clubs, and other outlets for students interested in working or doing an internship in the subject.

HOW TO USE THIS BOOK

There are three ways you can find information in *Social Science Resources in the Electronic Age: U.S. History*. First you can look at the detailed table of contents. If you are researching a particular topic in U.S. history, you can immediately go to the alphabetical listing of topics in chapter 2. You can also use the index, which expands the coverage significantly. Because we had to limit the number of topics in chapter 2, we added as much detail as possible to our site reviews. The detail includes names of people and countries, events, and other topics covered in the Web site but not included in our topic list. All of these details have been indexed. Don't forget to consult "The Basics" section in Volume I of this set for general information and sites.

1

————

Resources in U.S. History

FORMATS OF RESOURCES

Library Electronic Services

Specialized Databases

A number of topic-specific databases are popular among U.S. history students and researchers. The following represent just a handful of those you might find at your library. Check with the library staff about which databases would be useful for your project.

America: History and Life. Includes information published after 1964 about topics spanning all time periods. This is a good general database for students at all levels.

Expanded Academic ASAP. Includes full text of key journals in American history; although user friendly, it is not designed for students younger than high school.

Periodicals Contents Index. Full text of several historical journals; indexes from the start of publication for every journal listed (if a journal were first printed in 1776, it indexes from that date).

JSTOR. Published by the University of Michigan. Full text of 15 major academic historical periodicals from their inception through the mid-1990s. For advanced students of history.

CD-ROMs

Although subject-specific CD-ROMs are gradually being phased out in favor of Web-based content, there are many CD-ROMs that will help you in your American history research. Use the *Dictionary of National Biography* to search for key historical figures. *The Transatlantic Slave Trade* offers detailed information about the rise of slavery in the Americas. Unlike print reference tools, CD-ROMs can cross-reference and link information together. *The Transatlantic Slave Trade,* for example, combines interactive maps and multimedia exhibits with informative text.

E-mail

If you have a specific question about American history and need an expert to answer it, check out *AllExperts.com* (http://www.allexperts. com/). Follow the links from "Higher Learning" to "History" to "U.S. History." You can choose among several scholars who have different areas of expertise.

Mailing Lists

Here are a few examples of American history-related mailing lists.

AMERICAN-REVOLUTION-L

> Genealogical and historical discussion of the French and Indian War, the American Revolution, and the War of 1812
>
> To subscribe, send mail to AMERICAN-REVOLUTION-L-request@ rootsweb.com with the command: SUBSCRIBE

AFRICAN-AMERICAN FORUM

> African-American history forum
>
> To subscribe, send mail to LISTSERV@ASHP.LISTERV.CUNY.EDU with the command: SUBSCRIBE AFRICAN-AMERICANFORUM

H-CIVWAR

> H-Net U.S. Civil War history discussion group
>
> To subscribe, send mail to LISTSERV@LIST.UVM.EDU with the command: SUBSCRIBE H-FORUM

INDIAN-ROOTS-L

> Native American history and genealogy discussion
>
> To subscribe, send mail to LISTSERV@LISTSERV.INDIANA.EDU with the command: SUBSCRIBE INDIAN-ROOTS-L

To find other mailing lists of interest, check these Web sites.

CataList: The Official Catalog of Listserv Lists http://www.lsoft.com/lists/ listref.html

Liszt: The Mailing List Directory http://www.liszt.com/

Topica: The Email You Want http://www.topica.com/

Usenet Newsgroups

Some newsgroups of interest to U.S. historians include the following.

soc.history.war.us-re Discussion about the Revolutionary War

alt.history General discussion about history topics

alt.history.colonial Discussion about early American history

To find and subscribe to newsgroups that interest you, check out these two Web sites.

Deja News http://www.deja.com/usenet/

CyberFiber Newsgroups http://www.cyberfiber.com/index.html

E-Journals

A few e-journals of interest to researchers in U.S. history include the following.

The Early America Review (http://www.earlyamerica.com/review/) provides papers, articles, dissertations, book reviews, and personal commentary focusing on personalities, issues, and events in eighteenth century America.

Historicom (http://www.geocities.com/historicom/) publishes articles on any aspect of world, national, or local history, written by laypeople and history academics.

Digital Libraries

Digital libraries are an exciting initiative taking place on the Internet. For example, the *American Memory* digital library (http://memory.loc.gov/ammem/ammemhome.html), which will be explained in greater detail in the section on government Web sites below, was created in an effort to capture digitally the distinctive, historical Americana holdings at the Library of Congress. These extensive collections include an almost incomprehensible amount of primary source material for the American history student.

A couple of other digitized collections that provide images of interest to U.S. history students and teachers are:

Documenting the American South http://metalab.unc.edu/docsouth.index.html

American Heritage Project http://sunsite.berkeley.edu/amher/

Digital Library.Net http://www.digitallibrary.net/

Berkeley Digital Library Sun Site http://sunsite.berkeley.edu/

Digital Libraries Resource Page http://www.interlog.com/~klt/digital/

Reference Books

You will find a great deal of both background information and specific topical material on U.S. history in dictionaries and encyclopedias. These include the *Encyclopedia of American History*, *American Heritage Encyclopedia of American History*, *Encyclopedia of the American Civil War: A Political, Social, and Military History*, *Encyclopedia of Women's History in America*, *Encyclopedia of Native American Tribes*, *Encyclopedia of African American Culture and History*, and *Encyclopedia of American Political History: Studies of the Principal Movements and Ideas*.

If you're looking for biographical information on important people in U.S. history, numerous biographical reference books exist. For general reference, try the *Dictionary of American Biography*, *American National Biography*, and *Notable Americans*. *Who Was Who in the American Revolution* and *Who Was Who in the Civil War* can help you with people who lived during those periods. There's also *Contemporary Black Biography*, *Notable Asian Americans*, *Distinguished Asian Americans*, *Notable Hispanic American Women*, *Notable Native Americans*, *Notable Caribbeans and Caribbean Americans*, and many other such books.

TYPES OF WORLD WIDE WEB RESOURCES

Reference Sites

StudyWeb
http://www.studyweb.com/

StudyWeb is a subject guide designed for an academic audience. With more than 141,000 quality Web links reviewed and categorized into numerous subject areas, you can zero in on a topic for a report, find background material for a project, begin research for a paper, or just increase your knowledge of a particular topic.

The home page for *StudyWeb* is clutter free and easy to navigate. For starters, click on the "American History" topic link under the "History and Culture" heading. You can then narrow your search according to a number of historical topics, such as "The Nineteenth Century," "Colonial Times," "Westward Expansion," or "The Lewis and Clark Expedition." You'll find an entire section on "American Wars" with links to the "Civil War," "Plains Indian Wars," "Spanish American War," the "War of 1812," and the "French Indian War." The "American History" section also allows you to research the history of minority communities in the United States. Simply select the "Ethnic America" heading, and then "African American," "Asian American," or "Latin American" to explore the history and culture of these groups. Within each of these listings, there are "General Resources" Web links, as well as a handful of links to sites about the specific topics. *StudyWeb* helps you decide if the link is appropriate for your research by giving the site a score for visual interest, describing its contents, and indicating what age group the material is geared toward.

InfoPlease
http://www.infoplease.com/

InfoPlease is the online spin-off from a company that's published almanacs and reference databases for more than 60 years. This colorful site lets you to tap into a massive collection of almanacs, encyclopedias, and dictionaries to find almost every imaginable topic—chock-full of millions of authoritative factoids. For instance, by using the site's nifty "20th Century Time Line," you can quickly discover key events that happened in each year, such as the Triangle Shirtwaist Company Fire in 1911 that killed 146 workers.

Click on the subject area "History and Government" and you'll find "World History," "U.S. History," "U.S. Presidents," "U.S. Elections," "U.S. Documents," "U.S. Government Countries," "U.S. Historical Monuments," and the "Supreme Court." Within "U.S. History," there's "High Crimes and Misdemeanors: A Short History of Impeachment," "States by Order of Entry into the Union," "Assassination and Attempts Since 1865." Simply choose one of the many headings to learn more. Within "U.S. Elections," you can find brief overviews of a number of topics, such as "Presidential Elections: 1789–1996" and "Participation in Elections for President and U.S. Representatives: 1930–1996." If you select the "U.S. Presidents" heading, you can read biographies of all the American presidents.

You can search for keywords within *InfoPlease's* almanac database and come up with an impressive amount of information—more than some general search engines provide. For example, entering the keywords "Richard Nixon" resulted in over 20 relevant hits in *InfoPlease's* dictionaries and encyclopedias, including brief articles on impeachment hearings, the Vietnam War, and political events of the times. If you know the kind of information you need, you can use a pull-down menu to restrict your search to *InfoPlease's* dictionary, biographies, or encyclopedia.

For more general research help, click on "Homework Center," a section designed to help K–12 students conduct their research and improve note-taking and writing techniques. This section will also direct students to other study aid Web resources.

Discovery School's A to Z History
http://school.discovery.com/homeworkhelp/worldbook/atozhistory/index.
  html

This Web site allows you to research topics in a fast and easy way. Let's say you're hunting for information on the baby boom. Click on *B* from the alphabet index on the home page. You can then scroll through a list of articles on terms, people, and events that are related to history that begin with the letter *b*.

Glossary of American History
http://www.coe.uh.edu/gliah/historyonline/glossary_af.html

This online glossary allows you to look up basic terms, people, and events in American history. It won't provide much detail, but it will make a helpful companion to your research. Click on the letter that begins the term you are looking for (*E* for Emancipation Proclamation, for instance).

Commercial Sites

The History Channel.com
http://www.thehistorychannel.com/

This Web site, which is a companion to the cable television channel of the same name, is comprehensive and easy to use. It is a great site to visit when you have a specific question about a topic or when you want to trigger ideas for research.

One of the site's most useful features is its search capacity. Click on "Search Any Topic In History" on the home page, and you'll access a wealth of information. If you already have a topic, simply type it in. For example, if you are researching the Native American Chief Joseph, enter his name. You can then click on several articles about him, one of which gives biographical data, another that provides some of his speeches. From here, you can opt to "Continue Your Search." You can search for "Related People," which will give you other important Native American leaders, or you can peruse "Related Historical Places" or "Related Web Sites." By clicking on this latter option, you can access an extensive list of *The History Channel's* recommended Web sites, which are organized by period (such as "The Nineteenth Century") and subject (including "Native Americans").

If you don't have a narrowly defined topic, and just want to look for material, you'll enjoy the "Search by Time line" feature on the home page. After choosing a decade that interests you, say 1800–10, the Web site compiles a detailed list of key events for each year. For instance, under "1800," you'll learn that John Chapman began circulating religious tracts across the American Midwest in this year. Want to learn more? No problem! Just click on the link to read a brief essay on Chapman himself.

Another invaluable aspect of this Web site is its "What Happened Today" section. This is a terrific resource for both students and teachers. Instead of just giving you one key event, *The History Channel* allows you to read about "This Day in Automotive History," "This Day in Civil War History," "This Day in Cold War History," "This Day in Crime History," "This Day in Literary History," "This Day in Old West History," "This Day in Technology History," "This Day in Vietnam War History," "This Day in Wall Street History," and "This Day in World War II History."

Because this is a commercial site, you'll have plenty of opportunities to buy videos and books related to *The History Channel* features. If you're not in the market for this material, just ignore the sales pitch.

The History Net
http://www.historynet.com/

The History Net lives up to its motto, "Where History Lives on the Web." This site, which is operated by Primedia History Group, the publisher of several history-related periodicals, offers you access to over 760 articles. Use this site to trawl for research ideas or to look for specific information.

If you're more in the market for a paper topic, you can start with *The History Net's* current articles, listed on the home page under "This Week's Features." These essays cover a range of topics—not all of them about U.S. history, but you'll find some interesting reading. If you are searching for some specific information, search the site's extensive archives. Just click on "Site Search" in the toolbar at the top of the home page. Although *The History Net* is not as comprehensive as is a pure reference site like the *Encyclopaedia Britannica,* you will find plenty of information. For instance, searching for the key words "Chief Joseph" brought up a list of useful articles, including a book review and general essays on the American West and Native Americans.

You can also browse the archives by topic. Click on the area that interests you in the toolbar on the left side of the home page. Topics that probably will be most relevant to you are "American History," "Civil War," "Personality Profiles," "Great Battles," "World War II," "Interviews," "Eye Witness Accounts," and "Aviation and Technology." Click on "Additional Articles" at the bottom of each of these subject articles to find a complete list of all *The History Net's* articles about that topic. For instance, the "Civil War" archives contain interesting essays on an array of topics such as "Civil War Railroads" and "An Englishman's Journey Through the Confederacy."

The site has other useful features, which you can access by clicking on the appropriate heading in the toolbar on the left side of the home page. "THN Recommends" provides links to other Web sites. "Talk about History" is an interactive forum where you can enter into a discussion with or pose questions to other students and the editors of the site. The "THN Picture Gallery" has an archive of photographs of events and people.

The History Net is trying to sell you the magazines from which it culls its material. It's easy to avoid the ads, though, and the site is a good resource.

Government Sites

America's Story
http://www.americaslibrary.gov/cgi-bin/page.cgi

This Library of Congress Web site is ideal for younger students starting their research. *America's Story* has biographies, online exhibits, and quick overview of eras in American history. Click on "Meet Amazing Americans" to read biographies of some famous historical figures, ranging from Thomas Jefferson to Harry Houdini. Select "Jump Back in Time" from the home page to pick from eleven periods in American history ranging from "Colonial America (1492–1763)" to "Modern Era (1946–present)." Each of these headings will take you to features that include online exhibits of items from the period. For specific history about an American state, go to "Explore the States" from the home page. Click on the state you want and read a quick overview of its history.

American Memory: Historical Connections for the National Digital Library
http://rs6.loc.gov/

If you need to find any kind of primary source—from pamphlets printed by abolitionists to photographs of famous authors to sound recordings of a busy street in nineteenth century New York City—chances are that this Web site will have it. *American Memory* contains multimedia collections of digitized documents, photographs, recorded sound, moving pictures, and text from the Library of Congress' Americana collections. There are currently more than 80 collections available.

While this Web site is the American history researcher's dream, be prepared to be a little overwhelmed by this site because it is jam-packed with information. The best way to use the *American Memory* Web site is to come prepared with a specific topic. This site is *really* not designed for browsing. If you do want to scan through some of the collections available, click on "Collection Finder" on the home page and choose the area that interests you. Of course, "History" will probably have the most pertinent information for your project.

To get the specific material you need, though, use the site's comprehensive search features. From the home page, choose the "Search" option. Type in the key words that relate to your topic. The narrower your search terms are, the better. For instance, if you are writing a paper about African American women in the Civil War era, search for specific names. If you search for Sojourner Truth, for example, you'll uncover a wealth of material: a portrait of her; the full text of her autobiography, *Book of Life*; some of her correspondence; the full text of a magazine article about her written by Harriet Beecher Stowe for the 1863 *Atlantic Monthly*; and a photo of her with Abraham Lincoln. You can also limit your search to one medium—documents, photographs, sound recordings, sheet music, or motion pictures. Click on "What American Memory Resources Are Included in This Search" (which is just below the search box), to obtain a list of which collections were incorporated in your search.

American Memory has a number of other helpful resources. If you would like to view documents and collections according to either their geographic location or their historical period, use the site's handy time line feature. Simply click on "Collection Finder" from the home page and then scroll down to the bottom of the screen. Click on the era that interests you on the time line or choose the geographic area. Also of interest is the site's "Learning Page" for both students and teachers. You can access this from the home page and find lesson ideas, quizzes, research tools, and activities.

Time Line of U.S. Diplomatic History
http://www.state.gov/www/about_state/history/

This Web site, which is maintained by the U.S. State Department's Office of the Historian, is a good source of information about the history of American foreign policy. Click on the "Time Line of U.S. Diplomatic History" to access the bulk of this useful material. Select the period of history that interests you: "Diplomacy of the American Revolution," "Diplomacy of the New Republic," "Jeffersonian Diplomacy," "Diplomacy and Westward Expansion," "Diplomacy of the Civil War," "Diplomacy and the Rise to Global Power," "Diplomacy of World War I," "Diplomacy of Isolationism," "Diplomacy of World War II," "Diplomacy of the Cold War," "Diplomacy and Détente," or "Diplomacy in a Multi-polar World."

Under each of these headings, you'll find a concise explanation of the major events that occurred in each period. For instance, in the "Diplomacy of Isolationism" segment, you'll learn that the central theme of the era was "Disarmament Efforts." Each entry also contains the key diplomatic policies of the periods and the people who played an important role in developing U.S. foreign policy.

The Web site also contains straightforward history about the State Department, past secretaries of state, the Foreign Service, and the role of women and minorities in the State Department. Click on "Frequently Asked Historical Questions" on the home page to view such topics. In addition, the "Frequently Asked Questions" section includes a list of "Diplomatic and Consular Posts: 1781–1997" and "Department Personnel: 1781–1997."

Smithsonian National Museum of American History
http://americanhistory.so.edu/

Don't overlook this Web site just because you might think museums are boring. This excellent resource, which was created as a companion to the Smithsonian National Museum of American History in Washington, D.C., is full of interesting exhibits, useful information, and quirky factoids—all without the crowds.

If you are hunting for a good research topic, or if you just want to take a walk back in time, view the site's extensive "Virtual Exhibitions," which you can access from the home page. These comprehensive exhibitions, which include written history, photographs, sound recordings, and interactive features, cover a range of topics. Interested in the history of time itself in the United States? Then select "On Time," a multimedia exploration of the changing ways Americans have measured, used, and conceived of time for the past 300 years. Or maybe you're curious about American labor issues. If so, check out "Between a Rock and a Hard Place," which examines the history of American sweatshops from 1820 to the present.

For those of you looking for information about the presidency, you'll appreciate this site's huge exhibit, "The American Presidency: A Glorious Burden." The link for this is on the home page. You can start with a general overview of the election process by reading "On the Campaign Trail." "The Foundations" explains how the Founding Fathers thought about the office and how they shaped it, as well as the responsibilities and limitations of the position. "Life and Death in the White House" provides anecdotes of everyday life in the world's most famous residence.

The exhibit also contains a section pertinent to those of you interested in the image-making process. In "Communicating the Presidency," you can dive into an essay on the role of the media and advertising in our perception of the president. Possibly the coolest aspect of this exhibit is its moving time line at the top of the page. Click on one of the pictures of the presidents, and you can read a brief biography of him as well as an essay on the era in which he led. You can also view objects from his term in office.

Although this Web site is not ideal for finding specific information (after all, would you expect your town's museum to keep data on every possible topic you might want to research?), you can search through the archives of past exhibits. Simply click on "Search" from the home page, and then enter key terms. Be sure to place any names in quotations because the search function is Boolean.

National Archives and Records Administration (NARA)
http://www.nara.gov/

NARA is an independent federal agency that oversees the management of *all* federal documents. Although NARA has made only a fraction of its archives available online, you will still find an immense amount of information—all in the form of original documents.

One way to locate documents is to enter into NARA's virtual "Exhibit Hall" (just click on the heading in the toolbar at the top of the home page). You can then browse NARA's considerable holdings. If you're curious about early American history, select "The Charters of Freedom" exhibit, where you can view digital versions of the original Declaration of Independence, Constitution, Bill of Rights, and Magna Carta. The "American Originals" and "American Originals II" exhibits contain some of the most famous documents in U.S. history. Peruse the Louisiana Purchase or view the police blotter that describes President Lincoln's assassination. You can read the soon-to-be-broken treaty of 1868 that recognized the Black Hills as part of the Great Sioux Reservation. Another great exhibit for history students is "The Treasures of Congress," where you can examine documents and photographs that are related to the many issues that played out in Congress over the course of the nation's history.

For a more focused document search, select the "Search" heading from the home page toolbar. Then simply type in the key words that relate to your topic. Expect to find loads of documents about well-known historical figures or events. For instance, a search for "Franklin Roosevelt" yielded an audio recording of his speech after the bombing of Pearl Harbor, telegrams he sent to Navy commanders, letters written to ambassadors, and more. Less renowned figures, however, will yield fewer results. A search for "Chief Joseph," for example, brought up nothing.

Teachers and students will both enjoy NARA's "Digital Classroom," which can be accessed from the home page. "Primary Sources and Activities" presents educators and students with thematic lesson plans that use specific documents (links to these documents are included). "General and National History Day Research" provides tips and assignments for searching NARA's Web site. There is additional information for teachers as well.

Also of interest here are the links to related sites, including sites with declassified satellite imagery from the U.S. Geological Survey and records from the National Archives and Records Administration.

Academic and Educational Sites

American and British History Resources on the Internet
http://www.libraries.rutgers.edu/rulib/socsci/hist/amhist3.htm

This is a gateway site that provides hundreds of links to Web sites about various aspects of American (and British) history. Created and maintained by the Rutgers University's library, the site strives to give history students of all levels a comprehensive, categorized entry to relevant sites, filling the gap between search engines and nonacademic subject directories. Although the site is bland, slightly disorganized, and difficult to navigate, its benefits outweigh these shortcomings. *American and British History Resources on the Internet* is *the* source to find other sources.

The site is organized into six major headings: "Reference," "History Gateways and Text Sites," "Sites by Subject," "Archival and MSS Guides," "Other Internet Resources," and "Library and Publisher Catalogues." Since the Web site is constructed like a giant outline, simply scroll down the homepage to reach these different categories. You will probably find "Reference" and "Sites by Subject" the most useful. The "Reference" category is further subdivided into different categories of Web sites: "Documents," "Treaties," "Maps," "Statistics," "American and British History Bibliographies," "Electronic Journals," "Book Reviews," "Biographies," and "Curricula and Syllabi." The sheer number of links to reference sites (such as Yale University's Avalon project) is astounding. Every Web site has a short synopsis to help you rate it. Be prepared to sort through them, though, because British sites are mixed in with the U.S. history ones.

"Sites by Subject" is easier to use. It, too, is divided into subcategories, such as "Afro-American History and Culture," "Civil War," "Colonial America and Revolution," "Intellectual History," "Law, Crime, and Police History," "Native American Resources," "Presidents and the Presidency," and "Women's History." Under each of these broad categories are dozens of links to excellent Web sites.

American Cultural History—The Twentieth Century
http://www.nhmccd.edu/contracts/lrc/kc/decades.html

All you students of modern American history will love this easy-to-use Web site created by the Kingwood College Library. It provides all the basic facts about the twentieth century in a decade-by-decade format. Best of all, it recommends Web sites, books, and other sources to round out your research.

On the home page, click on the decade that interests you. The guides to each decade begin with some quick facts—the American population of the decade, the average salary, and so forth—to get you on your way. Then you can home in on one of the six cultural history topics available: "Art and Architecture," "Books and Literature," "Fashions and Fads," "Events and People," "Music," "Theater, Film and Radio." You can read about the major players, events, forces, and problems relevant to these topics. For instance in "Art and Architecture of the 1920s," you'll learn about early modernism and abstract expressionism, as well as about Georgia O'Keefe, William de Kooning, and Frank Lloyd Wright.

A great many of the names, events, and concepts are linked to other Web site, so you can learn more with ease. Click on "Abstract Expressionism," for example, and you'll link to the *World Wide Art Resource* site, where major artistic movements are defined. Within the "Art and Architecture" essay, you'll also find recommended print sources and even the Library of Congress numbers for easy browsing in the library. Links to "People and Events" of the decade (in case you need to brush up on your political chronology) are located at the bottom of each decade's guide.

American History Resources
http://www.mcps.k12.md.us/curriculum/socialstd/American_bookmarks.
    html

This Web site serves as a clearinghouse for American history-related Web site. It contains tons of links to other Web sites, which are conveniently arranged according to subject. *American History Resources* even provides capsule reviews for most of the linked sites. All you have to do is scroll down the screen, look under the heading that relates to your topic, and click on the sites that interest you.

A Biography of America
http://www.learner.org/biographyofamerica/index.html

This site, maintained by the Annenberg Foundation and the Corpo-ration for Public Broadcasting, is a companion to a video instruction series on American history. But you don't need the video series to find this site useful. A *Biography of America* divides U.S. history chronolog-ically into 26 chapters. Each includes a time line of key events, a map, and links to primary and secondary source materials for the period. You'll also find the full transcript of the video program, which gives you an overview of the period.

The Digital Librarian
http://www.digital-librarian.com/history.html

This site, maintained by Margaret Vail Anderson, a librarian in Cort-land, New York, provides hundreds of links to great resources in Amer-ican history. It is a little awkward to use. The American history sites are included in a long list that contains European history material as well, and because the site does not have search capability, you have to scroll to find what you want. Some of the topics also may be hard to find. George Washington's papers, for example, are listed under "Papers of George Washington." Despite the downside, this is a site well worth visiting.

Making of America (MOA)
http://moa.umdl.umich.edu/

This site is the result of an ongoing collaboration between the Uni-versity of Michigan and Cornell University to create a digital library of primary sources in American social history from the antebellum period through reconstruction. While sites such as *NARA* and *American Mem-ory* sport massive collections of documents pertinent to U.S. history, MOA is unique because it focuses on *social* history. MOA's strength is not in political documents, but in its wealth of sources about religion, education, science, and technology in America. True, you won't find a copy of the Declaration of Independence on this Web site. But you will find the full text of a book, *Baptists, The Only Religious Reformers*, by U.S. President John Quincy Adams.

MOA is set up to make both browsing and specific searching easy. Click on "Browse" from the home page if you want to explore the stacks of this digital library. You can then look through the MOA Journal Collection, which contains *full-text* versions of 11 periodicals, including *Catholic World* from 1865 to 1901 and the *Southern Quarterly Review* from 1842 to 1857. You can even read *Vanity Fair* issues dating from 1860. For a more organized browsing session, scan MOA's complete bib-liography of books and authors, which is arranged alphabetically.

If you're searching for a specific document, select the "Search" function on the home page. Once there, you can opt to conduct your search in books, journals, or both. You can also impose date restrictions. Keep in mind that MOA does *not* search according to subjects—it will pull up *every* book, journal, sermon, or pamphlet that contains your search term(s). So, for example, typing in "Missouri Compromise" will bring up 965 matches in 129 books. Luckily, you can use the "Advanced Search" feature to look for works in which a term appears a specified number of times. Therefore if you want to avoid, say, every magazine article from the nineteenth century that just mentions the Missouri Compromise in passing, you can search for sources that use the term 15 times or more. In this way, you can find primary source material that is really about the Missouri Compromise.

Presidents of the United States
http://www.ipl.org/ref/POTUS/

Chances are that, at some point, American history researchers will need to learn about an American president. This general Web site is the place to get basic information, as well as referrals on where to look to learn more. All you have to do is click in the index on the name of the president in whom you're interested. You'll then get a brief overview of his administration, along with links to Internet biographies.

United States History
http://www.tntech.edu/www/acad/hist/usa.html

Managed by the history department of Tennessee Technological University, this site contains hundreds of links organized topically and chronologically. We've included it because of the large number and wide variety of sites you can find here, but it has significant downsides. It has no search function, so you have to scroll to find what you want; the sites in each category are not arranged in any order; and, there are no annotations, so you frequently have to guess at what's in the site. Yet, despite its limitations, this is can be a good research shortcut for anyone with patience.

USA: Outline of American History
http://odur.let.rug.nl/~usa/H/1994/index.htm

Use this Web site to see the broad brushstrokes of a period in American history. *USA: Outline of American History* is divided into 13 eras of American history, starting with "Early America" and ending with "Towards the Twenty-first Century." Select the period you want to read about, and you'll automatically be taken to another index with a list of topics related to that period. Click on the "Colonial Period," for instance, and you'll be able to choose from among brief essays that include "Emergence of a Colonial Government," "French and Indian War," and "Witches of Salem." The site also has an excellent bibliography section if you're looking for print resources.

Interactive and Practical Sites

Practice Quizzes and Crosswords in U.S. History
http://home.earthlink.net/~gfeldmeth/quizzes.html

This site is a great resource for high school students wanting to quiz themselves on various topics in American history. Designed by high school history teacher Greg Feldman to offer his students extra help in their studies, the site has 32 quizzes to choose from. You can test your mettle in topics that include "Colonial Beginnings and Puritanism," the "Federalist Era," the "Jacksonian Era," "Expansionism and Manifest Destiny," the "Gilded Age," and the "1950s." If you choose the wrong answer in the test, look at the top of the screen to read a brief explanation of the correct answer.

In addition to the quizzes, this Web site also has a number of crossword puzzles for you to try. Again, the list of topics is comprehensive, ranging from the "American Revolution" to the "Federalist Era" to the "Civil War."

One word of warning is in order for this Web site—it is definitely a little advanced for middle school students. But the information is accurate and derived from a number of good sources (including the textbooks *A People and a Place*, *American History*, and *Enduring Vision*). The only downside is that the Web site doesn't have any bells and whistles.

U.S. History Interactive
http://www.geocities.com/heartland/pointe/3048/roadmap.html

Here's a fun Web site to test your knowledge on U.S. history topics. Scroll down the home page screen to find the "U.S. History Interactive Game." Choose one of the three relevant topics—"U.S. Presidents," "U.S. Constitution," or "U.S. History"—from the pull-down menu in the top half of your screen. Click on "next question" to start each quiz. If you answer wrong, you can click on "more information" to get a short synopsis of the answer. To brush up on your presidential history, choose the "Identify the President Quiz," which you'll find near the bottom of the home page. After viewing a picture of the president, you type in your guess at who he is.

The rest of this site is an American history potpourri, probably reflecting the intellectual interests of its author. If you're interested in learning more about the Civil War, this site provides an excellent overview. After taking one of the quizzes, you can read up on the Civil War (while music from the period plays in the background). Click on "Civil War Page" from the home page. You'll find biographies of key figures on both sides, a section on causes of the war, an overview of the abolitionist movement, and a biography of Lincoln. You can also access information on the "State of the Union" and the "U.S. Constitution," as well as an extensive biography of Theodore Roosevelt.

EPU: All-American Quiz
http://hagen.let.rug.nl/~epu/usmaze/

This Web site is the brainchild of one Peter Meindertsma, a member of the American Studies Student Association at the University of Groningen, the Netherlands. While Meindertsma may not be an American, he has constructed a tough test for any student of U.S. history. His quiz is a four-level test that includes questions about U.S. presidents, geography, key events, and state history. You proceed through the levels until you finish. Beware, though, Meindertsma has given you an extra incentive to get it right. Answer *any* question wrong, and you are sent back to the beginning of the level. You keep getting sent back until you answer correctly. At first you'll enjoy the funny graphics that pop up with each incorrect answer, but they lose their appeal rather quickly.

"The Early American History Interactive Crossword Puzzle"
http://www.earlyamerica.com/crossword/index.html

If you're into early American history, you'll love this site's extensive selection of crossword puzzles. Where else can you get your fix for a crossword with clues like "Founded Rhode Island," and "English-speaking Indian"? You can play the current puzzle online, print the current puzzle to work on at your leisure, or access the archives of past puzzles.

Since the puzzles are only one feature of the Web site, *Archiving Early America,* you'll be able to research the crosswords' clues by searching the Web site's vast archives of Early American documents. Simply click on "Home" at the bottom of the crossword puzzle page to access the main Web site.

Map Collections

Historical Atlas of the Twentieth Century
http://users.erols.com/mwhite28/20centry.htm

If you want a good general atlas of the twentieth century, turn to this site. It has hundreds of maps, charts, and graphs dealing with historical topics worldwide. The number of American maps is small, but we have included the site because it links to a superb collection of other sites that are very useful for American history. To find the sites, click on "Links" under "Broad Outline" at the left of the home page. Then scroll down to "America" under "Human History Organized by Place Rather Than Time" and click on "United States."

Images of American Political History
http://teachpol.tcnj.edu/amer_pol_hist/_browse_maps.htm

Images of American Political History concentrates on maps illustrating border changes or showing the results of presidential elections. While the territorial change maps are inclusive, running from 1768 to 1920, the election maps span only 1796 to 1968. The collection also contains a few demographic maps, but this is not the site for demographic information.

Map Collections: 1500–1999
http://memory.loc.gov/ammem/grndhtml/gmdhome.html

Map Collections offers a small fraction of the American maps and atlases in the Library of Congress. But *small fraction* is a relative phrase; the Library's Geography and Map Division holds more than 4.5 million items. There are hundreds of maps available for downloading from this wonderful site. The site is divided into six collections: "Cities and Towns"; "Conservation and Environment"; "Discovery and Exploration"; "Cultural Landscapes"; "Military Battles and Campaigns"; and "Transportation and Railroads." Each collection contains an overview, as well as a history of, mapping the topic. You can search *Map Collections* by keyword, geographic location, subject, map creator, and title.

Perry-Castañeda Library Map Collection: Historical Maps of the United States
http://www.lib.utexas.edu/maps/histus.html

The University of Texas at Austin has a wonderful online collection of maps that cover American history from pre-Columbian Indian tribes through the twentieth century. Maps in the site are organized under six broad categories: "Early Inhabitants"; "Exploration and Settlement"; "U.S. Territorial Growth"; "Military History Maps"; "Later Historical Maps"; and "Maps of National Historic Parks." The collection is particularly strong on military maps. The site also links to hundreds of maps on other Web sites.

West Point Atlas
http://www.dean.usma.edu/history/dhistorymaps/MapsHome.htm

This online atlas, developed by the history department of the U.S. Military Academy, is based on a series of print atlases that the department created over the years for its course on the history of military art. It includes detailed campaign maps of most of America's wars. *West Point Atlas,* which is still under construction, covers U.S. conflicts from the colonial period through the 1992–93 Somalia campaign. The site does not include any narrative, so you will have to look elsewhere to put the battles in historical context.

Primary Sources

African-American Mosaic
http://www.loc.gov/exhibits/african/intro.html

Part of the Library of Congress's *Exhibitions* site, *African-American Mosaic* is a great resource for primary material in four areas of African American history: abolition and slavery; the controversy over colonization of free blacks in Africa; the migration of African Americans to the West following the Civil War; and the Great Migration to the North during the early twentieth century. It also contains a large amount of material from WPA (Works Projects Administration) programs in the 1930s including ex-slave narratives. Although the focus is on primary documents, the text accompanying the exhibit gives you an excellent overview of the topics.

The American Colonist's Library: A Treasury of Primary Documents
http://personal.pitnet.net/primarysources/

This is an extraordinary site that is a must visit for anyone interested in colonial history. Compiled by Rick Gardiner, a history teacher, it is a comprehensive gateway to colonial American primary documents on the Web. The site states, "[I]f it isn't here, it probably is not available online anywhere." That's not an idea boast. *Colonist's Library* is massive. But what makes it invaluable is not just the size but the scope of the material. This is not just another "key documents" site where you find important government documents and political literature. Gardiner has linked any document available online that is relevant to the colonists' lives. Thus the user gets a deep understanding of what molded colonial culture and ideals as well as politics. The Mayflower Compact, the Stamp Act and the Declaration of Independence are all here, but there's much, much more. You'll find links to the classical and medieval authors such as Livy and Calvin who influenced colonial thought as well as the texts of Jonathan Edwards' sermons, letters of Plymouth settlers, the transcripts of the Salem Witchcraft Trials, and Daniel Boone's journal. It's all here. This is an incredible site!

American Memory
http://lcweb2.loc.gov/ammem/amhome.html

American Memory is gateway to the incredible collection of primary resources in American history and culture at the Library of Congress. It offers access to more than 7 million digital items—from documents and letters to films, photos, and sheet music. The site is easily searchable by collection, keyword, or format. *American Memory* also contains online versions of exhibits at the Library of Congress that are an excellent first stop for research in the topics covered.

Archiving Early America
http://earlyamerica.com/

Archiving Early America contains a wealth of primary source material from eighteenth century America, often displayed in its original format. This site sets itself apart from other primary document collections by emphasizing newspapers, maps, magazines, writings, and art rather than just government documents. The documents are here, but you'll also find contemporary reactions to important events. The site is a little frustrating to use. You get to the material either through "The World of Early America," a topical index with very broad and sometimes meaningless categories, or through the "Search" feature, which often generates numerous duplicates. But be patient. You'll find primary material here that you can't find in most other document sites.

Avalon Project at the Yale Law School
http://www.yale.edu/lawweb/avalon/avalon.htm

The site features documents from around the world in law, history, economics, politics, diplomacy, and government from ancient times to the twenty-first century. Although the site is international, it has an extensive collection of U.S. documents including colonial charters, Madison's notes on the Constitutional Convention, treaties between the United States and other nations as well as between the U.S. government and Native American tribes, and annual messages from the president. There is also a collection of documents related to the September 11, 2001, attack on the United States. You can access the material by time period, keyword or collection. If you don't know the formal name of the document you want, the easiest way to get to the American material is by clicking on "Major Document Collection" or by going through the "Chronology of American History" found under each time period. The chronology lists the U.S. documents in date order.

Chronology of the United States Historical Documents
http://hamilton.law.ou.edu/hist/

This collection, compiled at the University of Oklahoma, contains hundreds of primary documents from the founding of the colonies to the twenty-first century. It is particularly strong on inaugural speeches and presidential declarations as well as key legislation. It also contains some poetry and songs such as the Ralph Waldo Emerson's *Concord Hymn* and *Yankee Doodle*. There are some downsides to this site. It has no search function; you have to scroll down the list of chronologically arranged documents. In addition, some of the links to documents in the late twentieth century are not live.

Core Documents in U.S. Democracy
http://www.access.gpo.gov/su_docs/locators/coredocs/index.html

This site, maintained by the Government Printing Office, is the first place to look for important government documents. The focus is on legal and legislative material, but you'll also find regulatory and some presidential items as well. Although the site takes you to eighteenth and nineteenth century documents, such as the *Federalist Papers* and Congressional Debates, the emphasis is on the twentieth century materials. Here you can be connected to Supreme Court decisions from 1937 to the present and public laws from 1996 to 2001. You can also research presidential proclamations and executive orders from 1945 to 1989.

Documents for the Study of American History
http://history.cc.ukans.edu/carrie/docs/amdocs_index.html

This site, created at the University of Kansas, is one of the best collections of American documents on the Web. It contains not only speeches, congressional reports, and foreign relations documents, but also party platforms, key Supreme Court decisions, and even the text of some popular songs. Here you'll find hundreds of documents including excerpts from Christopher Columbus' journal, the Iroquois Constitution, the text of W. J. Bryan's "Cross of Gold" speech, and the words to "Lili Marlene." The site has no search function, so you'll have to scroll down the list of documents, which is organized chronologically. This is a great collection, but beware: a lot of the links to material from the 1980s and 1990s are dead.

Nineteenth Century Documents Project
http://www.furman.edu~benson/docs/

This gateway leads you to an extensive collection of primary sources that concentrates on speeches, editorials, and political documents important for understanding sectional conflict and evolving regional identity from the 1830s through Reconstruction. Among the wealth of material you'll find abolitionist Angelina Grimké's "Appeal to the Christian Women of the South," statistics on slaves and slave families, maps of the 1856 presidential election, the 1860 Republican Party platform, and South Carolina's Secession Declaration.

Nineteenth Century Documents Project is a very basic site. Documents are organized chronologically under general heads: "Early National Politics," "Slavery/Sectionalism," "Secession Era Editorials," 1850 Statistical Almanac," "The Election of 1860," "The War Begins," and "Post Civil War Documents." The site does not contain a search function, but you can use your browser's "Find" function to locate what you want.

Nineteenth Century Documents Project also has a great list of links to related sites. To reach them, just go to the bottom of the page and click on "Lloyd Benson's Past Connections." (Benson is the professor of history at Furman University who compiled the site.)

Speeches
http://www.historychannel.com/speeches/index.html

Here's a great place to hear some of the most important broadcasts and recordings in twentieth century history. Although the site is international, the emphasis is on American history. You can hear Martin Luther King's "I Have a Dream" speech or listen to Amelia Earhart discuss the future of women in flying. From the home page you can access the speech through the "Search" function at the left or by browsing the categories: "Politics and Government"; "Science and Technology"; "Arts, Entertainment, and Culture"; and "War and Diplomacy." Don't try to access material through "Speech Archives." You'll get a message asking you to use the search function.

United States Historical Census Data
http://fisher.lib.virginia.edu/census/

This site provides demographic and economic data for states and counties from 1790 to 1960. Each census can be searched by a number of variables depending on how the particular census was collected and organized. The site also contains a history of the census.

READY TO RESEARCH

Formats for Electronic Source Citations

See also "The Basics" section in Volume 1 of this set.

Citing Electronic Information in History Papers
http://www.people.memphis.edu/~mcrouse/elcite.html

This site focuses specifically on citation in academic history papers. It includes recommendations for an electronic source citation style that is derived from the traditional Chicago (Turabian) style.

2

Researching Individual U.S. History Topics on the Internet

Researching a specific topic on the Internet can be overwhelming. Type a topic such as "Lewis and Clark" into a search engine, and you'll pull up hundreds—if not thousands—of Web pages, some of which are only remotely connected to your subject.

This section of the book is designed to help you over this major hurdle to online research. In it, you'll find a list of about 150 topics in American history, such as the "Growth of Industry," the "Spanish-American War," and "Women's Suffrage." For each of these topics, you'll see several key terms listed that will make searching the Internet a little easier. For instance, under the "Spanish-American War," you'll learn that it might be helpful to search by keywords like *imperialism*, the *Rough Riders*, or the USS *Maine*. The best search engine to use is also listed.

Some of the Web sites give basic overviews, some are multimedia extravaganzas, and some make primary source material available to you. Because each main topic is so broad, some of these Web sites deal with a particular facet of the topic. Use these tried-and-true sites as a jumping-off point, and then follow the links to your heart's content—and your paper topic comes into crystal-clear focus.

ABOLITION

Best Search Engine:	http://www.google.com/
Key Search Terms:	Abolitionist movement + history
	Slavery + history + United States

Abolition, Anti-Slavery Movements, and the Rise of Sectional Controversy
http://memory.loc.gov/ammem/aaohtml/exhibit/aopart3.html
high school and up

The Web site, part of the Library of Congress's *African American Odyssey*, gives you a good overview of the abolition movement and growing sectionalism in the years before the Civil War. The site is very plain vanilla. It's divided into two parts. Part 1 offers you information on "Anti-Slavery Activists" and "'Popularizing Anti-Slavery Sentiment." Click on the former if you want to learn more about abolitionist groups and their leaders, such as Anthony Benezet and William Lloyd Garrison, or about their philosophy. Click on the latter if you want to see examples of abolitionist literature and songs. Part 2 discusses the Fugitive Slave Law of 1850, growing sectionalism in the 1850s, and the rise of militant abolition, particularly John Brown's raid in 1859. It also has a section on Harriet Beecher Stowe's *Uncle Tom's Cabin*, which it calls "The Book That Made This Mighty War."

The site has some limitations. There are no links to people and terms, and it doesn't list what's in Part 2 when you are in Part 1 and vice versa. But stick to it, and you'll find a lot of first class information here.

ALAMO

Best Search Engine:	http://www.google.com/
Key Search Term:	the Alamo

The Alamo
http://www.thealamo.org
high school and up

Here's a good one-stop source for information on the Alamo, the siege and battle of the Alamo, and the Alamo's defenders. Maintained by the Daughters of the Republic of Texas, it's really easy to use.

From the home page you can click on "The Alamo's Historic Past" to get an overview of its history. Click on "The Alamo in 1836," and you get a detailed chronology of the siege and battle with links to biographies and events important to the story. In addition, the 1836 section gives you weather conditions during the siege, as well as letters from two of the defenders. One of the best features of the 1836 section is "Alamo Myths and Misconceptions," which debunks some of the legends that have grown up around the battle. The Web site also contains short biographies of the mission's defenders. To reach them just click on

"The Defenders" at the home page. Doing so leads you to an alphabetical list of defenders' names with their birthplaces.

Finally the site allows you to take a virtual walking tour of the Alamo battlefield and offers links to other resources on Texas history.

ALGER HISS CASE

Best Search Engine: http://www.google.com/

Key Search Terms: Alger Hiss + McCarthyism

Alger Hiss + history

1948: The Alger Hiss Spy Case
http://www.thehistorynet.com/AmericanHistory/articles/1998/0698_cover.
  htm
high school and up

This excellent Web page, which consists of an article that first appeared in *American History* magazine, provides a detailed analysis of the contentious Alger Hiss case, along with all the background information you'll need to understand it. Hiss, who was convicted of perjury in 1950, was accused of being a member of a Communist espionage ring. The furor surrounding the Hiss case lent credence to McCarthy's claim that Communists had infiltrated the State Department.

Select the "Full Text" link from the home page to read the article. If you want to view the *New York Times* front page from the day of his perjury conviction, simply click on the image of the newspaper from the home page.

ALIEN AND SEDITION ACTS

Best Search Engine: http://www.google.com/

Key Search Terms: Alien + Sedition Acts + history

Sedition Act + history

John Adams + Sedition Act

Virginia Resolution

Sedition Act of 1798
http://www.studyworld.com/sedition_act_of_1798.htm
middle school and up

Think of this no-frills Web site as your first research stop. It doesn't have pictures, links to primary sources, multimedia exhibits, or interactive features. But what it does have is a thorough and tidy description of the Sedition Act of 1798, the events that led to its passage, and the Act's consequences. *Sedition Act of 1798* hits on all the related topics— Federalism, the Alien Acts, and the Virginia and Kentucky Resolutions. So while you might miss having some bells and whistles on this site, you'll appreciate its careful and understandable examination of the Sedition Act. It's also a no-brainer to navigate. Just scroll down the screen.

> *Virginia Report of 1799–1800, Touching on the Alien and Sedition Laws, Together with the Virginia Resolutions of December 21, 1798*
> http://www.constitution.org/rf/vr.htm
> high school and up

This Web site is probably the most comprehensive one about the Alien and Sedition Acts that you could possibly find. It has full text versions of all three Alien Acts, the Sedition Act, the Virginia Resolution, and the Kentucky Resolution. It also contains the transcripts of the debates held in the Virginia House of Delegates in 1798 regarding the Virginia Resolution, the full text of the Virginia Report of 1799, James Madison's commentary on the Virginia Report of 1799, and letters Madison wrote about it.

How are all these documents related? The "Introduction" by Jon Roland explains. Roland links these documents to the feud between the Federalists and the anti-Federalists, a disagreement that colored the creation of the Constitution and jeopardized the early unity of the nation. To access the "Introduction," scroll down the home page until you see the table of contents. It's the first item in the index.

This site also contains explanatory information written by J. W. Randolph, who published the Virginia Report in 1850. Randolph's "Preface" goes over the history behind all these documents, as does his "Analysis." You'll find both in the table of contents on the home page.

Like the *Sedition Act of 1798* site, this one could use some sprucing up. There are no visual materials whatsoever. It's tough to criticize a site that is so helpful, though. Also keep in mind that the *Virginia Report of 1799–1800* is probably too advanced for younger students. They can get a simpler version of the events in the *Sedition Act of 1798*.

AMISTAD

Best Search Engine: http://www.google.com/
Key Search Terms: Amistad

Exploring Amistad *at Mystic Seaport*
http://amistad.mysticseaport.org/main/welcome.html
high school and up

This is a really great Web site that covers the *Amistad* revolt of 1839 and its aftermath that continued into 1842, a shipboard uprising of slaves that set off an intense political, legal, and popular debate over slavery. Here you'll find a detailed narrative of the revolt as well as a concise time line of events. Both these features put the revolt in historical context so you learn about slavery and the slave trade while researching the *Amistad* incident. Click on "Discovery" at the home page to connect to a section that presents the story of the *Amistad* and offers essays by historians on the various themes surrounding the incident. Essays cover topics such as the navy and the slave trade and precursors to the *Amistad* incident. You can link to biographies of key players such as Cinque, who led the revolt, and descriptions of places such as Cuba, important in the incident.

The site is incredibly easy to navigate because the text tells you exactly how to find what you want. There's no guessing at what you will get when you click on a link, so you're saved a lot of frustration. The site has an extraordinary amount of detail and draws you into the story. You'll want to spend a lot of time here.

ANGEL ISLAND

Best Search Engine: http://www.google.com/
Key Search Terms: Angel Island

Angel Island: The Pacific Gateway
http://www.internationalchannel.com/education/angelisland/
high school and up

Angel Island is known as the "Ellis Island of the West." Here more than a million immigrants, mostly Chinese, first entered the United States. This easy-to-use site tells the story of their experience, which was very different from that of immigrants coming through Ellis Island. While Ellis Island was a processing center through which most people passed in a few hours, Angel Island was a detention center. There immigrants spent weeks or months while trying to prove they had a legal right to enter the United States under restrictive laws designed to exclude most Asians.

This site offers an overview of immigration through the island as well as information highlighting the Chinese experience. Here you'll also find descriptions of living conditions as well as the medical examinations and interrogations immigrants underwent. Just click on the appropriate topic at the home page to access the information. One of the most moving sections of the site offers samples of the poetry immigrants carved into the barrack walls. You can also hear audio clips of the poetry by clicking at the bottom of each page.

Angel Island
http://www.angelisland.org/
middle school and up

Once you've read about the immigrant experience on Angel Island, you might want to learn more about the island and its immigration station facilities. If so, this site, maintained by the Angel Island Association, is perfect. Here you can read a history of the island and take a tour of its historic buildings. The site also includes a live Webcam that takes photos between sunrise and sunset every day.

Angel Island is really easy to use; everything is accessible from the home page. The best way to access the history of the island is to click on "Early History" under Points of Interest and continue reading the text through the section on "Immigration Station."

ANTEBELLUM SOUTH

Best Search Engine: http://www.google.com/

Key Search Terms: Antebellum + history

                         Antebellum period

First-Person Narratives of the American South
http://docsouth.unc.edu/fpn/fpnmain.html
high school and up

First-Person Narratives of the American South, developed by the library of the University of North Carolina at Chapel Hill, is a wonderful site for studying the history of the antebellum and Civil War South through the eyes of Southerners. The site focuses on the experience of the often-overlooked populations: women, African Americans, Native Americans, laborers, and Confederate soldiers. These people tell their stories through diaries, autobiographies, memoirs, travel accounts, and narratives of former slaves. Here you can read an account of a girl's life on a plantation, recollections of a Confederate sailor, and the diary of Mary B. Chestnut, the wife of an aide to Jefferson Davis. There are over 100 documents in the site.

The site is fascinating, but a little frustrating to use. There is no topical search function. You have to scroll to find what you need. But be patient. This is a great site for studying social history.

ANTI-FEDERALISTS

Best Search Engine: http://www.google.com/
Key Search Terms: Anti-federalists
                        Federalism + history

The Anti-Federalist Papers
http://odur.let.rug.nl/~usa/D/1776-1880/federalist/antixx.htm
high school and up

In 1778 the states debated the merits of the proposed Constitution. Those who supported the Constitution defended it in *The Federalist Papers*, which became a classic of American political thought. Those who opposed ratification also presented their position in papers, leaflets, and discussions in the Continental Congress. Because their arguments never appeared in one body of work, it's hard to find a good collection of Anti-Federalist thought. If you are studying these views, go to this simple site. Here you'll find almost 50 documents that present Anti-Federalist concerns on issues such as states rights, direct elections, suffrage, and slavery.

The Anti-Federalist Papers site is very simple and easy to use. Documents are organized chronologically under to main heads, "The Federal Convention of 1787" and "Ratification of the Constitution." Just click on the document you need.

ARTICLES OF CONFEDERATION

Best Search Engine: http://www.goggle.com/
Key Search Terms: U.S. Constitution + history
                        Articles of Confederation + history
                        Founding fathers + Constitution

The U.S. Constitution Online
http://www.usconstitution.net/articles.html
middle school and up

Use this Web site to learn about the Articles of Confederation, the basis of U.S. central government prior to the Constitution, and the important role this document played in American history. You can start by clicking on a "Constitutional Topic Page," which leads you to an essay that gives you historical background on the Articles and summarizes each of the document's provisions. It also includes a list of men, such as John Hancock, who served as president of Congress under the Articles. You can then go back to the home page to read the entire text of the Articles. Finally you can compare the Articles of Confederation with the Constitution by clicking on "Comparison of the Articles and the Constitution" at the top of the home page. This site is virtually all text, and not very exciting to look at, but it's a great resource for exploring how the Constitution came about.

To Form a More Perfect Union
http://memory.loc.gov/ammem/bdsds/bdexhome.html
high school and up

See **Continental Congress** for description.

ATOM BOMB

Best Search Engine: http://www.google.com/
Key Search Terms: Atomic bomb + history
                      World War II + weapons

The Atomic Archive
http://www.atomicarchive.com/main.shtml
middle school and up

If you are looking for information about the atom bomb, this site has it all. *The Atomic Archive,* which is international in scope and encompasses the whole nuclear age, contains biographies of the scientists and political figures who made the invention of the bomb possible, eyewitness accounts of nuclear tests, a detailed history of the nuclear age, explanations of the science behind the bomb, photograph and video archives, and primary documents about the making of the bomb and its aftermath. In addition to being chock-full of the information you need, *The Atomic Archive* is easy to navigate and well-organized.

Use the straightforward menu on the left side of the home page to track down the material you want. For a general overview of the history of the atom bomb—from the scientific discoveries that made the bomb possible to the 1999 nuclear tests in Pakistan and India—click on "Time Line" from the main menu. The time line is broken down by decade, so click on the appropriate time span at the bottom of the screen. If you're in the market for detailed biographies of the key players in the atomic age, click on "Biographies" from the main menu. To read what some of these folks had to say about the atom bomb itself, go to "Reflections" from the main menu where you'll find extensive excerpts. If you are looking for further primary source material for a research project, click on "Documents" from the main menu to enter a virtual library of historical papers. You'll find digital copies of Albert Einstein's 1939 letter to President Franklin Roosevelt, the White House press release on the bombing of Hiroshima, eyewitness accounts of the bombing of Nagasaki, and much more.

The Atomic Archive has a ton of other material to help you in your research. Use the "Glossary" to find definitions and explanations of scientific terms related to the atom bomb. For further help in understanding the technical aspects of this topic, click on "Nuclear Fission and Nuclear Fusion" from the main menu. The "Nuclear Data" section gives specific information about nuclear stockpiles, nuclear weapons accidents, and nuclear test sites. If you're interested in the history of arms control, choose "Treaties" from the main menu. You'll find brief summaries of arms control treaties from 1959 to 1996. In the "Photos and Videos" sections, you can access one-of-a-kind visual material. The most chilling part of The Atomic Archive is the "Examples" section, which explains what would happen if an atom bomb went off today in New York City.

Atomic Bomb: Decision
http://www.dannen.com/decision/
high school and up

Atomic Bomb: Decision concentrates on a narrow area of this unique history—the decision by the United States to drop atomic bombs on Japan. What is especially interesting for you researchers is that Atomic Bomb: Decision chooses to examine this subject exclusively through primary source material.

The site presents 21 documents that provide various perspectives on this crucial decision—beginning with minutes from the 1945 Target Committee of the Manhattan Project. You can find the digital copies of a petition sent by scientist Leo Szilard to President Harry S. Truman urging that the atomic bomb never be used, the radiation monitoring results from the Trinity Test, excerpts from President Truman's diary, and an audio copy of Truman's radio address to the American people about dropping the bomb on Hiroshima.

BAY OF PIGS

Best Search Engine: http://www.google.com/
Key Search Terms: Bay of Pigs + history
                               John Kennedy + Fidel Castro
                               John Kennedy + Cuba

The Timetable History of Cuba
http://www.historyofcuba.com/history/baypigs/pigs.htm
middle school and up

This site provides a terrific overview of the Bay of Pigs invasion and helps you put this event into the broader framework of Cuban history. Although it doesn't have many photographs or other visual aids, the site is easy to navigate, clearly written, and quite informative. You can read the entire essay, or you can select a subject heading that interests you on the home page ("Introduction," "The Plan," "Invasion, Victory," and "Aftermath"). The piece does a great job of explaining why President John F. Kennedy undertook an invasion and what the consequences were for both Cuba and the United States. If you want to get Cuba's perspective on the event, read the speech Fidel Castro delivered just a couple of weeks after Bay of Pigs (scroll down to the bottom of the screen and click on "Speech"). If you're looking for further research material, this site has a fairly comprehensive print bibliography. Click on "References" from the Bay of Pigs subject headings to access it.

The Bay of Pigs Invasion
http://web.cs.mun.ca/~david12/papers/bayofpigs.html
middle school and up

While *The Timetable History of Cuba* helps you place the Bay of Pigs invasion into the context of Cuban history, *The Bay of Pigs Invasion* offers you a more detailed view of the invasion's impact on the United States. *The Bay of Pigs Invasion* is a very straightforward, no frills site. Just scroll down the screen to read the historical essay. Don't let its plainness put you off, though. The site provides useful material for student researchers. You'll learn about the origins of the invasion, the plan of attack used, and the consequences of its failure.

If you need more research material, use the site's long bibliography of print sources. You'll find it at the bottom of the essay. Near the end of the essay, you'll also find an "Update" on the relations between the United States and Cuba. Follow the links to read the text of the Helms-

Burton bill, background on the bill, and the text of the Cuban Liberty and Democratic Solidarity Act.

Documents Relating to American Foreign Policy
http://www.mtholyoke.edu/acad/intrel/cuba.htm
high school and up

Web sites like this one give the Internet a good name! *Documents Relating to American Foreign Policy* is a researcher's dream. Those of you looking for documents about the Bay of Pigs invasion will love this site, which has tons of useful material. This site provides access to hundreds of primary source documents about the Bay of Pigs invasion, much of it recently declassified, as well as a number of thoughtful secondary source articles.

Approximately a third of the articles on this Web site are directly related to the Bay of Pigs invasion. The remaining articles deal with the fallout from the failed attack—especially the Cuban missile crisis. *Documents Relating to American Foreign Policy* is incredibly easy to use. Simply click on the document that interests you, and away you go! The first link is to the National Security Council's (NSC) *Archive of Declassified Files on the Cuban Missile Crisis*. Among the many articles and memos that are part of the NSA's *Archive* are ones that shed some light on the buildup of tension between the United States and Cuba in the months preceding the Bay of Pigs.

As you scan the list of resources in *Documents Relating to American Foreign Policy*, you'll find memos sent to President Kennedy urging him to launch the invasion (and many others pleading with him not to) from the Central Intelligence Agency (CIA), the Joint Chiefs of Staff, and the secretary of state (to name just a few). There are also letters from President Kennedy to Soviet Premier Nikita Khrushchev. Don't overlook the link to the Department of State's treasure trove of material. Click on "Foreign Relations of the United States: 1961–1962" to access 443 documents and memos dealing with Cuba, including papers prepared by the CIA.

The secondary source material is also helpful. There are links to several recent *New York Times* articles discussing the invasion in light of emerging declassified information, as well as several more scholarly pieces from periodicals such as *Foreign Affairs* and *Diplomatic History*. Although these articles are interpretive, they don't provide a lot of background. So if you need to review basic facts, use *The Timetable History of Cuba* or *The Bay of Pigs Invasion* in conjunction with *Documents Relating to American Foreign Policy*.

BILL OF RIGHTS

Best Search Engine: http://www.google.com/
Key Search Terms: Bill of Rights + history
                        James Madison + Bill of Rights
                        Bill of Rights + Constitution + history

The Constitution of the United States
http://www.nara.gov/exhall/charters/constitution/conmain.html
middle school and up

This Web site, which is part of the National Archives and Records Administration's vast holdings, is a great place to start your research on the Bill of Rights. Although it doesn't go into a lot of detail, it explains the Bill of Rights in the context of how the Constitution was created. You'll find biographies of all the major players involved, the story of the Bill of Rights, and a digital version of the original copy of the Bill of Rights.

The best way to dive into this subject matter is to check out this Web site's long (but easy-to-read) essay, "A More Perfect Union" (you'll see the link from the home page), which is an in-depth look at the ratification process of the Constitution. There is a section on the Bill of Rights and the role that these first amendments played in getting enough delegates to accept the Constitution. This essay introduces you to the important figures related to the Bill of Rights—James Madison, George Mason, Thomas Jefferson, and Patrick Henry—and also to the major themes underlying these first 10 amendments to the Constitution.

The link "Bill of Rights" at the bottom of "A More Perfect Union" (and also at the bottom of the home page) allows you to access more specific information. You'll find another short essay, as well as links, that enable you to read the full text of the Bill of Rights (click on "Amendments 1–10" to view the original document). Click on "Virginia Declaration of Rights" to learn more about this precursor to the Bill of Rights that Mason wrote for the Virginia Constitutional Convention in 1776 and that served as a model for Madison when he drafted the Bill of Rights.

The Bill of Rights: A Brief History
http://www.aclu.org/library/pbp9.html
middle school and up

This informative Web site, which is part of the American Civil Liberties Union's (ACLU) site, contains an essay by the scholar Ira Glasser that provides basic information about the Bill of Rights. The site also gives some background information on the Bill of Rights and why it was so important to getting the Constitution accepted (although the explanation is not as complete as the one you'll find at *The Constitution of the United States*). The real strength of this Web site is that it makes the Bill of Rights come alive! It helps you understand that the Bill of Rights is a *living* document that is recreated and reinterpreted in American courts every day. As this site makes clear, the Bill of Rights isn't just about James Madison and George Mason arguing over long-since-outdated issues. *The Bill of Rights: A Brief History* explains how the document impacts you and everyone around you. You also learn about the people who were *left out* of the Bill of Rights—women, Native Americans, and African Americans—and how the struggle to apply the Bill of Rights to *all* Americans has been hard fought and even harder won.

In addition to the informative main essay, this site provides opportunities for you to get more information. For those of you who want to see just *how* the Bill of Rights is still being fought over, go to the ACLU's home page (the link is at the very bottom of *The Bill of Rights: A Brief History*). From here, select issues from the Bill of Rights that interest you, say religious liberty or freedom of speech, and then read about current cases and legislation that impact this Constitutional right. If you want to learn more about the freedoms protected by the Bill of Rights, click on the links under the "Certain Unalienable Rights" section. You can read "ACLU Briefing Papers" on the freedom of religion, press, speech, petition, assembly, as well as on equality before the law.

James Madison: His Legacy
http://www.jmu.edu/madison/madison.htm#Top
middle school and up

This Web site sheds light on the important role Madison played in incorporating the Bill of Rights into the U.S. Constitution. *James Madison: His Legacy* is a fairly large site, so be sure to concentrate on specific topics, unless you have time to browse and learn.

To focus on Madison's writing of the Bill of Rights, click on "Bill of Rights" from the home page. From here, you can view several important documents. If you are interested in the background of the concepts he laid out in the Bill of Rights, read the documents listed under "Antecedents" in the "Bill of Rights" section. To read the text of the speech that Madison gave to the Constitutional Convention recommending the adoption of a Bill of Rights, select that link under "James Madison Proposes the Bill of Rights." The "Introduction" to this speech is especially helpful in explaining *why* Madison felt compelled to advocate the Bill of Rights. If you click on "The Document" you can access a digital copy of the original Bill of Rights, read the full text version, and listen to the first 10 amendments being read aloud. If you want to chart Madison's thinking about some of these concepts after he wrote the Bill of Rights, go to the "Epilogue" heading in the "Bill of Rights" section, where you can read an article on the separation of church and state that Madison published in 1813.

Documentary History of the Bill of Rights
http://www.constitution.org/dhbr.htm
middle school and up

If you're searching for primary source material about the Bill of Rights, this is your Web site. It explains the history of the Bill of Rights through documents. Beginning with the "English Bill of Rights," you can chart the development of the ideas that were eventually incorporated in the Bill of Rights. Reading the documents that influenced men like James Madison and George Mason gives you a unique historical perspective on the Bill of Rights. You can also find the text of the "Virginia Bill of Rights," which served as an example for Madison when he drafted the Bill of Rights. This Web site also allows you to track conflicts that took place in incorporating the Bill of Rights into the U.S. Constitution. You can read amendments proposed by the ratifying commissions of various states, as well as a letter written by Madison to Thomas Jefferson.

BOSTON MASSACRE

Best Search Engine:	http://www.ajkids.com/
Key Search Terms:	Boston Massacre + history
	Crispus Attucks
	American Revolution + Boston Massacre + causes

The Murder of Crispus Attucks
http://rs7.loc.gov/exhibits/treasures/trr046.html
middle school and up

Do you like watching legal shows on television? If so, you might appreciate this view of the Boston Massacre, the 1770 account of the trial of the eight British soldiers who killed five Boston civilians. Keep in mind that this is a digital copy of the original manuscript, so it might take some time to work your way through the archaic dialect and flowery font. It's worth the effort, though.

The Murder of Crispus Attucks is part of the online exhibit, *The American Treasures of the Library of Congress*. You can read the Library of

Congress's overview of the document, and then proceed to the court-room drama itself. You have to click on each individual page you want to see from the home page.

Remember that Crispus Attucks was an African American (indeed the son of a slave), so reading this testimony is also likely to provoke some interesting questions to take to the classroom. Was it typical in colonial American for the murder of a black man to receive such attention? How was the death of Crispus Attucks treated compared to that of other New England African Americans?

The Boston Massacre
http://www.earlyamerica.com/review/winter96/massacre.html
middle school and up

This Web page is part of the excellent *Early America* site that is dedicated to making available primary sources related to the revolutionary period. After you read the brief but informative overview of the Boston Massacre, scroll to the bottom of the screen where you will find links to two primary documents. You can access an account of the Massacre written in 1770 in the *Boston Gazette and Country Journal* as well as the actual obituaries of the slain colonists (Samuel Gray, Samuel Maverick, James Caldwell, and Crispus Attucks). What's especially cool is that you can view digital copies of the original papers, which helps make the event seem all the more real and timely. If you have any questions about the Boston Massacre, join one or both of *Early America's* online discussions by clicking on "The Town Crier" or "Early America's E-mail Discussion Group" from the home page.

Transcript of the Trial of Thomas Preston
http://www.ilt.columbia.edu/k12/history/blacks/masacre.html
middle school and up

This Web site gives you a more accessible entry into the same trial as the one in *The Murder of Crispus Attucks*. Unlike that site, these accounts have been transcribed into modern English and are much easier to read. After you read an excerpt from Thomas Preston's deposition (you can find the full account at *Captain Thomas Preston's Account of the Boston Massacre* below), you can scan the testimony of witnesses called, all of whom offer their own unique perspective on the massacre. This site is a terrific primary source for all of you looking for material for research papers.

Captain Thomas Preston's Account of the Boston Massacre
http://odur.let.rug.nl/~usa/D/1751-1775/bostonmassacre/prest.htm
middle school and up

There are two sides to every story, and often the most effective way to learn the "truth" about something is to hear both sides. This Web site offers you a terrific resource—the ability to "hear" both sides of the Boston Massacre. Start by reading Captain Thomas Preston's account of what went on that fateful day in Boston. It gives you the British perspective since Preston was the commander of the British troops, some of whom fired on the American civilians. This viewpoint is a whole lot different from the one Paul Revere depicted in his famous engraving. Preston said, "The mob still increased and were more outrageous, striking their clubs or bludgeons one against another, calling out, 'Come on you rascals, you bloody backs, you lobster scoundrels, fire if you dare. . . .'"

At the top of this page, you'll find a link to an *Anonymous Account of the Boston Massacre*, which presents the opposite view of Preston's testimony. This author claims that the soldiers of Preston's detachment "attacked people with their bayonets" while the members of the crowd had their backs to the soldiers. Both accounts provide links to related topics that you can follow for more information.

BOSTON TEA PARTY

Best Search Engine: http://www.google.com/
Key Search Terms: Boston Tea Party + history

                              American Revolution + history

                              Samuel Adams + American Revolution + history

                              Intolerable Acts + history

American Revolution Home Page
http://www.americanrevwar.homestead.com/files/INDEX2.htm
middle school and up

This Web site is the place to get the basics about the Boston Tea Party—who was involved, why this act of rebellion took place, and what the consequences were. What's also great about the *American Revolution Home Page* is that it allows you to place the Boston Tea Party in the context of the rest of the events that led up to the American Revolution. This site is informative, easy to navigate, and clearly written. It's a little dull, though, since it doesn't have any interactive features or interesting illustrations.

To read the site's essay on the Boston Tea Party itself, simply click on "Boston Tea Party" from the subject index on the home page. The piece gives you the nuts and bolts of the raid and provides links for more information on related topics. Click on key figures involved in the Boston Tea Party, including Samuel Adams, Governor Thomas Hutchinson, and John Hancock, or on other events, such as the passage of the Intolerable Acts, to learn more.

If you want to get a sense of the chronology of the American Revolution and how the Boston Tea Party fit into it, explore the other topic headings in the index. "The End of Compromise," "The Stamp Act," "The Townshend Acts," "The Boston Massacre," and "The Burning of the HMS *Gaspee*" will all shed some light on why the Boston Tea Party took place. "The Intolerable Acts" and "Lexington and Concord" will sketch out the ultimate results of the Boston Tea Party.

The History Place
http://www.historyplace.com/unitedstates/revolution/teaparty.htm
middle school and up

Sometimes, the best way to learn about an important historical event is to read what people who experienced it had to say about it. So if you're looking for primary source material on the Boston Tea Party, you'll love this site. From the home page, select "1763–1775: Prelude to the Revolution" from the main index at the top of the screen. This will take you to an easy-to-read and detailed chronology of the events leading up to the American Revolution. You can scroll through this time line if you like, or proceed directly to 1773, where you'll see a link to "The Boston Tea Party." If you click on this, you can access a description of the event written by a man named George Hewes, who participated in dumping the tea into the Boston Harbor.

Perhaps you need primary documents about events that took place before or after the Tea Party. Then you can simply click on the links from the "Prelude to the Revolution" chronology. Are you interested in the build-up of tensions prior to the Tea Party? Then check out the 1765 "Resolution" that colonists sent to King George III requesting a repeal of the Stamp Act. If you want to explore some of the fallout from the Tea Party, scroll down to 1774, where you can follow the link to read a declaration drafted by the First Continental Congress disputing taxes imposed by the British.

BROWN V. BOARD OF EDUCATION

Best Search Engine:	http://www.google.com/
Key Search Terms:	Brown + Board of Education + history
	Desegregation + Brown + Board of Education

Brown v. Board of Education (1954)
http://www.civnet.org/resources/teach/basic/part6/36.htm
middle school and up

This straightforward Web site provides a clear overview of the landmark *Brown v. Board of Education* case along with a lengthy excerpt from the Supreme Court's decision. The introduction covers the cases before the Supreme Court about segregated schools that had preceded *Brown*, including *Plessy v. Ferguson, McLaurin v. Oklahoma State Regents,* and *Sweatt v. Painter.* This site is decidedly unglamorous. In fact, with the exception of one small picture, it's all text. But it will give you a lot of useful information about *Brown.* Just scroll down the home page to read it.

Brown vs. Board of Education: *The Interactive Experience*
http://www.digisys.net/users/hootie/Brown/
middle school and up

The emphasis in this site is on making the case of *Brown v. Board of Education* understandable. No legal jargon here. Instead, this site gives you the basic information about the landmark case with a lot of interactive features that makes learning about it fun. This site won't provide enough detailed information to be a single source for more advanced students. But it's perfect for younger students or for those of you just getting started on your research.

The site is divided into five main sections: "Background," "Linda Brown," "The Case," "Thurgood Marshall," and "Conclusion." Each of these contains a multimedia feature that illustrates the topic of the section. In "Background" you can listen to an audio clip of Martin Luther King Jr.'s "I Have a Dream" speech. Under "The Case" there's an audio clip of Earl Warren announcing the Court's decision in *Brown v. Board of Education.*

African-American Odyssey: *The Quest for Full Citizenship*
http://lcweb2.loc.gov/ammem/aaohtml/exhibit/aointro.html
middle school and up

This terrific site from the Library of Congress's *America's Story* online exhibits looks at the history of African Americans in the United States through primary documents and photographs. Most of you won't need to use the entire site, which begins its narrative with the introduction of slavery into the United States. However, one section of the site focuses specifically on *Brown v. Board of Education* and the subsequent desegregation of American schools.

To access the material about *Brown* and desegregation, select "Civil Rights" from the menu on the left side of the home page. Then click on "Desegregation" and scroll down the screen to read the excellent essay. As you work your way down the page, you'll encounter documents that illustrate the essay's points. Among other items, there's a letter from Thurgood Marshall to the National Association for the Advancement of Colored People (NAACP), a photograph of Marshall celebrating after the *Brown* decision, and material about James Meredith's heroic efforts to attend the University of Mississippi.

CHILD LABOR

Best Search Engine: http://www.goggle.com/

Key Search Terms: Child labor + American history

Child Labor in America 1908–1912
http://www.historyplace.com/unitedstates/childlabor
middle school and up

This site is a reminder of the bleak conditions under which children worked during the early twentieth century. Part of *The History Place*, it is a collection of photographs by Lewis W. Hine, a reformer who used photography to document the lives of child workers. The site contains a short overview of child labor and attempts at reform, which you can reach by clicking on "About These Photos" at the home page. However, the photos and captions are the major feature of this site. These reveal the horrible conditions under which children worked in a variety of jobs. Here you'll meet *newsies*, small children forced to sell newspapers late into the night, and boys working 10-hour days in mines. This is a very simple site. You have to scroll down to see the collection, and the photographs are in black and white; but the site clearly presents the tragedy of these children's lives.

CIVIL RIGHTS

Best Search Engine: http://www.goggle.com/

Key Search Terms: Civil rights + black history

Civil rights + history

Spartacus Encyclopedia: *Civil Rights 1860–1980*
http://www.spartacus.schoolnet.co.uk/USAcivilrights.htm
middle school and up

This site can tell you almost anything you'd ever want to know about the struggle for civil rights in the United States from the beginning of the Civil War to the dawn of the Reagan era! It has a huge number of links to essays about key figures, organizations, events, and issues in this long-running American morality play. You could spend hours on this site—and because it's so well designed, you'd never get lost.

Spartacus Encyclopedia: Civil Rights 1860–1980 breaks up its offerings both chronologically and between people and events/issues. But all of the information is accessible from the home page. You just need to scroll down to get to the sections that interest you. To learn about the NAACP, for example, look for the heading "1900–1980: Issues and Events" and find NAACP in the alphabetically arranged list. Following the link takes you to an essay about the history of the organization that has a tremendous number of links to articles on the people and issues important to the organization.

Another cool feature of many—but not all—of the other essays on the site is the selections from primary source documents at end of them. You can read comments from various contemporary figures (including Frederick Douglass, Abraham Lincoln, Andrew Johnson, and Supreme Court Justice Salmon P. Chase) on whether African Americans should be allowed to vote.

Civil Rights
http://www.wld.com/conbus/weal/wcivilri.htm
high school and up

You've heard the phrase *civil rights* used a whole lot, but have you ever stopped to wonder exactly what it means? This page can tell you. It's an entry on civil rights from the *West Legal Dictionary* that covers a whole lot more than just a simple definition of these words. Starting with a look at the meaning of the phrase, the essay goes on to explain how that meaning relates to the enactment of civil rights legislation.

But that's not all. The essay presents a comprehensive overview of the history of American civil rights legislation, starting with the drafting of the Constitution and the adoption of the Bill of Rights, through the Civil Rights Act of 1866 and the U.S. Supreme Court's decision in *Plessy v Ferguson*, which effectively took civil rights *away* from African Americans, all the way up to the Civil Rights Act of 1991. Although the essay is too complex for younger students, more advanced researchers will get a lot from it.

CIVIL RIGHTS ACTS

Best Search Engine: http://www.google.com/
Key Search Terms: Civil rights acts + history
                        Civil rights act + 1866
                        Civil rights act + 1875
                        Civil rights act + 1957
                        Civil rights act + 1960
                        Civil rights act + 1964
                        Civil rights act + 1968
                        Civil rights act + 1991
                        Lyndon Baines Johnson + civil rights + history

Spartacus Encyclopedia: *Civil Rights 1860–1980*
http://www.spartacus.schoolnet.co.uk/USAcivilrights.htm
middle school and up

If you're interested in the modern civil rights legislation, you'll probably want to approach this site by cruising down to the heading "1900–1980: Issues, Events, and Organizations" (it's most of the way down the very long home page). There you can click on the links that interest you. Obviously you'll want to hit "Civil Rights Act (1957)," "Civil Rights Act (1960)," and "Civil Rights Act (1964)." The 1964 act receives the most coverage here, but the essay on the 1960 act has a link you should follow to learn more about President Lyndon Baines Johnson, who was instrumental in securing the passage of the Civil Rights Act of 1964. Just click on the "Lyndon Baines Johnson" hypertext in the essay. You should also take a look at some of the other key laws, such as the "Voting Rights Act (1965)" and the "Immigration Act (1965)," passed during this period. And don't skip links such as "NAACP," which tell you about groups that played important roles in working to enact and put into practice the guarantees made by the civil rights acts.

As you did on this site if you investigated civil rights in the nineteenth century, you should then back up to the section dealing with key people of the era. Look for the "Campaigners: 1900–1980" heading and click away. Most of the essays have embedded links to the key people, places, and events that are involved in the issues the essays discuss, and you'll quickly come to recognize how interconnected the various twentieth century efforts to achieve civil rights were. Keep in mind that because this site ends its coverage in 1980, it has no information about

the Civil Rights Act of 1991. Oddly, it also overlooks the Civil Rights
Act of 1968. But given the breadth of *Spartacus Encyclopedia: Civil Rights
1860–1980*'s other offerings, these are only minor inconveniences.

EEOC: 35th Anniversary
http://www.eeoc.gov/35th/index.html
middle school and up

This site is filled with information to help you research this topic. It
was launched by the Equal Opportunity Employment Commission
(EEOC)—the government agency that was created by the Civil Rights
Act of 1964—to celebrate its history. *EEOC: 35th Anniversary* provides
a comprehensive overview of civil rights legislation in America. This
site draws material from a variety of perspectives. The photographs,
video clips, and other primary source documents make the subject come
alive. The time lines, essays, and interpretive material help you understand the significance of the civil rights acts and put the historic legislation into their historical contexts.

To begin your online journey into the history of civil rights legislation,
choose one of the topic headings—"History," "Milestones," "The Law,"
"Voices," or "Visions"—from the home page. You'll probably find the
"History" section to be the best place to learn the specifics about the
various civil rights acts. The "History" section is further subdivided into
eras so that you can focus your research more closely. Select from among
"Pre-1965," "1965–1971," "The 1970s," "The 1980s," "The 1990s," and
"The 2000s." Within each of these areas, you'll find photographs, videos,
and links to other documents. For instance, you can read the Civil
Rights Acts of 1964 and 1991, the Equal Employment Opportunity Act
of 1972, excerpts from President Kennedy's famous 1963 speech about
civil rights, and the audio file of the elder President Bush's speech before
he signed the Americans with Disabilities Act.

The other sections are also good resources. If you select "Milestones"
from the home page, you can access an excellent interactive time line.
For a brief look at the laws enforced by the EEOC, click on "The Law"
from the home page. The "Voices" section (click on the heading from
the home page) gives you a cool behind-the-scenes look at the EEOC's
history. You can read (or listen to) several oral history projects in which
EEOC personnel and people outside the agency reminisce about important events.

EEOC: 35th Anniversary is clearly written, easy-to-use, and a breeze
to navigate. It's also one of the few Web sites out there that concentrates
on the history of modern civil rights legislation as a whole. The only
downside is that it sometimes focuses a little *too* closely on important

events within the EEOC (especially in the "History" section) that might be of less interest to the general reader. Nevertheless, you'll love the breadth and depth of this site's offerings and its many interactive features. Just remember that it doesn't cover the two nineteenth century civil rights acts. For information on those, use a site like *Spartacus Encyclopedia: 1860–1980* (discussed previously).

CIVIL RIGHTS MOVEMENT

Best Search Engine: http://www.google.com/

Key Search Terms: Civil rights movement + history

Martin Luther King Jr. + civil rights

Civil Rights: A Status Report
http://www.ghgcorp.com/hollaway/civil.htm
high school and up

This vast Web site provides a detailed history of the Civil Rights movement in America. While most people think of the Civil Rights movement as having begun in the 1950s, this site charts the nearly 400-year struggle of African Americans for civil rights in the United States. As the author says in his introduction, "We would be remiss if we ignore the earlier struggles that laid an immovable foundation for freedom and equality in America." *Civil Rights: A Status Report* is definitely for more advanced students. The site is dense, comprised almost entirely of plain text, and written at a high level. It's worth the effort, though. *Civil Rights: A Status Report* is an excellent resource that is both thoughtful and encyclopedic. But remember that this is not the ideal Web site to use if you want to find information in a hurry.

When you enter the site, you are automatically taken to an introductory page. Scroll to the bottom of that screen to access the "Table of Contents," which contains many "chapter" headings (arranged chronologically). The site begins with the "Discovery of the New World," and devotes a lot of attention to the history of slavery, the Compromise of 1850, and the rise of the Ku Klux Klan in the South. Although you might want to skip this material because it's not directly relevant to the modern Civil Rights movement, these chapters do a lot to help put the modern movement in context. It's only when you have a sense of the persecution that African Americans have endured that you begin to understand the significance of the quest for equality during the modern Civil Rights movement.

If you do want to limit your reading to the modern Civil Rights movement, scroll down the "Table of Contents" until you reach "The Democratic Convention of 1948." The next 25 or so chapters cover the period you want. Near the end of the "Table of Contents," you'll see "Opinion" essays on a variety of topics. These are interesting, but not terribly informative. Farther below is another section, "Final Analysis," that contains links to essays that give a quicker synopsis of various eras. The most relevant essays to the modern Civil Rights movement are "WWII and the Beginnings of Change," "The New Movement Begins," "Change Finally Comes," and "Non-Violence Yields to Chaos."

Timeline of the American Civil Rights Movement
http://www.wmich.edu/politics/mlk/
middle school and up

This is a great site if you just want to get a handle on the key events of the modern Civil Rights movement! Unlike *Civil Rights: A Status Report,* this site is perfect for younger students—or anyone who wants to learn the basics about the Civil Rights movement. As its name suggests, *Timeline of the American Civil Rights Movement* condenses the Civil Rights movement into an easy-to-digest time line that highlights the key events of the period.

The time line runs down the left side of the home page. Just click on the events that interest you. The topics are *"Brown v. the Board of Education,"* "Montgomery Bus Boycott," "Desegregation at Little Rock," "Sit-in Campaign," "Freedom Rides," "Mississippi Riot," "Birmingham," "March on Washington," and "Selma." When you click on a topic, a short essay with photographs appears on the right side of the screen. You can access primary source material from some of the essays. For instance from the "Birmingham" section, you can click on a link to read Martin Luther King Jr.'s "I Have a Dream" speech.

Martin Luther King Jr.
http://www.seattletimes.com/mlk/index.html
middle school and up

No one person defined the Civil Rights movement more clearly than Martin Luther King Jr. This Web site focuses on King's life, his accomplishments, and his role as the leader of the Civil Rights movement. This site is particularly terrific because it incorporates multimedia exhibits that really make the topic come alive! You can listen to excerpts from King's speeches and view a number of photographs. Also it's a good resource for younger students or those searching for basic information about King because although it is fairly comprehensive, the site doesn't go into too much detail.

To navigate the site, use the menu on the left side of the home page. To find out how King influenced the Civil Rights movement, click on "Civil Rights Timeline" from the main menu. King was also a fabulous public speaker, and this site lets you actually hear (rather than just read) some of his words. Click on "In His Own Voice," which contains audio clips, to listen to clips from his two most famous speeches—"I Have a Dream" and "Let Freedom Ring." For pictures of King and scenes from the Civil Rights movement, go to "Photo Gallery" from the main menu.

The site has several other good features as well. If you're trying to get a sense of King's impact on both the Civil Rights movement and American society, check out the "Legacy" section where you can read first-hand accounts by people inspired by King. If you want to test your King I.Q., go to the "Interactive Classroom" where you can take an interactive quiz and use an online study guide.

CIVIL WAR

Best Search Engine: http://www.google.com/
Key Search Terms: Civil War + American + history
                     Confederate States of America + Civil War
                     Abraham Lincoln + Civil War

Shotgun's Home of the American Civil War
http://www.civilwarhome.com/
middle school and up

This enormous site is one of the best general Web sites about the Civil War. Not only does it have a vast amount of information on many topics, it's well-organized, clearly written, and fun. There aren't many other places where you can find material on subjects ranging from the rations given to Confederate soldiers to the role of women in the war.

Shotgun's Home of the American Civil War is organized into topic headings so that you can easily browse the site. You'll find these subject headings on the home page. Those that will probably be most helpful include "Civil War Battles," "Civil War Biographies," "Civil War Medicine," "Civil War Potpourri," "Confederate States of America," "Essays on the Civil War," "Letters About the Civil War," "Overview of the Civil War," "Naval War," and "The Armies."

If you're just beginning your research and are looking for an easy-to-follow overview of the major events of the Civil War, you'll find "Overview of the Civil War" an invaluable asset. Many Web sites on the Civil War tend to get bogged down in a lot of details. With this "Overview" you simply select the time period that interests you, and you can read a simple—yet comprehensive—review of the events. You'll also find links within the text to access more information on key people and events.

Another helpful section is "Civil War Biographies" that provides short biographies of key players. Each essay includes a picture and concentrates on the individual's role in the Civil War. All you military historians will like "Civil War Battles." This section not only gives you a description of the major and the minor battles, but also contains the "Official Records of the War of the Rebellion," which are the reports filed by the officers involved in the battles. These first-hand accounts of the battles make them a lot more interesting and relevant! For more military information read the "Civil War Medicine," "Naval War," and "The Armies." If you need to find some short secondary source material, check out "Essays on the Civil War."

One of the great things about this site is that it provides background on the war and events beyond the battlefield. You find most of this information by clicking on "Civil War Potpourri" that contains information on such topics as states rights, the Missouri Compromise, and the New York City draft riots. The "Civil War Potpourri" section has a wealth of material on a lot of other subjects as well, such as Civil War weapons and even General Robert E. Lee's horse Traveller. If you don't find the information you are looking for in other sections, check out "Potpourri."

AmericanCivilWar.com
http://www.americancivilwar.com/
middle school and up

This is another great Web site about the Civil War. While it doesn't have the variety of information you can find in *Shotgun's Home of the American Civil War*, it does give you information on topics that *Shotgun's* glosses over or doesn't cover. If you need information on African American troops, just go to "Colored Troops" under "Featured Indexes" on the home page, and you'll find a short history of their role in the war. You'll even find a list of African Americans who won the Medal of Honor. You can also get information on "Women in the War." Read the reminiscence of Ida Baker, a South Carolina woman, or a biography of Rose O'Neal Greenhow, who spied for the Confederacy. The site also has a really great time line of the war.

Just like *Shotgun's*, *AmericanCivilWar.com* has a list of Civil War battles. Unlike *Shotgun's* narratives of the battles, *AmericanCivilWar.com* presents a quick overview. Each battle entry includes a short description of battle, its location, the results, date of battle, principal commanders, forces engaged, and estimated casualties. The site also includes suggested "Additional Reading."

Ulysses S. Grant Home Page
http://www.mscomm.com/~ulysses/
middle school and up

What better way to learn about the Civil War than through the life of one of its key participants? This Web site provides an incredibly detailed biography of Ulysses S. Grant, with whole sections dedicated to his role as a general in the Union Army during the Civil War. There are loads of photos, transcripts of interviews from people acquainted with Grant, and excerpts from his diary.

To learn about the Civil War, scroll down the biographical menu on the left side of the home page until you find the "Civil War" heading. Beneath this heading is a list of more specific topics, such as "His Battles," "Great Soldier," "Military Genius," "Grant and Lee," "Appomattox," and "Secession," to help you hone your search. If you select "His Battles," you'll find a wealth of information about major Civil War battles, including battle summaries, maps, Grant's recollections, photographs, and an explanation of the significance of each battle. "Grant and Lee" provides an analysis of the similarities and differences between these two leaders, while "Appomattox" includes Grant's account of Lee's final surrender.

Keep in mind that this Web site doesn't give an overview of the Civil War or provide more general information as does *Shotgun's Home of the American Civil War*. But *Ulysses S. Grant Home Page* does offer you an in-depth view of one of the most important figures of the Civil War.

COLD WAR

Best Search Engine: http://www.google.com/
Key Search Terms: Cold War + history

The Cold War
http://cnn.com/SPECIALS/cold.war/guides/about.series/
middle school and up

Web sites like this one give the Internet a good name! This site, which is a companion to CNN's critically acclaimed television series, has everything you need to research the Cold War—essays, biographies, interactive time lines, video and audio clips, primary documents, interactive maps. Many of the Web sites that are part of television specials try to do one, and only one, thing—get you or your teacher to watch the program. *The Cold War,* on the other hand, is like the original documentary series on steroids. It has everything the program did—and a whole lot more!

The best way to approach this giant site is to use the "Episode-By-Episode" guide (look in the menu on the left side of the home page). You can pick the period that interests you, or you can explore all 24 episodes of *The Cold War* (which cover from 1917 to 1991). If you want a quick overview of the period you've selected, click on "Episode Recap." For those of you with more time on your hands, check out "Episode Script." After you've gotten down the basics, you can dive into the wealth of information available to you on each episode.

For instance, if you're surfing the section on Episode Nine, "The Wall," you can view an interactive image of Checkpoint Charlie on the Berlin Wall, listen to the radio-on-the-scene report as the wall went up, and look at an interactive map on "How the Wall Worked." You can also read interviews with people who lived in both East Berlin and West Berlin when the wall was up. If you need historical documents, look no further than the episode screen. You can access President Kennedy's speech on the Berlin Crisis, Soviet Premier Khrushchev's response to that speech, and several other documents. Each episode screen also provides background information for the installment. In "The Wall" section, for instance, you can easily access biographies of U.S. Secretary of State John Foster Dulles and others. You can also click on the "Cold War Timeline" from this screen. Each online episode guide also has "Online Spotlights." In "The Wall," you can check out the differences in media coverage on the Berlin Wall between the United States and the Soviet Union. Don't forget to use the "Message Board" (also available on each episode screen) if you have questions or comments.

The Cold War has other incredible—and easy to access—material that is just a click away. "The Cold War Experience" (look in the menu on the left of the site's home page) provides multimedia media journeys on a variety of Cold War topics such as "Culture," "Technology," "Espionage," and "The Bomb."

If you approach this site looking for specific information, say a particular document, photograph, or biography, go directly to the "Knowledge Bank" (in the same menu as "The Cold War Experience"). From here, you can access the "Cold War Chronology," a handy interactive time line (simply click on the year that interests you), "Interactive Maps" (pick the one that applies to your research), "Historical Documents" (you can scroll through the list), and "Interactive Images." Better yet is "Profiles," which provides biographies of key figures in the Cold War, and "The Cold War Glossary," which allows you to search terms and subjects.

When you're done mining this site, perhaps you'd like to test your Cold War I.Q. If so, take the "Cold War Challenge," an interactive game that'll test whether you've really learned the subject. You'll find the link to the game from the menu on the left side of the home page. Teachers will like "Educator's Guide," which can be found in the same menu as the "Cold War Challenge."

The Cold War Museum
http://www.coldwar.org/index.html
middle school and up

Like CNN's *The Cold War*, this Web site offers you a broad range of material on the Cold War. It's well organized—all you have to do is pick the decade that interests you—and easy to understand. You might want to begin your research on this Web site with a visit to *The Cold War Museum*'s special feature, its "Online Exhibits." Simply click on the topic from the toolbar on the left side of the home page. Then you can browse the virtual halls of an exhibit of CIA posters from the Cold War era, an exhibit on the Berlin Wall, a collection of Cold War patches, a photo gallery, and a reconnaissance aircraft exhibit.

When you're ready to home in on your topic, use the "Timeline" menu from the bottom of the home page. After you pick a decade, you'll be presented with a list of topics. For instance, under the 1940s, you can choose the "Separation of Berlin," the "Marshall Plan," or the "Berlin Blockade" from a number of subject headings. Click on one to access a brief but thorough essay on the topic. What's really cool about *The Cold War Museum* site is that it makes tons of links available to you. At the bottom of each essay, you'll see a place to click if you want more information. If you select this button, you can access a vast list of other Web sites that provide extra material.

Although most of the rest of *The Cold War Museum* is devoted to talking about the museum itself, there are a couple of other great resources. If you like computer games, click on "Trivia Game" from the menu at the top of the home page. You can play one of three games, the best of which is the "Interactive Cold War Trivia Quiz." If you'd like to join an online conversation about the Cold War, click on "Discussion Forum" from the same menu on which you found "Trivia Game."

COLONIAL AMERICA

Best Search Engine: http://www.google.com/

Key Search Terms: Colonial America + history

Early America + history

13 Originals: Founding the American Colonies
http://www.timepage.org/spl/13colony.html
middle school and up

Although this Web site is somewhat disorganized, it does provide a lot of useful information about colonial American history. It's a good place to start your research, especially since it has a lot of links to other Web sites that can give you further information.

If you're looking for maps, check out the top of the home page, where you'll find links to various maps of colonial America. The rest of the Web site is organized according to colony. Below each of the thirteen colony entries, you'll find a very brief overview of that colony's history. You'll almost certainly need to know more than this snippet provides, so scan through the helpful links that follow. Under "New York," for instance, you can link to several great sites, including the "New York History Net," "The New Netherland Project," and "Drums Along the Mohawk." The "1621 Charter of the Dutch West India Company" and the "New York Constitution" are also only a click away.

Because *13 Originals* acts as a portal to Internet resources about colonial America, it can point you in the right direction to complete your research. However since the site is arranged by colony, you won't find much material on colonial America as a whole.

The American Colonist's Library: A Treasury of Primary Documents
http://personal.pitnet.net/primarysources/
middle school and up

Are you looking for primary source documents to support your research on colonial America? If you are, this Web site is a must visit. It has everything!

The Web site is arranged chronologically. Just scroll down the home page to move forward in time. The first part of the site lists books and papers that the American colonists themselves read. You can check out the documents that contributed to the formation of American politics, culture, and ideals—from the Vulgate Bible to Copernicus's *On Revolutions of the Heavenly Bodies*.

Most of you are probably looking for the documents that the colonists wrote. To view these, scroll down the home page screen until you find the heading "Seventeenth Century Documents Relating to American History." Choose the ones that interest you from the dozens available. The Settlement of Jamestown (1607), the Mayflower Compact (1620), and the Harvard College Admissions and Graduation Requirements (1642–1700) are just a few of the gems you'll find. Mixed in with these American works are writings by European authors of this period that influenced the colonists. Continue down the screen to find "Eighteenth Century Sources," such as *The Selling of Joseph* (1700), an early argument against the slave trade, Cotton Mather's sermons from 1709, and the Constitution of the Iroquois Confederacy.

The Web site doesn't have a search feature, but you can use your browser's "Find" function to search the library.

COLUMBUS, VOYAGES OF

Best Search Engine: http://www.google.com/
Key Search Terms: Christopher Columbus + history
Discovering America
Christopher Columbus + Native Americans

1492: An Ongoing Voyage
http://www.ibiblio.org/expo/1492.exhibit/Intro.html
middle school and up

This excellent online exhibit from the Library of Congress examines the collision of cultures that resulted from Christopher Columbus's historic voyage into the New World. The site is divided into six sections: "What Came to Be Called America," "The Mediterranean World," "Christopher Columbus: Man and Myth," "Inventing America," "Europe Claims America," and "Epilogue." Each section sheds light on a unique facet of Europe's "discovery" of America. You can read the whole exhibit (simply follow the prompts at the bottom of the screens) or you can pick and choose the topics that interest you from the site's outline (to find the outline, click on "Jump Ship" at the bottom of any page).

We all know that "in 1492 Columbus sailed the ocean blue," but what was life like in the Americas before he and his colleagues showed up? Read "What Came to be Called America" to find out. In this section you'll find a brief overview of the native cultures throughout the New World. There is a different Web page for each region (such as "Caribbean Societies" and "North America"), so be sure to follow the links at the bottom of the pages to get the full picture. In addition to the text, you'll find links to view objects, maps, pictures, and documents. "The

Mediterranean World" gives you some background on Columbus's roots. You'll learn what his world was like and why Europe was expanding its horizons.

"Christopher Columbus: Man and Myth" focuses on the explorer himself. You can read his biography and learn how he got the commission to set sail. Don't forget to check out his *Book of Privileges*, which is the collection of agreements between him and the Spanish crown. "Inventing America" and "Europe Claims America" deal with the impact of Europeans on native cultures, how the explorers thought of the natives, and how they established their dominance on the continent. You'll learn how the Spaniards virtually wiped out Caribbean tribes within 20 years of their arrival. These sections also discuss the introduction of African culture (as the first slaves were brought over) to the New World. The "Epilogue" reveals the legacy of European discovery and settlement of the Americas.

1492: An Ongoing Voyage is a terrific resource because it is comprehensive and easy to use. Even better, it tells the story of European discovery from different perspectives: Columbus, the Europeans, and the Native Americans who suffered and lost a great deal because of this "progress."

The Columbus Navigation Home Page
http://www1.minn.net/~keithp/
middle school and up

Like *1492: An Ongoing Voyage*, this Web site is comprehensive, authoritative, and quite helpful—especially for all you intrepid explorers. This site's special strength is that it explains *how*, with limited technology, Columbus was able to complete his journeys to the New World. The site doesn't have much biographical material on Columbus, but it more than makes up for this with its vast array of material on the voyages themselves.

The Columbus Navigation Home Page is organized into three main sections: "Columbus's Navigation," "Columbus History," and "Columbus Special Topics." The "Navigation" section, which is further divided by topic, deals with the types of navigation Columbus used on his voyages. It also has sections on how distances were measured in his time and on his ships (what their dimensions were and why they were constructed as they were). Although this section deals with fairly complex material, it is clearly written and easy to understand.

"Columbus History" provides some information about Columbus's life. Click on the "Timeline" to access it. The rest of the section is dedicated to describing his voyages. (It is divided according to voyage, so click on the one that interests you.) "Columbus History" provides detailed descriptions of each voyage, and uses maps to analyze the routes he took. If you want to read Columbus's thoughts on his trips, follow the links to obtain a summary of his logbooks. The "Columbus Special Topics" section has a number of interesting essays. "Who Really Discovered America?" discusses the explorers who preceded Columbus to the Americas, which brings into question Columbus's status in history textbooks. "Columbus and the Destruction of Native Peoples" casts a different sort of doubt on Columbus's heroic status. At the bottom of the Web site, you can access links to other Columbus-related Web sites.

CONFEDERATE STATES OF AMERICA

Best Search Engine: http://www.google.com/

Key Search Terms: Confederate States of America + Civil War
                         Civil War + American History

Shotgun's Home of the American Civil War
http://www.civilwarhome.com/
middle school and up

This enormous site is one of the best general Web sites about the Civil War on the Internet. Not only does it have a vast amount of information on many topics, it's well-organized, clearly written, and fun. Although most of the site is devoted to the war and military topics (explained previously), it is also a great place to learn about the politics of the Confederate States of America.

Shotgun's Home of the American Civil War is organized into topic headings so that you can easily browse the site. To find the information on the Confederacy scroll to "Confederate States of America" on the home page. This gives you a list of links to both military and political information. The links you will find most helpful are "Overview of the Confederacy," "Causes of the Civil War" (as viewed by Confederates), "Confederate Heads of State" (the Confederate Cabinet), and "Confederate Senators." There is also a section that provides background information on the Confederate constitution as well as a copy of the constitution marked to show differences between it and the U.S. Constitution.

Documenting the American South
"The Southern Home Front: 1861–1865"
http://docsouth.unc.edu/imls/index.html
high school and up

This excellent Web site from the University of North Carolina at Chapel Hill Libraries will enable you to grasp the Civil War from the perspective of the Confederacy. You can read all sorts of primary texts from this unique period in southern American history. You'll find a collection of the Confederate government's laws and other official documents, examples of Confederate currencies, copies of sermons delivered during this period, excerpts from letter, diaries, almanacs, and magazines, and official documents from the various state governments. Not only is this Web site incredibly rich, it is also really easy to use!

From the home page, click on "Topical Access to the Collection" to find a list of the various collections of primary documents you can browse. In addition to "Belles-Lettres" (an introduction to the novels and poetry of the Confederacy) and "Economic Affairs" (proceedings and reports from companies and first-hand accounts of business conditions in the Confederacy), you can access collections on "Education" (examples of Confederate textbooks), "Confederate Official Documents," "Politics and Social Issues" (speeches and opinions published in the Confederacy), "Home Life" (personal letters and diaries), "Religion," "Science and Medicine," and "State Official Documents."

Once you've selected a collection, you can spend hours reading and browsing. For example, if you're looking in "Confederate Official Documents," you'll find "An Act Relative to Prisoners of War (1861)," "The Statutes-at-Large of the Confederate States of America," and "A Bill to Prohibit Dealing in the Paper Currency of the Enemy." In the "Politics and Social Issues," you can read "Remarks on the Subject of the Ownership of Slaves (1863)" and the "Guide for the Claimants of Deceased Soldiers (1864)."

Although *Documenting the American South* is an ideal Web site for finding first-hand accounts and primary source material on life in the Confederate States of America, it doesn't give you second-hand interpretations of the material it provides. Use other Web sites, such as *Shotgun's Home of the American Civil War*, to place these documents in their historical context.

CONSERVATION MOVEMENT

Best Search Engine: http://www.google.com/

Key Search Terms: Conservation movement + history

The Evolution of the Conservation Movement 1850–1920
http://memory.loc.gov/ammem/amrevhtml/conshome.html
high school and up

The Evolution of the Conservation Movement is a great source for background and documents on the reform movement formed to conserve and protect America's natural heritage. Here you'll find almost 800 books, pamphlets, government documents, manuscripts, and photos on the subject. The site is part of the *American Memory Project* of the Library of Congress, so the focus is on primary sources; but it also contains an excellent chronology. To access that, scroll to "Chronology of Selected Events" at the bottom of the home page and choose the time period you need. Reading the entire chronology gives you a great overview of the movement. The chronology includes links to key documents and players such as Henry David Thoreau, Albert Bierstadt, and John Muir.

If you need only documents, you can access them directly from the home page, either by key word search, subject, author, or title. The collection includes a tremendous amount of material including samples of Bierstadt's paintings to the text of the law creating Yosemite National Park to rare films of Theodore Roosevelt.

CONSTITUTION, U.S.

Best Search Engine: http://www.goggle.com/
Key Search Terms: U.S. Constitution + history
Founding fathers + Constitution

A Roadmap to the U.S. Constitution
http://library.thinkquest.org/11572/
middle school and up

This fantastic Web site explores the U.S. Constitution from lots of different angles—and it does so in a straightforward style that will make sense to all students. In easy to understand language, *A Roadmap to the U.S. Constitution* discusses the history behind the famous document and gives a detailed look at the creation of the Constitution. The site also presents the Constitution as a living document. You can read about contemporary Constitutional issues and Supreme Court cases that affect everyone.

A Roadmap to the U.S. Constitution is divided into five major sections. To read the Constitution, click on "Constitution" from the main menu on the left side of the home page. You'll have the option to "Browse the Constitution," or if you're in a hurry, you can get an overview of the "Important Sections." If you click on "Origins" from the main menu, you can trace the people, events, and concepts that influenced the Constitution's framers. Within this section, you can select the period that interests you: "When in Rome" (impact of Classical thinkers), "English Influences" (such as the Magna Carta), "Colonial Influences" (like the Mayflower Compact), or "Philosophers" (Locke, Montesquieu, and Rousseau).

If you want to learn the nitty-gritty of how the Constitution was hammered out, click on "Creation" from the main menu. In this section, there are several good pieces. Select "Delegate Dossiers" for biographies of some of the Constitutional delegates. "Virginia and New Jersey Plans" talks about the two competing blueprints for the Constitution. "Smoothing Out the Bumps" discusses the many conflicts that arose at the convention and explains how they were resolved. "Federalists and Anti-Federalists" explores how these conflicts continued after the document was written.

Are you interested in the Constitution's history once it was down on paper? If so, look at "Issues and Cases" from the main menu. The "Issues" section discusses Constitutional issues from the past to the present, such as abortion, affirmative action, capital punishment, judicial review, and slavery. "Cases" provides a brief history of the most important cases of the Supreme Court.

If you already have a sense of what you're looking for, you can skip browsing entirely and just go directly to the site's handy search engine (you'll find it at the center of the home page). Those of you with questions and comments will like the site's two online bulletin boards. Click on "Messages" to access these.

This Web site has a lot of information—and it's fun and easy to navigate. However, A Roadmap to the U.S. Constitution doesn't go into a tremendous amount of detail. More advanced students will want to bolster their research with material from sites such as The Constitution of the United States.

The Constitution of the United States
http://www.nara.gov/exhall/charters/constitution/conmain.html
middle school and up

Like A Roadmap to the U.S. Constitution, this Web site is comprehensive. However, it goes into a lot more detail, making it a better choice for high school and college students. One bonus feature of this Web site is that you can view digital copies of the Constitution itself.

The Constitution of the United States is organized into several sections, which you can access from the main menu on the home page. Click on "The Founding Fathers" to access biographies of all 55 delegates to the Constitutional Convention. To read the Constitution, select "Transcription" from the home page. As you browse the document you'll find links to the biographies of the 39 delegates who signed it. Amended passages are also linked, so you can see how the Constitution has changed over the years.

For an in-depth view of the Constitutional Convention and the ratification process, check out the long essay in the "More Perfect Union" section. There is also a helpful short essay on George Mason and why he opposed the adoption of the Constitution. For fast and fun facts about the document, click on "Questions and Answers Pertaining to the Constitution." In addition, the site has a transcript of a speech by Dr. Michael Beschloss explaining how the actual document that was drafted in 1787 has been protected and preserved over the years. To feast your eyes on an original copy, simply scroll down the screen until you have the option to download digital copies of the document a page at a time.

James Madison: His Legacy
http://www.jmu.edu/madison/
middle school and up

James Madison is often called the Father of the Constitution because of the important role he played in writing the document and getting it ratified. You can learn a lot about the political thought, issues, and events surrounding the Constitution by studying his life. This encyclopedic Web site can tell you everything you've ever wanted to know about James Madison—and then some! But don't worry. The site is a snap to navigate, and it's easy to find the information on Madison and the Constitution.

For a basic overview of Madison's life, click on "Biography" from the menu on the home page. If you want to focus your research more specifically on Madison and his relationship to the Constitution, just browse the following sections of the site: "American Confederations," "Constitution," "Federalist Papers," and "Bill of Rights." Of course if you're interested in Madison's presidency, you can click on "President James Madison" from the main menu.

In "American Confederations," you can read Madison's notes on the Articles of Confederation, the basis of U.S. central government prior to the Constitution. In these notes, Madison outlines the weaknesses of the Articles and lays out the themes that he would return to in more detail in the *Federalist Papers*. In the "Constitution" section, you can read both Madison's letters about the Constitutional Convention and his notes on the debates there. These letters are particularly helpful if you want to explore the clash between Federalists and Anti-Federalists at the Convention. The "Federalist Papers" allows you to read the full text of the document. In this section you can also access a letter Madison wrote to Thomas Jefferson about the Constitution. In the "Bill of Rights" section you'll find several documents written (at least in part) by Madison in which he again addresses federalist issues. Remember that the Bill of Rights was a compromise measure incorporated into the Constitution so that Anti-Federalists would accept the document. The Virginia Declaration of Rights was a precursor to the Constitutional Bill of Rights. There's also an "Introduction" to the Bill of Rights and Madison's speech when he proposed the Bill of Rights to the Constitutional Convention.

To Form a More Perfect Union
http://memory.loc.gov/ammem/bdsds/bdexhome.html
high school and up

See **Continental Congress** for description.

CONSTITUTIONAL HISTORY

Best Search Engine: http://www.google.com/

Key Search Terms: American constitutional history

                     American legal history

FindLaw
http://www.findlaw.com/casecode/constitution
upper high school and up

If you are looking for a comprehensive site on constitutional law, *FindLaw* is the place for you. Here you will find commentary, called annotations, for each of the articles and amendments. These annotations provide an overview of judicial thought on the various issues generated by constitutional provisions. The site breaks down annotations into general areas, which are further divided into specific topics. For example general areas under "First Amendment" include "Free Exercise of Religion," "Freedom of Belief," and "Maintenance of National Security and the First Amendment." Specific topics include school prayer, obscenity, right of association, and seditious libel.

The site is simple to use. Just click on the article or amendment and then chose the area or topic you want to research. Be aware, however, that the writing is scholarly; but for upper-level students, this site is a goldmine.

CONTAINMENT

Best Search Engine: http://www.google.com/

Key Search Terms: Truman Doctrine + history

Harry Truman + foreign policy + history

Truman + containment

Containment: 1947–1949
http://history.acusd.edu/gen/20th/truman47.html
middle school and up

Containment became the dominant American foreign policy in the late 1940s and early 1950s. The policy was based on the notion that the best way to handle the Soviet Union was to recognize that it had expansionist goals (that it wanted to export Communism around the world) and to construct a policy aimed at thwarting that effort. In other words, rather than aiming to stamp out Communism in the Soviet Union itself, the containment doctrine was geared toward making sure that the Soviets couldn't put a Communist system in place elsewhere.

Containment: 1947–1949 lists the major applications of this foreign policy in an easy-to-follow outline format. It proceeds chronologically, starting with the Truman Doctrine and the Marshall Plan and goes through Truman's Point Four Program. Within the text are links to more information or to view primary texts. You can read Truman's speech on the need to give aid to Turkey and Greece to prevent a Communist takeover. You can also follow the links to learn about the Marshall Plan, the formation of NATO, Truman's Loyalty Program, and the National Security Act. Off to the right side of the screen are photographs, political cartoons, and magazine illustrations about containment. Don't miss the copy of the cover from the 1948 *US News* that explained why the American government should provide aid to Turkey.

CONTINENTAL CONGRESS

Best Search Engine: http://www.google.com/

Key Search Terms: American + Continental Congress

To Form a More Perfect Union
http://memory.loc.gov/ammem/bdsds/bdexhome.html
high school and up

Here's a great site for researching the Continental Congress, which governed the United States from 1774 to the adoption of the Constitution in 1789. You can learn how the Congress organized the Revolutionary War and inspired citizens to support independence. The site also provides background on the key issues facing the Congress after the war, particularly the problem of incorporating western territories that led to the passage of the Northwest Ordinance of 1787. Finally, you can review the limitations of the Articles of Confederation, the basis of U.S. central government prior to the Constitution, and trace the steps in the creation of the Constitution.

The site is primarily text with links to key players and important documents. To get to the era you want, simply click on the appropriate topic at the opening page. If you just want documents, you can scroll to "Continental Congress and Constitutional Convention Broadsides" at the bottom of the screen. From there you can access 274 documents, either by keyword or subject. The documents include treaties, laws, congressional reports, resolutions, and proclamations as well as the Declaration of Independence and the Constitution. If you just want a flavor of some of the documents, use the links in the text. Such links will transfer you to broadsides, such as one signed "Constitutional Mechanic," addressing criticism of the Congress. "Suffer not yourselves to be misled by partial representation; not to be deluded by the false clamours of designing men: but consult the real interest of the State and the happiness of your country." The language is eighteenth century, but the thoughts are very modern. The site also contains a concise chronology that you can access through "Continental Congress and Constitutional Convention Broadsides" at the bottom of each screen.

CUBAN MISSILE CRISIS

Best Search Engine: http://www.google.com/
Key Search Terms: Cuban missile crisis + history
                       Cuban missile crisis + documents
                       Fidel Castro + Cuban missile crisis

14 Days in October: The Cuban Missile Crisis
http://library.thinkquest.org/11046/
middle school and up

This fantastic site takes you about as close as you can get to the Cuban missile crisis without wanting to head for a bomb shelter. Divided into six sections—"Crisis Center," "Briefing," "Situation Room," "The Players," "Recon Room," and "Debriefing"—*14 Days in October* is a research bonanza. "Crisis Center" fills you in on all the events surrounding the crisis. The "Situation Room" contains some great primary source materials—including letters from President John F. Kennedy and Soviet Premier Nikita Khrushchev, diplomatic cables, and audio and video files of President Kennedy's speech to the American people warning them about the unfolding events. Learn about the men who played crucial roles during the crisis in "The Players." With offerings like these, you could (and should) spend a lot of time browsing this site; but if you're in a hurry, just go straight to "Briefing Room" where you'll get a condensed version of what the site can do for you.

Getting around *14 Days in October* is a breeze. You can link to any of the six sections from the introductory paragraph at the top of the home page, or just scroll down for a while (you'll need to skip over a rather lengthy recitation of the site's own history and accolades) until you get to the heading "Where Can I Go On This Site?" Then just click and go. You don't even need to hop back to the home page to move among the sections. Just use the buttons on the left side of each screen.

Foreign Relations of the United States
"Vol. XI, Cuban Missile Crisis and Aftermath"
http://www.state.gov/www/about_state/history/frusXI/index.html
high school and up

If you want to find primary source documents that show exactly what the American foreign policy team knew and did during these dark days of 1962 and afterwards, you've got to check out this site. This State Department site gives you access to all kinds of official documents— minutes of meetings that included President John F. Kennedy and his national security team, letters between Kennedy and Khrushchev, digests of intelligence reports, and a whole lot more. Unfortunately, the site is horribly organized. There's no way to search for specific documents or even to pick out individual documents from among the longer threads the site presents. But if you spend some time browsing, you'll be rewarded with an unparalleled sense of how the decision makers handled the crisis.

Cuban Missile Crisis Revisited: October 16, 1997
http://www.pbs.org/newshour/bb/latin_america/July-dec97/cuba_10-16a.
    html
middle school and up

Unlike *14 Days in October*, which presents its background information with an eye toward making you feel like you're there, this site tries to put the event into a more historical perspective. The transcript of a PBS television news program commemorating the 25th anniversary of the crisis, *Cuban Missile Crisis Revisited* consists of a brief overview of the crisis and a panel discussion among several historians and Premier Khrushchev's son.

When you go to this site, you'll first see the overview page. Read through it and then scroll back to the top to find the link to the roundtable discussion. The discussion is particularly useful because it gives you a sense of how ordinary Americans reacted to the crisis.

The Challenge of Democracy
http://www.hpol.org/jfk/cuban/
middle school and up

This site takes advantage of one of the Internet's best features for researchers—it's not limited just to text. At this site, you can access audio files of recordings made in the Oval Office during the crisis. In other words, you can hear President Kennedy talking with his advisors and reviewing his options *in his own voice*. This site is also great because, unlike the State Department site, it actually helps you find what you want. There's a brief introductory essay that gives an overview of the crisis, and then the essay is replaced by an audio file on a detailed time line that traces the course of the crisis. The site even summarizes the material contained in the audio files in handy blurbs just after each individual link. It's a phenomenal resource.

D DAY

Best Search Engine:	http://www.yahoo.com/
Key Search Terms:	D day + history
	Normandy invasion + history
	World War II + D day
	Eisenhower + D day

Normandy: 1944
http://normandy.eb.com/
middle school and up

If you are looking for information on the Allied invasion of Normandy (or D day), *Normandy: 1944* has everything you'll need. It contains detailed descriptions of D day and its aftermath, photographs, maps, documentary clips, newsreels, audio files, online special exhibits, personal histories, documents, and biographies of key figures. It even has a link to a feature on the history behind the blockbuster D day movie *Saving Private Ryan*.

The site is divided into five main sections: "Build-Up," "Invasion," "Fighting Inland," "Breakout," and "Normandy in Memory." Each section has an excellent essay about the specific topic written by renowned military historian John Keegan. "Build-Up" discusses the year before the invasion and goes into the planning of D day. "Invasion" describes the Allied troop landing at the Normandy beachhead, while "Fighting Inland" describes the postinvasion battles in June and July of 1944, and "Breaking Out" covers the drive to the river Seine and the liberation of Paris. "Normandy in Memory" discusses the legacy of D day and its significance. You'll see links in the articles to more information on the people and places mentioned.

Reading these essays is only the beginning, though. Look to the left side of each screen for the fun stuff. There are "Special Exhibits" in each section. Just click on the links to access them. For instance in the "Build-Up" section, you can view multipage exhibits on "The Leaders and the Generals," "Training Fortress Europa (The Führer's Dream)," and "Seven Soldiers in Normandy." Each of these exhibits has its own set of "Related Articles" to read. But there's even more. Each section has several video documentary excerpts for you to watch on topics ranging from troops battling seasickness during the crossing of the English Channel to Stalin, Roosevelt, and Churchill meeting in Tehran. There are also radio clips to access. You'll see links to newspaper clippings, the personal histories of Allied and German soldiers, and war documents. And don't overlook the interactive "World War II Study Guide" that you can access from the top of every page except the home page.

The amount of material contained in this site is almost mind-boggling. The only downside to *Normandy: 1944* is that it doesn't have a search feature in case you want to look for a particular document or fact. There are a couple of ways to target your searches on this site, though. At the very bottom of every screen, you'll see a menu. Click on "People" for an index to all the biographies on the site; "Places" lists all the locations described. You can do the same to inventory "Weapons and Tactics," "Documents," and "Maps." Just click on items in the indexes to read about them. But you will definitely get the most out of this site by browsing each section.

The American Experience
D Day
http://www.pbs.org/wgbh/amex/dday/
middle school and up

Although this PBS site is not nearly as vast as *Normandy: 1944*, it is more manageable. One word of caution, though—it provides a whole lot less background information. But it does a great job of presenting some primary source material you might not find elsewhere. A companion to the *American Experience* movie on D day, the *D Day* Web site uses personal narratives of D day participants to tell its story.

You might want to begin exploring *D Day* by clicking on "About the Program" from the menu on the home page. This introductory piece explains the purpose of the film and the Web site, and also has some background material. The second main section is "Hot Off the Presses," which contains contemporary news accounts of the D day invasion. "The Paratrooper Experience" focuses on a group often overlooked in D day summaries—the paratroopers who were dropped behind enemy lines before the naval assault began. Click on *D day* from within the text to read a short synopsis of the invasion. "Letters from the Front" lets you read letters written by soldiers to their friends and family at home. This section in particular provides excellent primary source material. And "Read More and Learn More" allows you to access an extensive print bibliography on D day.

Message Drafted by General Eisenhower
http://www.nara.gov/education/cc/dday.html
middle school and up

This Web has a very basic—yet very thorough—description of D day that is perfect for younger students who might be overwhelmed by a site such as *Normandy: 1944*. The site is actually part of a lesson plan about the Constitution on the National Archives and Records Administration's Web site. To focus on D day, just ignore the lesson plan and stick to reading the information. More advanced students will get a lot more out *Normandy: 1944* or the PBS site, though.

To navigate the site, scroll down the home page. You might want to put off looking at the documents until you have read the "Historical Background" section. When you're ready, return to the "List of Documents" (directly above "Historical Background"). There're a couple of photographs to check out. But don't overlook the message Eisenhower prepared the day before the assault in case the D day invasion failed. This site helps drive home the message that history really could have come out differently. Just imagine how the course of World War II would have changed if the Allied invasion on D day had failed.

Normandy
http://replica.eb.mirror-image.com/normandy/index.html
middle school and up

This *Encyclopedia Britannica* Web site has a wealth of information about the Allied invasion of Normandy, which proved to be the decisive attack of World War II. The Web site includes so many types of resources—photos, radio clips and newsreels from the 1940s, maps, and first-hand accounts from soldiers and every day folks—that learning about the invasion won't seem like work at all! The Web site is designed around an essay written by military historian John Keegan.

In the "Build-Up" section, you'll find a detailed essay on the factors that led the Allied Forces to launch the Normandy invasion. Scroll down through the essay until you reach the "Allied Commanders" section for biographies of key political and military figures in the Allied effort. Click on the links within the essay to learn more about specific players. You can access additional biographies in "The Leaders and the Generals" section by clicking on the heading on the left side of your screen. Also in the "Build-Up" section, you will find documents about the Allied planning to launch the offensive.

The "Invasion" section gives you a detailed overview of the Normandy invasion, and you can access "Special Exhibits" (on the left side of the screen) about the events that occurred at specific sites, such as Omaha Beach, Pointe du Hoc, and the Orne Beach. You can even listen to radio broadcasts and read first-hand accounts of the invasion. The Web site also provides links to other World War II sites. Scroll to the bottom of the page and click on "World War II on the Web."

DECLARATION OF INDEPENDENCE

Best Search Engine: http://www.google.com/
Key Search Terms: Declaration of Independence + history

The Declaration of Independence
http://www.ushistory.org/declaration/
middle school and up

This Web page tells you all about the Declaration of Independence—why it was written, who was involved in the writing, and what the Declaration accomplished. The page is simple, focused, and easy to use. Simply scroll down the screen to navigate it.

The page includes links to biographical information about the signers of the Declaration of Independence, an excerpt from Thomas Jefferson's autobiography that talks about the days leading up to the signing of the Declaration, and a copy of the Declaration itself so that you can read it for yourself. You can even visit the Graff House, where Jefferson wrote the Declaration.

The excellent, though small, list of links includes a site from the National Archives and Records Administration that outlines the history of the Declaration from 1776 to the present.

DONNER PARTY

Best Search Engine: http://www.google.com/
Key Search Terms: Donner party

The Donner Party
http://www.teleport.com/~mhaller/index.shtml
middle school and up

Even though this Web page isn't completely finished, it's still one of the best places on the Internet to learn about the Donner party, which on its way to California got trapped in the Sierra Nevada mountains during the winter. Half of the party died, and some survivors resorted to cannibalism.

Although the site is well organized, it's a bit drab since there are no pictures, illustrations, or photographs. But it will tell you what you need to know. For a history of the Donner party—along with a look at the broader issue of westward expansion—go to the "Overview" section listed in the table of contents on the home page. Below the essay is a substantial set of links to other Web sites about the topic.

The best part of this site is its historical documents. Select "Primary Documents" to access two first-hand accounts of the ordeal. "Patrick Breen's Diary" was written during the trip and recounts the events of the winter before the survivors' rescue in the spring. "Across the Plains in the Donner Party" is a three-part memoir by a survivor written many years later. Equally interesting are the secondary sources written in the nineteenth century about the Donner expedition. Click on "Secondary Sources" from the main menu to read these.

DRED SCOTT DECISION

Best Search Engine: http://www.google.com/
Key Search Terms: Dred Scott

The Dred Scott Case
http://library.wustl.edu/vlib/dredscott/index.htm
high school and up

The Supreme Court decision in the Dred Scott case, which declared that Congress had no power to limit slavery in the territories, inflamed sectional conflicts and led to the Civil War. This simple site offers a detailed chronology of events surrounding the case as well as the court records. To access the documents from the trial and appeals courts just click on "Dred Scott Case Exhibit Table of Contents." To read the Supreme Court decision, go to bottom of the chronology and click on "*Scott v. Stanford.*"

DUST BOWL

Best Search Engine: http://www.google.com/
Key Search Terms: Dust Bowl + history
                        Dust Bowl + Roosevelt
                        Farm Security Administration + history
                        Farm crisis + Roosevelt

The Day of the Black Blizzard
http://www.discovery.com/area/history/dustbowl/dustbowlopener.html
middle school and up

This Web site, which is part of the Discovery Channel Online, is an excellent place to learn about the Dust Bowl. Although it's short on text, this site will be especially useful for younger students who don't need highly detailed material. *The Day of the Black Blizzard* examines the Dust Bowl by focusing on one of its worst days—April 14, 1935. It uses nifty graphics, lots of photographs, audio and video clips, and text to tell its powerful story.

The site is divided into specific times on that fateful day in 1935. As you enter the site, you are automatically taken to the first section, "8 A.M." Here you'll get some background information about the Dust Bowl. Look for the links off to the side of the screen to read more about certain topics or to listen to audio clips. For instance from "8 A.M.," you can click on "What Were the Dust Blues?" to learn about the depression and listlessness people endured because of effects of the Dust Bowl. If you select "How Bad Was the Dust?," you can look at pictures, read about just how bad the dust was, and hear audio clips of old timers talking about the dust piling into their homes, covering their cars, and choking them as they slept. The most shocking exhibits are the video clips. Watch "Dust Battles" to get a sense of how horrible the experience was.

After you've worked your way down to the bottom of the "8 A.M." screen, you can choose the time of the day you want to learn about next: "2:40 P.M.," "3:00 P.M.," or "6 P.M." It makes sense to proceed sequentially so you can get the whole story. Like the "8 A.M." section, the others describe the day's unfolding events, giving you a sense of the broader picture. For instance, in "6 P.M." you can click on a link, "Did Most People Give Up?," to read about the farmers who abandoned their homes and their land in search of better opportunities.

If you just want to listen to or view the audio and video clips, go to "Audio Gallery" at the bottom of any screen. You can scan the headings and select the clips you want to view. The site also has a "Web Links" section (you'll see the link at the bottom of any screen) with recommendations for more Internet resources on the Dust Bowl.

Surviving the Dust Bowl
http://www.pbs.org/wgbh/amex/dustbowl/
middle school and up

While *The Day of the Black Blizzard*'s greatest strength is its tremendous visuals and other multimedia offerings, *Surviving the Dust Bowl* is the place to go if you're looking for really in-depth information. This site goes into a ton of detail and covers aspects of the Dust Bowl that are overlooked by *The Day of the Black Blizzard*. *Surviving the Dust Bowl* was created as a companion to a film of the same name produced by PBS's *American Experience*. The Web site presents all the material covered in the film—along with some interactive extras!

The best way to navigate *Surviving the Dust Bowl* is with the menu on the left side of the home page. Click on "The Film and More" to read a program description and access an "enhanced transcript" of the film, which contains the text of the program and has links to related topics. You can also listen to interviews with program participants and the producer and use a fairly comprehensive bibliography of print sources. The "Special Features" section (second heading in the main menu) consists of two long pieces. The first is "An Eyewitness Account" of the Dust Bowl years told by a Kansas farmer. The second discusses "New Deal Remedies"—the steps the government took to aid Dust Bowl farmers. Each of these essays is accompanied by lots of photographs and links to more information.

Another helpful feature of this site is its "Timeline" section, which can help you organize the information you've learned. It gives a month-by-month chronological record of Dust Bowl-related events. The "Maps" section illustrates the parts of the country directly affected by the Dust Bowl. "People and Events" lists the key figures and events of the Dust Bowl, such as "President Roosevelt," "Black Sunday," and "The New Deal." Simply click on the ones you want to learn more about. Educators and students will find the "Teacher's Guide" helpful as well. It presents a number of questions to test your Dust Bowl knowledge.

Voices from the Dust Bowl
http://memory.loc.gov/ammem/afctshtml/tshome.html
middle school and up

What happened to the farmers and their families who lost their homes and their farms in the wake of the Dust Bowl? What was life like for them? Where did they go, and what did they do? This Library of Congress online exhibition can tell you. *Voices from the Dust Bowl* contains 18 hours of audio recordings from 1940 and 1941 that were made in the Farm Security Administration (FSA) camps for migrant Dust Bowl refugees.

While Web sites like the *Day of the Black Blizzard* and *Surviving the Dust Bowl* contain good secondary source material about the Dust Bowl and the people who endured it, *Voices from the Dust Bowl* lets you hear Dust Bowl refugees tell their own stories. It contains interviews, songs, camp meetings, storytelling sessions, and camp court proceedings. These unique perspectives make *Voices from the Dust Bowl* an incredible resource.

A good place to begin your journey into the everyday life of Dust Bowl refugees is to read the site's explanatory essay, "The Migrant Experience." Scroll down the home page until you see the heading (it's right below "Research Materials"). After you gain some general information about the Dust Bowl and the FSA camps, you can begin to explore the world of Dust Bowl survivors.

The site is vast, though, so you'll need to be careful not to get lost. There are four ways to browse its massive collections—you'll see these options at the top of the home page. If you're looking for the text of songs performed at the camps (but don't actually want to listen to them being sung), click on "Song Text." If you want to scan the hundreds of audio files, select "Audio Titles." The range of material available is mind-boggling. You can listen to an announcement giving the results of camp election; you can eavesdrop on a camp council meeting in which residents discuss speed limits and security for their weekly Saturday night dance; you can hear songs and performances at the camps; and you can hear people discuss their lives, hopes, and dreams in interviews. If you are looking for a photograph, browse the collection by clicking on "Photographs." You can also scan the collection by the name of the "Performer/Interviewee."

As you have probably guessed, browsing an online exhibit the size of *Voices from the Dust Bowl* can be pretty time consuming. One way to expedite the process, if you have an idea of specific documents you'll need, is to use the keyword search feature. Click on "Search" from the top of the home page.

Like most of the Library of Congress's exhibits, *Voices from the Dust Bowl* is truly a one-of-a-kind resource and will prove invaluable to your research. But you might need some help interpreting the documents you find on it. If so, both *Day of the Black Blizzard* and *Surviving the Dust Bowl* will do the job.

1876, ELECTION OF

Best Search Engine: http://www.google.com/
Key Search Terms: Election of 1876

Hayes vs Tilden

Finding Precedent: Hayes vs. Tilden, The Electoral College Controversy of 1876–1877
http://elections.harpweek.com/controversy.htm
high school and up

This is a good site for background on the 1876 presidential election, one of the most controversial in American history. Because neither the Democratic candidate, Samuel J. Tilden, nor the Republican, Rutherford B. Hayes, won an electoral majority, the election was thrown into the U.S. House of Representatives where the outcome was determined by political dealing. The House decided the election in favor of Hayes, despite the fact that Tilden had won the popular vote.

The site provides an excellent overview of the election as well as a day-by-day account of the controversy from the presidential nominations in June 1876 through the final outcome in early March of 1877 just days before Inauguration Day. You can also browse through contemporary political cartoons on the issue and search biographies of the key players in the controversy.

ELLIS ISLAND

Best Search Engine: http://www.google.com/
Key Search Terms: Ellis Island + history

Immigration + history + United States

Immigrant experience + America

Ellis Island
http://www.historychannel.com/ellisisland/index2.html
middle school and up

This Web site, which is part of the History Channel's site, does an incredibly good job of conveying the experience of the 12 million immigrants who passed through Ellis Island. The site uses video and audio clips, photographs, and essays to help you understand what it was like trying to enter the United States. You can even fill out the same form the immigrants did to prove they were fit to enter the country.

A good way to begin your online journey is by watching a video that explains how immigrants saw America as they first arrived through Ellis Island. Click on the "Video" heading in the center of the home page. As you watch the brief interviews, you'll understand that the America the immigrants saw was not always the country that they had hoped for and expected. Right below the "Video" link, you'll see red links to audio clips. Each of these interviews is with an immigrant from a different country, so you can get a sense of how different nationalities experienced Ellis Island.

The easiest way to navigate the rest of the Web site is by using the menu on the left side of the home page. Click on "Timeline" for a complete history of Ellis Island. There you can watch another video about the island, or just click on the period that interests you to read an overview of the immigration-related events that took place then. There are plenty of photographs to look at in each historical synopsis.

The other sections of the Web site are designed to put you into an immigrant's shoes—and teach you about Ellis Island at the same time. Click on "Who Are You?" from the main menu, and you can complete a form to see if you are eligible to enter the United States. The key question on the form is your nationality. When you complete the form, click on "Submit," and you'll be presented with a short overview of the history of immigration from the country/region you selected. To learn about the experiences of immigrants from other nations, select "Try Again" from the bottom of the screen, and fill out the form with a different country.

The "Gateway" section takes you from the boat through the various checkpoints on Ellis Island. To make this part more interesting, "Gateway" tells this story from the perspective of Frank Martocci, an inspector at Ellis Island. Select an area of Ellis Island from the menu at the bottom of the screen, and you'll be shown a map of it. There's also a brief synopsis of what took place there. Make sure to follow the "Click here for more information" link, which will take you to video interviews of

Martocci (you can also just listen to audio interviews with him) discussing the significance of the various areas of Ellis Island. There are also some photographs. At the bottom of each of the screens, you can click on "View Entire Story" if you want to read the inspector's entire narrative at once.

The other sections of the main menu are less helpful. "Heritage" allows you to fill out a genealogical tree and has links for online genealogical sources. "Passages" is where the History Channel sells its video about Ellis Island. If you don't want a sales pitch, skip this section entirely.

Ellis Island: Through America's Gateway
http://www.I-Channel.com/features/ellis/index.html
middle school and up

This Web site, which is part of the broader *International Channel* site, really complements the *Ellis Island* site. Although both sites cover much of the same material, such as what happened when an immigrant arrived at Ellis Island, *Ellis Island: Through America's Gateway* tells the story in a totally different way.

Ellis Island: Through America's Gateway is divided into six sections, of which only the first three are historically oriented. You'll find the main menu on the home page. The site mainly uses audio clips from immigrants to present its material. Click on the portrait icons to listen to these first-hand accounts.

The first section, "Historical Overview," lays out the basic history of Ellis Island. It's far less detailed than the "Timeline" on the *Ellis Island* site, but the audio excerpts and the photographs are truly fascinating. "The Journey" covers material completely left out of the *Ellis Island* site—what the trip to the United States from the Old World was like. Again, click on the portrait icons for first-hand audio accounts. "Through America's Gateway" gives a step-by-step summary of what new arrivals experienced on Ellis Island. This section is further divided into six subtopics: "Arrival," "Medical Inspection," "Mental Inspection," "Legal Inspection," "Detention," and "Free to Land." Make sure to listen to the interviews to get the whole story.

EMANCIPATION PROCLAMATION

Best Search Engine:	http://www.google.com/
Key Search Terms:	Emancipation Proclamation + history
	Abraham Lincoln + Emancipation Proclamation

Slavery + United States + history

Abraham Lincoln + slavery + history

The Emancipation Proclamation
http://www.nara.gov/exhall/featured-document/eman/emanproc.html
middle school and up

This is a really helpful Web site because it gives you a number of perspectives on the significance of the Emancipation Proclamation. It also lets you read a transcript of the text and view the original document. *The Emancipation Proclamation* is part of the National Archives and Records Administration's (NARA) *Online Exhibit Hall.*

To get a quick overview of what the Emancipation Proclamation meant, read the short essay in the middle of the home page. As you work your way down, you can click on the individual pages to get a close-up of the original document in Lincoln's handwriting. If you want to read the entire Emancipation Proclamation, select "Transcript of the Proclamation" from the menu on the left side of the home page.

The Web site also allows you to access a first-rate article about the Emancipation Proclamation, with a discussion of both its triumphs and its shortcomings. Click on "The Emancipation Proclamation: An Act of Justice" from the menu on the home page. The piece was written by historian John Hope Franklin and initially appeared in *Prologue: Quarterly of the National Archives and Records Administration.* There are even lots of illustrations to make the article more lively. When you've gotten a sense of how history has judged the Emancipation Proclamation, it's time to learn how the famous document changed—or didn't change— the lives of former slaves. Click on "Audio" from the main menu to check out the audio file of Charlie Smith, a former slave, talking about his life after the Proclamation.

Abraham Lincoln Papers at the Library of Congress
http://memory.loc.gov/ammem/alhtml/malhome.html
middle school and up

This Library of Congress online collection offers insight into what President Abraham Lincoln thought about emancipation, slavery, and his own Emancipation Proclamation. Since the collection is still a work in progress, some material might not yet be available. But the site is a one-of-a-kind resource.

To concentrate on the Emancipation Proclamation, scroll down the home page to "Special Presentations." Directly below this is a link called the "Emancipation Proclamation." Click on this link to be taken to the "Introduction" of the section, which discusses events leading up to Lincoln's historic issuance of the Emancipation Proclamation. At the bottom of the screen is a menu with other information, "Timeline" and "Gallery" on the Proclamation. The time line is a year-by-year chronology of the Lincoln presidency that highlights the various events leading up to the Proclamation. The "Gallery" allows you to view various drafts of the document as well as a letter in which Lincoln sums up his thoughts on emancipation.

The only major downside to *Abraham Lincoln Papers at the Library of Congress* is that it doesn't provide much interpretive help. So once you've found your primary documents, you might want to turn to other sites, such as *The Emancipation Proclamation,* to place them in their historical context.

Emancipation Proclamation
"From the View of a 1903 South Carolina Secondary School Textbook"
http://www.geocities.com/Heartland/Hills/6240/emancipation.html
middle school and up

How did proslavery Southerners feel about Lincoln's Emancipation Proclamation? Did they quickly learn to accept their slaves' freedom? This Web site, which is nothing more than an excerpt from a 1903 textbook, conveys how little Southerners liked the notion of freed slaves, much less of racial equality. This site is an interesting (and sad) comparison to the account of the life of the former slave found on the NARA site (*The Emancipation Proclamation*). The geocities site doesn't have any bells or whistles, so all you have to do is scroll down and read. Nevertheless the perspective it provides could be helpful in your research.

EUROPEAN VOYAGES OF EXPLORATION

Best Search Engine: http://www.google.com/
Key Search Terms: Age of Discovery + history
                        European explorers + New World
                        Christopher Columbus + history
                        Henry the Navigator + history

Discoverers Web
http://www.win.tue.nl/cs/fm/engels/discovery/#age
middle school and up

This rambling metasite is a great place to begin researching the European Age of Discovery. *Discoverers Web* allows you to access loads of useful information—time lines of voyages, biographies of key explorers, and links to dozens of Web sites. Although this Web site covers more than the history of exploration during the vaunted Age of Discovery (1400–1520), the bulk of the material is related to this topic. Because the site is so vast and contains so many links, it might take you a little time to find what you need at this site. But the extra effort will pay off. You can expect *Discoverers Web* to point you in the right direction to find information about a specific topic related to the Age of Discovery. If you haven't yet settled on a topic, don't worry. *Discoverers Web* will help you navigate your way to a topic that interests you.

To find your way around this site, scroll down the home page and select the links that you need. The first set of links is listed under the heading, "Apart from this page on this site there are." Beneath this wordy header, you'll find a number of useful links, such as one to a "Special page for multipage sites on voyages of discovery." In other words, follow this link if you want to view an index of other big sites related to the topic of exploration. Keep in mind that these links are *not* just to other sites about the Age of Discovery. You'll find an array of Web sites listed here—from the *Polynesian Voyaging Society* to the *Columbus Navigation Homepage* to the *History of Cartography Gateway*. If you're looking for print sources to use in your research, select "A list of primary and secondary sources" from the home page. Also in this section are a substantial number of links to biographies of key explorers, many of whom sailed the high seas during the Age of Discovery. Keep scrolling through the list, and chances are you'll find the name you need.

You can navigate the remainder of the site by either scrolling down the screen or by using the topical index you'll find right below the links to the biographies. Simply click on "Age of Discovery" in this index, and you'll be able to scan through a list of links that is impressively comprehensive. You can access a paper about the Spice Trade, dozens of additional biographical sites about explorers, charts and maps, and much more. All you have to do is point and click.

Unfortunately, material from the Age of Discovery is scattered in some of the other sections on this site. So, if you don't find what you need under "Age of Discovery" scroll through the other sections as well. Although it's disorganized, you'll appreciate the site's breadth.

1492: An Ongoing Voyage
http://www.loc.gov/exhibits/1492/
middle school and up

Christopher Columbus is one of the most familiar names from the Age of Discovery. This site—one of the Library of Congress's many excellent online exhibits—uses Columbus's famed voyage to America as the starting point for further discussion. *1492: An Ongoing Voyage* examines the world that existed before European explorers arrived. You can examine the Age of Discovery from the perspective of the native peoples whose lives were irrevocably changed when the Europeans reached their shores. The site also provides an overview of the Mediterranean world and worldview from which Columbus and other explorers emerged. There's detailed information about Columbus, as well as a look at how explorers "invented" America.

One of the coolest features of this site is that you can view objects and manuscripts from the holdings of the Library of Congress. As you read through the different sections, you'll be able to examine maps from medieval Spain, a digitized copy of Columbus's *Book of Privileges*, sketches of native communities made by fifteenth century explorers, and much more. Simply click on the small pictures to get a larger view.

Like other Library of Congress sites, *1492: An Ongoing Voyage* is well-organized, clearly written, and a snap to navigate. The main menu, found at the top of the home page, directs you to the site's different sections. The first section, "What Came to Be Called America,"discusses the native peoples (and their communities) as they existed before Columbus showed up. "Mediterranean World," the second main section, provides a background for understanding why Columbus and others of his ilk began to venture beyond the confines of their known world. This section has some especially useful material on the European worldview of the time. "Christopher Columbus: Man and Myth" covers the biography of Columbus. The last two sections—"Inventing America" and "Europe Claims America"—deal with the imposition of European policies and philosophies on the New World. Check out the "Epilogue" for some final thoughts on these subjects. See also the **Voyages of Columbus** entry in this volume.

FEDERALIST PAPERS

Best Search Engine: http://www.google.com/

Key Search Terms: Federalist Papers

The Federalist Papers
http://www.vote-smart.org/reference/histdocs/fedlist/
high school and up

Alexander Hamilton, John Jay, and James Madison wrote the *Federalist Papers* in 1787 to gain support for the ratification of the recently drafted Constitution. This Web site allows you to read the *Federalist Papers* in their entirety.

The Federalist Papers is a bare-bones site, simply providing links to each of the 85 individual entries that comprise the *Papers*. Simply click on individual paper you want to read from the index on the home page. (You can browse, but it'll be a whole lot easier if you already know what you're looking for.) As you read these famous documents, you'll learn about the problems the young republic had under the Articles of Confederation. For example, since the Articles gave the federal government only very limited powers, the United States struggled to repay its war debts and fund its budget. The themes outlined in the *Federalist Papers* were the same ones that motivated federalist politicians during the Federalist era.

While this is a good site if you're already somewhat familiar with the period, or are just looking for primary source material, it has no background information. You'll be able to read the *Federalist Papers*, but there's nothing to help you interpret the document. Use the *Federalist Era* Web site to place the *Papers* in their historical and political context.

FEDERALISTS

Best Search Engine: http://www.google.com/

Key Search Terms: Federalist era + history

The Gilder Lehrman Institute: History Online
http://www.hfac.uh.edu/gl/contents.htm
middle school and up

Although this site is a complete history of America from the Revolution to the end of the Civil War, it is a good place to get a quick introduction to the Federalist era. The Federalist era is the period in American history generally defined as 1787 to 1801, from the writing of the Constitution through the presidency of John Adams. Just scroll down to the first link, "Critical Issues in American History." When you get to that page, scroll down to the section called "The First New Nation" and begin reading there. You'll see links to short essays on "The Formative Decade," "The Birth of Political Parties," "The Presidency of John Adams," and much more.

Return to the home page for an "Interactive Timeline of the American Revolution" or a "Glossary of American History." There's also a list of succinct essay on major historical controversies and several online quizzes you can take to test your command of this period in U.S. history.

FREEDMAN'S BUREAU

Best Search Engine: http://www.google.com/
Key Search Terms: Freedmen's Bureau

                                     Reconstruction + American history

The Freedmen's Bureau Online
http://www.freedmensbureau.com/
middle school and up

What was life like for African Americans in the reconstructed South? What sorts of employment options did the recently freed African Americans have? Were they the victims of violence from bitter whites who resented losing the Civil War? This Web site helps you answer questions like these. It looks at Reconstruction through the documents of the Bureau of Refugees, Freedmen, and Abandoned Lands—better known simply as the Freedmen's Bureau.

As the name indicates, the Freedmen's Bureau was responsible for providing relief to refugees and freedmen. The organization kept detailed records on all sorts of issues, such as violence and labor disputes, that confronted African Americans in the South. This site makes a lot of these records available to you. It also provides a link to civil rights activist W. E. B. DuBois's book on the organization—*Freedmen's Bureau.*

For a history of the violence perpetrated against African Americans, click on "Records Relating to Murder and Outrages" under the "Contents" heading. You'll be shocked at the level and scope of the brutality. For a look at what sort of work African Americans did, check out the "Records Relating to Freedmen's Labor." This section also contains reports about labor disputes stemming from indentured servitude contracts.

To read the full text of W. E. B. DuBois's analysis of the Freedmen's Bureau, click on the link under "Related Sites" on the right side of the home page. Also be sure to look at the documents listed under "Recent Additions" in the center of the home page.

FRENCH AND INDIAN WAR

Best Search Engine: http://www.google.com/
Key Search Terms: French and Indian War

The French and Indian War
http://digitalhistory.org/wolfe.html
high school and up

This is one of the few okay Web sites on the French and Indian War, which was the war between England and France for control of North America. Here you can learn about the troops, battles, and forts involved in the conflict as well as get some background on the weapons used. On the home page you can click on "Montcalm" or "Wolfe" to read biographies of the two major commanders in the war. The biography of Montcalm is great, with lots of information on the French general's role in the war. Unfortunately, Wolfe's biography is a general overview of the English commander's career and his personality with almost no specifics on the conflict.

If you want to learn about what troops fought in the war, just scroll down to "British Troops" or "French Soldiers" and click on the units you want to investigate. Scrolling farther down the home page enables you to access information on forts and battles. A word of caution: Researching battles is not easy because you have to know the year that the battle was fought to access the information. Each year begins with a summary of events, so by moving from year to year, you can get a good overview of the military action. By clicking on "Digital History LTD," you can access a glossary of eighteenth century military terms. The site also contains a time line of the eighteenth century, but it's not much help in researching the French and Indian War.

French and Indian Wars
http://odur.let.rug.nl/~usa/E/7yearswar/fiwxx.htm
high school and up

The site, prepared by the University of Groningen in the Netherlands, provides a quick summary of the political background and the effects of the French and Indian Wars. It's really simple to use. At the home page just click on "Prelude to War," "Development of the War," or "Effects of the War" to find the information you need. There are a few links in the essays to people important in the war, such as British Prime Minister William Pitt, and events that were generated by the war, such as the passage of the Stamp Act and the Sugar Act.

FUGITIVE SLAVE LAWS

Best Search Engine:	http://www.google.com/
Key Search Terms:	Fugitive Slave Laws + history
	Slavery + history + U.S.

Fugitive Slave Acts
http://blackhistory.eb.com/micro/222/8.html
middle school and up

Although this Web site doesn't go into a lot of detail, it provides some good basic background information on the Fugitive Slave Acts of 1793 and 1850. It also explains the consequences of both acts and how they are related. In particular, this site makes the good point that the 1850 Fugitive Slave Act was really a reaffirmation of its 1793 predecessor. You can learn why the 1850 Fugitive Slave Act was enacted just by scrolling down the essay on the home page. The site also contains links to articles on related topics, including the "Underground Railroad" and "Slavery." Although this site is in no way comprehensive (and isn't that visually interesting either), it is the perfect place to start your research on this topic.

Fugitive Slave Law of 1793
http://www.ukans.edu/carrie/docs/texts/fugslave.htm
middle school and up

Don't overlook this brief Web page, which contains the text of the Fugitive Slave Act of 1793. It won't take you long to read, but it's an important resource in your research of this topic.

Effects of the Anthony Burns Affair
http://spider.georgetowncollege.edu/htallant/courses/his312/klivingo/
    aburns12.htm
middle school and up

This Web site concentrates on the life of Anthony Burns, a Virginia slave who escaped to Boston. He was captured, tried in a Massachusetts court, and then returned to his owners in Virginia in accordance with the Fugitive Slave Acts of 1793 and 1850. After he was jailed in Virginia, Burns's friends in Boston purchased his freedom. His case had a huge impact on relations between northerners and southerners and catalyzed northerners to defy the Fugitive Slave Laws.

Use the menu on the left side of the home page to navigate the site. Within the text, you'll see links to primary source material by or about Burns.

FUR TRADE

Best Search Engine:	http://www.google.com/
Key Search Terms:	Fur trade + American history
	American mountain men

Mountain Men and the Fur Trade
http://www.xmission.com/~drudy/amm.html
high school and up

Mountain Men and the Fur Trade provides a good introduction to the trappers, explorers, and traders in the Rocky Mountain region of the United States from 1800 to 1850. Here you can read approximately 40 historical documents—primary sources as well as contemporary works by authors such as Washington Irving. You can also view business records from the fur trade and images from the era including contemporary maps and portraits of mountain men such as Kit Carson, James Beckworth, and Merriweather Clark. Unfortunately the site does not contain biographical information on these men. *Mountain Men* also contains a great glossary of terms, words, and expressions as well as good links to related sites. The bibliography, on the other hand, is very limited.

The site is very easy to use. You can access virtually everything you need from the home page. The glossary, however, is a little tricky to find. Just click on "Miscellaneous Items of Interest" and scroll down the list of entries.

GILDED AGE

Best Search Engine: http://www.google.com/

Key Search Terms: Gilded Age + history

America's Story from America's Library
http://www.americaslibrary.gov/cgi-bin/page.cgi/jb/1878-1889
middle school and up

This Web site makes learning about the major events of the Gilded Age fun and easy! It's definitely designed with younger students in mind—it's broken down into bite-sized sections with catchy titles—but it still conveys a lot of information. It's also highly interactive.

To get a sense of the period called the Gilded Age, read the overview on the home page. There's a time line at the top of the page, so you can easily put this era into its historical context. The best part of the Web site, though, is its lighthearted synopses of key Gilded Age events. You'll see links to a few of them on the right side of the home page. Farther down is a link labeled "More." Click on it to get the full list of sections.

From the sections list just click your way back into the Gilded Age.

Some of the pieces deal with big issues, such as "A Woman on the Dollar," which talks about Susan B. Anthony and her quest for women's suffrage. "Wash Those Hands!" deals with the assassination of President James Garfield, while "Lady Liberty Sets Foot in America" discusses the flood of immigrants into America during the Gilded Age. Pieces like these tend to be several pages long; you just need to click on the "Next" link at the bottom of each page to keep reading. Other sections are more lighthearted, such as those dealing with the birth of athlete Jim Thorpe and songwriter Jim Cohan.

The Gilded Age Web Quest
http://www.oswego.org/staff/tcaswell/wq/gildedage/student.htm
middle school and up

This Web site uses an innovative strategy to get you to think about the Gilded Age. It proposes that you make documentary segments about certain aspects of the Gilded Age. Don't worry, though—we're not trying to give you more work by recommending this site. You don't *have* to mess around making a documentary. Whether you choose to or not (it *could* be fun), this site does a great job laying out the major events and themes of the era. It's also one of the few Web sites that provides a truly comprehensive look at the Gilded Age.

The site is pretty straightforward. It is broken down into sections about the big themes of the period: technological innovation, big business, urbanization, immigration, and reaction to the period. You'll see the links to these themes in the *middle* of the home page (not in the menu on the left side of the screen).

Each of the sections is actually a detailed outline that lists the people, places, and events related to the topic. So in the big business section for example, you find an easily digestible outline of specific material about big business in the Gilded Age, such as the "Forms of Business Organization" (monopoly, conglomerate, pool, trust, holding company) or "Entrepreneurs: Robber Barons or Captains of Industry?" (Andrew Carnegie, John D. Rockefeller, J. Pierpont Morgan, Jay Gould, and Henry Ford).

Remember, because this site is an outline, you'll have to use other resources to flesh out the picture.

The Gilded Page
http://www.wm.edu/~srnels/giltext.html
middle school and up

If you're hunting for primary source material about the Gilded Age, look no further! This Web site provides easy access to the full text of dozens of books, speeches, and articles written during the Gilded Age. And it's incredibly easy to use. *The Gilded Page* automatically takes you to other online sites where you can download complete books. Just click on "Documents" from the menu at the top of the home page for the complete list.

Almost every aspect of the Gilded Age that was reduced to writing is covered here. Do you want the primary sources that spawned the rags-to-riches myth that played such a key role in the psychology of the era? If so, check out the books by Horatio Alger. Maybe you want to examine the inaugural addresses of Gilded Age presidents to see what tone they set for the country? No problem. You'll find links to the speeches of Grover Cleveland, James Garfield, and Ulysses Grant. Or perhaps you're interested in influential philosophical texts. Then check out Karl Marx's *Communist Manifesto* or Herbert Spencer's *Man Versus State*. What about African American voices? Sure. There's Booker T. Washington's *Up from Slavery* and W. E. B. DuBois's *The Freedman's Bureau*.

The Gilded Page even recognizes that it can't quite link to everything. If you're looking for a text that's not available through this site, go to "Other Places" from the home page for a list of additional Internet locations to obtain e-texts. But remember that *The Gilded Page* doesn't provide any interpretive materials—these are all primary source documents. If you need background information, or help making sense of these sources, or help putting them in context, use a site such as *America's Story*.

GOLD RUSH (CALIFORNIA)

Best Search Engine: http://www.google.com/
Key Search Terms: California gold rush

Gold Fever!
http://www.museumca.org/goldrush/fever.html
middle school and up

This incredible Web site can be your personal guide to the history of the California gold rush. Be sure to set aside plenty of time to fully explore this Web site—it's part movie theater, part museum, and part book, and it's huge! Created by the Oakland Museum of California, *Gold*

Fever! makes learning about the history of the West an interactive adventure. For an overview of the exhibits, as well as a brief history of the major themes of the gold rush in California, select "Gold Rush" from the menu that runs down the left side of the home page.

Once you've previewed the site and this history, you might want to start your multimedia journey by watching the site's film, "Stories of the Lure and the Legacy." Unlike a lot of Internet films that last for only a few minutes, this multipart documentary covers the history of the gold rush from different angles. It has segments on the land, the people, and the life of the gold rush, with a special section on women who came to California during the gold rush. To get to the documentary, click on "Experience the Gold Rush" from the menu that runs across the top of the home page. You can either watch the entire film or select the segments that interest you from the menu that will pop up on the left side of the screen. (You'll need a Shockwave plug-in to access the film; the page has a link to get one.)

You can also take a virtual tour of some of the Oakland Museum's most popular exhibits about the gold rush. To get there, select "Onsite Adventures" from the menu at the top of the home page. These panoramic photographs (that you get to control) are accompanied by detailed text that tells you what you're looking at. You can take virtual tours of mines and towns from the gold rush. There are also more general exhibits about prospecting and life in California during this period.

While you're browsing around the menu at the top of the page, you can test your knowledge with the "Gold Rush Quiz." You should also stop and read "More Tales from the Mine," which are historical essays on different topics related to California history and the gold rush, such as "Gold Districts of California."

And there's more! If you're interested in the history of the people who came to California during the gold rush, use the menu that runs down the left side of the home page. "Silver and Gold" is an online exhibit of historic photographs in the museum's collection. You can check out some amazing pictures of Native Americans, Forty-Niners, and stern-faced women, and read a short essay on each one that puts the pictures in their historical context. If you select "Natives and Immigrants" from the menu on the left side, you'll see this period of California history through the eyes of four different cultures—California Indians, African Americans, Chinese, and Californio/Latinos. "Art of the Gold Rush," an online exhibit of the paintings and fine arts of the period, is also worth at least a look.

GREAT DEPRESSION

Best Search Engine: http://www.google.com/

Key Search Terms: Great Depression + history

Stock market crash + 1929 + history

Looking Back at the Crash of '29
http://www.nytimes.com/library/financial/index-1929-crash.html
middle school and up

This *New York Times* online special feature does a good job of explaining the stock market crash of 1929. It covers the causes of the crash as well as its long-term consequences. There are some interesting photographs, and you can even check out articles about the crash that the *New York Times* ran in 1929.

For those of you interested in reading an interpretive article about the crash, check out the main article by Floyd Norris on the home page. The bulk of the historical material is in the second part of the essay. You'll need to click on "More" at the bottom of the home page to access it. There are lots of photographs mixed in with the text.

When you're ready for some primary source material on the crash, turn to the original *Times* articles. The site lets you read *every* article printed in the *Times* from the week of October 28, 1929, as well as the front pages. This material helps you understand how people viewed the stock market collapse as it happened. The articles also reveal something about the tenor of the times. For instance, one article declares, "Women Traders Going Back to Bridge Games; Say They Are through Forever." To view these articles simply click on the titles from the menu on the right side of the home page (look under the heading "A Bad Week").

Slouching Towards Utopia? The Economic History of the Twentieth Century
"The Great Crash and the Great Slump"
http://econ161.berkeley.edu/TCEH/Slouch_Crash14.html
high school and up

You won't find a better place about the economic history of the crash of 1929 and the Great Depression on the Internet than this terrific site by J. Bradford DeLong, an economics professor at the University of California at Berkeley. Don't use *Slouching Towards Utopia?* to research the social and political history of the Great Depression, though. This site's focus is on the economic events of the period and why they happened. *Slouching Toward Utopia?* is clearly written, easy to understand, and chock full of graphs and charts to help you make sense of the material.

To navigate the site, simply scroll down the screen as though you're reading a book chapter. When you reach the end, you have the option of going to the next chapter. De Long does an excellent job of looking at the consequences of the Great Depression in this chapter, though, so don't feel obligated to read more.

Voices from the Thirties: Life Histories from the Federal Writers' Project
http://memory.loc.gov/ammem/wpaintro/exhome.html
middle school and up

After exploring *Slouching Towards Utopia?* and *Looking Back at the Crash of '29*, you probably have a good sense of the causes and the consequences of the stock market crash and the Great Depression. But what was *life* like during the Depression for everyday folks? This wonderful Web site, which is part of the Library of Congress's *American Memory Project*, will help you find out.

In the late 1930s, when one out of every four Americans was out of work, President Franklin Roosevelt launched the Works Project Administration (WPA) that employed people to use their skills for the public good. Unemployed authors were placed in a Federal Writers' Project (FWP) and assigned the task of recording the life stories of Americans. Before the project was discontinued in the mid-1940s, the FWP had conducted interviews with more than 10 thousand men and women from different regions, occupations, and ethnic groups. This Web site makes their stories available to you.

If you want to read an overview of the FWP, click on the "Introduction" from the menu on the right side of the home page. To save yourself from sorting through more than 10 thousand documents, you probably want to start your research by first looking at the excerpted interviews. Click on "Excerpts from Sample Interviews" from the home page menu. The sample interviews are divided by occupational type: "All in a Day's Work: Industrial Lore"; "Rank and File"; "Hard Times in the City"; "Testifying"; and "Making Do: Women and Work." There are several excerpts under each of these categories. The interviews include the subjects' occupations and wages to help you better understand their economic status during the Depression.

If you don't find the material you want in these samples, you can dive into the main collection. Remember that the FWP collection contains interviews recorded up to 1940 (when the Depression had technically ended). To access the main collection, click on "WPA Life Histories Home Page" from the bottom of the *Voices from the Thirties* home page. You can then either search for documents by keyword or by state. If you choose to search by state, you can conduct keyword searches of the documents in that state, or you can browse all the documents from that state.

GULF OF TONKIN RESOLUTION

Best Search Engine: http://www.google.com/
Key Search Terms: Gulf of Tonkin Resolution
                              Vietnam War + Tonkin Resolution

Tonkin Gulf Incident; 1964
http://www.yale.edu/lawweb/avalon/tonkin-g.htm
middle school and up

You might not think that a Web site consisting of just the full text of President Lyndon Johnson's "Message to Congress" about the Tonkin Gulf incident and Congress's Joint Resolution would make a great research tool. But you'd be wrong. What's unique about this particular site, which is part of Yale Law School's Avalon Project, is that it provides links to the treaties, resolutions, and protocols that are referred to in both Johnson's address and the resolution. In this way, you get access to an entire collection of Vietnam War government documents. So if you're not sure what the Southeast Asia Collective Defense Treaty that Johnson cites is, simply click on the link to read that treaty.

If you want to look at the Avalon Project's collection of Vietnam War official documents, scroll to the bottom of the "Tonkin Gulf Incident" page and click on "Indochina—Vietnam, Cambodia, and Laos." This link takes you to an index of documents. All you have to do is select the ones you want to read.

There's no doubt that this site is a terrific resource. Remember, though, that it doesn't provide any secondary material *about* the Gulf of Tonkin Resolution. If you need help understanding the document, use another Web site such as *Battlefield: Vietnam*.

Foreign Relations of the United States: 1964–1968
"U.S. Reaction to the Events in the Tonkin Gulf, August 1–10, 1964"
http://www.state.gov/www/about_state/history/vol_i/255_308.html
middle school and up

Like the Avalon Project site, this one, maintained by the U.S. State Department, provides primary source material about the American response to the Tonkin Gulf incident. But unlike the Avalon site, *Foreign Relations of the United States* doesn't look at *official* documents. Instead it makes available the transcripts of telephone conversations, telegrams, and memoranda circulated among various government departments, embassies, and individuals. The site takes you into the minds of U.S. officials and lets you examine their motivations, strategies, and goals.

To navigate this site, all you have to do is scroll down the home page. Instead of just bombarding you with documents, the site gives background information about what was taking place in helpful sections called "Editorial Notes." And the documents themselves are truly fascinating. You can find the transcript of a telegram sent by the Joint Chiefs of Staff to the commander in chief of the Pacific, the transcript of a telegram from the U.S. embassy in Vietnam to the Department of State, and the memorandum of a telephone conversation between the secretary of state and the secretary of defense (and much else).

HARLEM RENAISSANCE

Best Search Engine: http://www.yahoo.com/

Key Search Terms: Harlem Renaissance + history + high school

　　　　　　　　　　　Jazz Age + history + high school

The Harlem Renaissance
http://harlem.eb.com/harlemhome.html
middle school and up

This *Encyclopaedia Britannica* site, complete with a backdrop of black-and-white photographs of Harlem in the twenties, is your ticket back in time. The writing is engaging, the format is easy to use, and the information is comprehensive. You'll get a history of what led to the cultural flowering in Harlem known as the Renaissance—in the words of those who lived it. Quotes come from famous Harlem personalities and even from characters in books written by Harlem Renaissance writers.

While the site gives you a fantastic overview, you may already have a specific subject to research. No problem. The main menu offers links to "Leadership," "Literature," "Art," "Entertainment," "Hot Spots," and "Timeline" that will take you directly to your subject, whether a business leader, a writer, an artist, a musician, or a famous Harlem landmark.

Click on "Link" for links to other Harlem Renaissance sites, or click on "Guide to Black History" to learn more about other eras in African American history.

Harlem Renaissance
http://www.wku.edu/~diesmanj/harlem.html
high school and up

If you'd like to join a mailing list about the Harlem Renaissance and correspond with others interested in the topic, this is your site. Just click on the link for "Mailserv Information."

There's a good general introduction to the period and some nice photos, but the real reason to visit this site is for the collections of complete poems and short stories by Harlem Renaissance writers and the galleries devoted to paintings by such renowned painters as William H. Johnson, Palmer Hayden, and Lois Mailou Jones.

PAL:Perspectives on American Literature: A Research and Reference Guide
"Chapter 9: The Harlem Renaissance—An Introduction"
http://www.csustan.edu/english/reuben/pal/chap9/9intro.html
high school and up

At this straightforward site, the chronology is the highlight. Spanning the years from 1919 to 1940, it's a comprehensive look at the significant events that shaped Harlem and created the Renaissance.

You can also click on "Important Features" to access a list of significant ideas during the Renaissance, an interesting feature not available at other sites. Links to pages on famous personalities and a lengthy list of novels published by writers who were associated with the Harlem Renaissance round out the offerings.

Harlem 1900–1940, An African-American Community
http://www.si.umich.edu/CHICO/Harlem
middle school and high school

Get a basic overview of the Renaissance here by clicking on "Timeline" and browsing or choose the searchable database of writers, artists, and performers to go directly to the subject of your research. Just type in your keywords, and the database takes you to the information it has on your subject.

Click on "Exhibition" to open a portfolio of photographic and graphic images from the Harlem Renaissance, including such subjects as political movements, education, sports, religion, music, and the Harlem Hospital, among others. Images are accompanied by informative text.

There's also a "Teacher Resources" link with information on incorporating oral histories into the history curriculum.

HAYMARKET AFFAIR

Best Search Engine: http://www.google.com/
Key Search Terms: Haymarket affair

The Dramas of Haymarket
http://www.chicagohistory.org/dramas/overview/over.htm
middle school and up

The Dramas of Haymarket tells the story of the Haymarket affair, a violent conflict between police and labor protestors in Chicago in 1886. The site combines excellent essays with primary source material, photographs, and illustrations.

The site is organized into seven sections (or acts) that you get to by selecting "Main Contents" from the menu on the left side of the home page. *The Dramas of Haymarket* uses the specific incident of the Haymarket affair as a lens through which to view the massive changes in work and industry taking place during the Gilded Age. The drama begins with the Chicago Fire and ends with the present day. Click on the act that interests you. In addition to the main essay in each section, you'll see links to additional material on the left side of the page. Most of these are to online exhibits that use archived material to craft a narrative.

HIROSHIMA AND NAGASAKI

Best Search Engine: http://www.google.com/
Key Search Terms: Hiroshima + history

A-Bomb WWW Museum
http://www.csi.ad.jp/ABOMB/
high school and up

This Web site focuses on the impact of the United States' decision to use the atom bomb against Japan in 1945. Although *A-Bomb WWW Museum* is disorganized and rather cumbersome to use, it does provide crucial information about the destruction caused by the atom bomb. *A-Bomb WWW Museum* uses visual materials and first-hand accounts to describe the effects the bombing of Hiroshima and Nagasaki had on Japan. The result is a moving, informative, and often disturbing Web site that can play a role in your research. As an online museum, this site is not going to provide you with reference material. Instead *A-Bomb WWW Museum* focuses on bringing you into contact with individual items from this one historical event. Be aware, however, that this site contains graphic images that are not appropriate for younger students.

To get to the heart of this site, scroll down the home page until you reach the heading "Welcome to the A-Bomb WWW Museum." Below this is the table of contents of the visual and written exhibits. Click on

"Introduction: About the A-Bomb" for a brief essay on the effects of the bomb in terms of the amount of heat and radiation emitted and the number of deaths caused. Select "From the Exhibits of the Peace Memorial Museum," "Things That Tell the Story," and "Record of the A-Bomb Disaster" from the main menu to view photographs that testify to the deadly force of the weapon used. Many of the images are photographs of items, such as a child's tricycle twisted and charred from the heat. To try to get a sense of what experiencing such an event would be like, click on "Voices of A-Bomb Survivors, A Child's Experience," and "Children of Hiroshima" from the main menu for first-hand accounts of the deadly days in Hiroshima and Nagasaki.

A third portion of this Web site is devoted to chronicling how current residents of Hiroshima and Nagasaki deal with the legacy of the past. Click on "Hiroshima Today," "The Second Generation," "Message from the Mayor of Hiroshima," and "Message from the Mayor of Nagasaki" from the main menu to read these perspectives. Click on "Related Work" for a lengthy print bibliography as well as links to several related Web sites.

HOLLYWOOD 10

Best Search Engine: http://www.google.com/
Key Search Terms: Hollywood 10

                      Hollywood ten + McCarthy

Blacklist
http://www.otal.umd.edu/~rccs/blacklist/welcome1.html
middle school and up

Beginning in 1947, the House Un-American Activities Committee (HUAC) investigated Communism in Hollywood. As Senator Joseph McCarthy would later, HUAC operated by getting witnesses to provide lists of other supposed Communists to secure more lenient treatment for themselves. Of the many people summoned before HUAC, the Hollywood 10 (10 influential screenwriters, novelists, directors, and producers) gained the most attention.

This site is about those 10 people. It tells their story by focusing on the case of one of the 10, Adrian Scott, a screenwriter and movie producer who refused to answer HUAC's questions, was imprisoned for this refusal, was blacklisted, and was unable to find work again in the United States until 1968.

For an overview of the Hollywood 10, the events, and their trials, read all three links in the "Hollywood Blacklisting" section of the table of contents. To learn about Adrian Scott and to read his testimony before HUAC, click on the links "A Brief Biography" and "HUAC Testimony" that are listed below his name in the table of contents on the home page. To access primary source material, including photographs and letters, go to the links in the "Archives and Resources" section.

HOLOCAUST AND AMERICA

Best Search Engine: http://www.google.com/

Key Search Terms: American + Nazi + holocaust

America and the Holocaust
http://www.pbs.org/wgbh/amex/holocaust/
middle school and up

Although you might not think of Hitler's effort to exterminate the Jews as an aspect of *American* history, this gripping site makes it clear that this country was not immune to the events surrounding the Holocaust. A companion to the PBS *American Experience* television program of the same name, *America and the Holocaust* provides a comprehensive look at America's response to the Holocaust and has several terrific features that will really make this period come alive for you. The site offers access to all the material that was included in the broadcast, plus a whole lot more!

America and the Holocaust is beautifully laid out and incredibly easy to navigate. There's a menu on the left side of the home page (and, conveniently, on every page you open on the site) from which you can select from the site's six sections: "The Film & More," "Special Feature," "Timeline," "Maps, People, and Events," and "Teacher's Guide." Each of these sections (except "Teacher's Guide," unless you're interested in some discussion questions on this topic) has a wealth of fascinating material, so unless you know exactly what you're looking for, you can browse in pretty much any order. "The Film & More" has a complete transcript of the TV show, but with an added bonus—key terms are in hypertext so that you can click on them to get more information. You can also find links to some great primary source material here, extended interview transcripts with participants in the program, and a bibliography of print sources connected to this aspect of America's World War II experience.

And do not miss the "Special Feature," which tells the heartbreaking story of Kurt Klein who immigrated to the United States from Germany in 1937. This section contains a narrative time line and links to copies of letters Klein and his parents (who remained in Germany) exchanged between 1937 and 1942 when Klein's parents were deported to Auschwitz and were killed. The tragic story is made even worse by the fact that it was the foot-dragging of the American State Department that prevented many people like Klein's parents from obtaining visas to come to this country and escape the Holocaust.

HOMESTEAD STRIKE

Best Search Engine: http://www.google.com/
Key Search Terms: Homestead strike

The Homestead Strike: 1892
http://www.geocities.com/CapitolHill/Senate/7672/homestead.html
high school and up

The Homestead Strike: 1892 focuses on the strike by the Amalgamated Association of Iron and Steel Workers at the Carnegie Steel Company. This Web site consists of three primary sources about the Homestead strike, written by three contemporaries of Carnegie who were wholly unsympathetic toward him: Louis Adamic, Emma Goldman, and Alexander Berkman. Simply scroll down the screen to read the excerpts.

At the bottom of the page, you'll find some useful links to other Web sites about the Homestead strike. The last listed (http://www.bgsu.edu/departments/acs/1890s/carnegie/strike.html) will take you to another excellent history of the strike that discusses the major events and that also has photographs, maps, and biographies.

HUTCHINSON, ANNE TRIAL

Best Search Engine: http://www.google.com/
Key Search Terms: Hutchinson + trial
                     Anne Hutchinson

Religious Freedom: The Trial of Anne Hutchinson
http://www.pbs.org/wgbh/amex/kids/civilrights/features_hutchison.html
middle school and up

This PBS site is geared towards younger students, and it does a great job of presenting material about Anne Hutchinson's sedition trial and her subsequent expulsion from the Massachusetts Bay Colony. The essay is informative and to the point, and there are a number of illustrations that liven things up. As an added bonus, the site presents the darker side of the Massachusetts Bay Colony. Even though its founders were looking for religious freedom, they weren't willing to extend that freedom to those who didn't agree with them. And the site is tremendously easy to navigate. All you have to do is scroll down the home page to read about Anne Hutchinson and look at the pictures.

IMMIGRATION

Best Search Engine: http://www.google.com/

Key Search Terms: American immigration + history

The Immigration Experience
http://members.tripod.com/~L_Alfano/immig.htm
middle school and up

Although this Web site isn't glitzy, it presents some fantastic material on the history of immigration to the United States from 1855. More advanced students will appreciate *The Immigration Experience* for its wealth of primary source documents.

To navigate this site, simply scroll down the home page. You can then follow the links to read various documents about immigration. Most of this material is first-hand accounts from newspapers and magazines. The site begins its history in 1855, when immigrants to New York City passed not through Ellis Island but through Castle Garden. You can even find a description of Castle Garden that appeared in the 1866 *New York Times*. Or scroll down the screen to find a link to an early account of Ellis Island (with the original drawings) in the *Illustrated American*. There's a ton of other good primary source articles to be found as well, so be sure to work your way down to the bottom of the screen. If you'd like to look at photographs of Ellis Island, click on the "Postcards" link.

American Immigration
http://www.bergen.org/AAST/Projects/Immigration/
middle school and up

If you need quick information on immigration use this site. You won't be able to research the topic in depth, but you will get an overview of immigration history that enables you to see broad patterns. Here you can find links to: "Reasons for Immigration"; "Who Were the Immigrants to the U.S.?"; "Peaks and Waves of Immigration"; "Methods of Transportation and Ports of Arrival"; "Process of Entering the U.S."; "Destination/Places Where They Settled"; "Treatment/Reception by Other Americans"; "Effects/Impact on America"; "Opportunities for and

Successes of Immigrants"; "Assimilation?"; "What Did Immigrants Find Distinctive about America?"; "Legal vs. Illegal Immigrants"; and "Laws Restricting Immigration."

The site is really easy to use. Just click on the type of information and time period you need. The text for each section is presented in bulleted items or very short paragraphs, so you can retrieve your information quickly. This site is really basic, both in design and content, but it provides a great outline from which to start your research.

> *Immigration and Naturalization Service (INS): History, Genealogy, and Education*
> http://www.ins.usdoj.gov/graphics/aboutins/history/index.htm
> high school and up

If you are looking for information on the evolution of U.S. immigration policy or historical statistics on immigration and immigrants, this is the place to turn. This site has it all. Here you can get an overview of INS history, view immigration and naturalization records, or read an essay on immigration control along the Mexican border. There is also a special section on "Chinese Immigrant Files." Clicking on "Historical Articles" on the home page leads you to great essays, including "Changing Immigrant Names," "Women and Naturalization 1802–1940," and "Why Isn't the Green Card Green?" If you're looking for a history of government policy, go to "An Immigrant Nation: The Regulation of Immigration, 1798–1991." To reach that link, click on "Historical Research Tools" on the left side of the home page. Then scroll down to a list of tools under "Subject History Research."

You can find some of the best material in the site by clicking on "Teacher Resources" on the home page. This leads you to a "List of Informational Resources for Teachers and Students" that offers information on immigration legislation as well as a wealth of historical statistics. "Coming to America" presents immigrant history through links to other sources. You can also find information on researching your own family's history. This is a very rich site. Plan to spend a lot of time here.

IMPEACHMENT OF ANDREW JOHNSON

Best Search Engine: http://www.google.com/

Key Search Terms: Impeachment + Johnson

Finding Precedent: The Impeachment of Andrew Johnson
http://www.impeach-andrewjohnson.com/
high school and up

This is a must visit site if you're researching the impeachment of Andrew Johnson. It's easy to use and a great blend of primary and secondary material. Here you'll find information on the political background of the impeachment, the arguments for and against impeachment, the articles and rules of impeachment, and a who's who of 28 important figures in the impeachment drama. You can also get an overview of Johnson's presidency with links to appropriate articles in *Harper's Weekly*, the most important periodical of the time.

The arguments surrounding impeachment come from *Harper's Weekly*, which gives you the contemporary flavor of the debate. The biographical section is particularly helpful because it covers a wide variety of individuals from Johnson and his major opponents and defenders to prominent journalists who covered the incident.

The site is extremely simple to navigate. Just click on the appropriate topic from the home page. The link from "Impeachment Arguments" brings you to a topical list of entries. This is a good outline of the kinds of arguments presented in the case. Clicking on an individual entry will get you to the *Harper's* editorial in which it is discussed.

IMPERIALISM

Best Search Engine: http://www.google.com/
Key Search Terms: Age of Imperialism + U.S. + history
                      American expansion + history
                      U.S. foreign policy + 19th century
                      U.S. + Latin America + history

The Age of Imperialism
http://www.smplanet.com/imperialism/toc.html
middle school and up

Think of this Web site as one-stop shopping for information about overseas expansion by the United States. You'll find material, including photographs, maps, notes on key figures, and time lines, on a range of topics. You name it, and this Web site has it!

The Age of Imperialism is organized into five main sections: "Expansion in the Pacific"; "Spanish-American War"; "Boxer Rebellion"; "Panama Canal"; and "U.S. Intervention in Latin America." Click on any of these topics from the home page to enter a world of interactive history. Each section gives you the pertinent historical information along with an easy-to-understand analysis of the events. You'll not only get the *who, what, when,* and *where* of each topic, but also the *why.*

The other fantastic aspect of this Web site is its links that put a wealth of information at your fingertips. You can click to access biographies of various American presidents, texts of treaties between the United States and other nations, detailed maps of areas, and time lines. For example in the section on the Boxer Rebellion, you can link to the "Background of Ch-ing China," "A Concise Political History of China," "John Hay's Open Door Notes," and various maps. Check out the links to outside resources too. Click on "Bibliography" from the home page for links to supplemental resources.

The Birth of U.S. Imperialism
http://www.geocities.com/Athens/Ithaca/9852/usimp.htm
high school and up

This Web site has loads of good information on U.S. expansion in the nineteenth century. However, it is much less comprehensive than *The Age of Imperialism,* and it is definitely written for an older audience. Expect more complicated writing. Definitely check out *The Age of Imperialism* first, and then use this Web site to fill in any gaps you might have. It's also more bland than *The Age of Imperialism,* so don't expect pictures or maps to help you with your research.

This Web site is arranged according to several key terms, such as the Monroe Doctrine and Dollar Diplomacy, that are related to the history of U.S. imperialism. After a brief discussion of the concepts, the site gives links to other sources. Click on these for good primary source material. For instance, if you click on the "Avalon Project" link under the "Monroe Doctrine," you can read the text of the Monroe Doctrine.

The Web site also includes an essay on the history of U.S. imperialism. The essay provides some good background, but parts of it are way too advanced for younger students. Click on "Bibliography" if you need to find books on the topic.

An Outline of American History
"Chapter 6: The Era of Expansion and Reform"
http://odur.let.rug.nl/~usa/H/1990/ch6_p8.htm
middle school and up

Are you looking for a basic Web site that can answer quick questions on U.S. imperialism? If so, this no-frills Web site is for you; but don't expect photographs or much supplementary material. The site hits the major points, but not much more.

An Outline of American History provides a brief explanation of the key events of this era—the Spanish-American War, Theodore Roosevelt's Rough Riders, and American involvement in China. Click on the links for additional information. For example, you can access Mark Twain's thoughts on U.S. intervention in the Philippines, read John Hay's "First Open Door Note," or take a look at the biographies of some U.S. presidents. Some of the links take you back to *The Age of Imperialism* site, though, so don't hope for too much new material here.

INDIAN WARS

Best Search Engine: http://www.google.com/

Key Search Terms: Indian wars

Indian Wars
http://www.encyclopedia.com/articles/06329.html
middle school and up

Indian Wars gives a great overview of the conflicts between native American and European settlers from the colonial period to the end of the nineteenth century. Here you can learn about the Pequot War of 1637, the Black Hawk War of 1832, or the campaigns against the Plains Indians following the Civil War. You'll also find material on famous generals such as Anthony Wayne and Indian leaders such as Tecumseh as well as information on important incidents including the battle of Tippecanoe and the massacre at Sand Creek. The site also gives you general background on specific tribes.

To begin your research just click on the appropriate time period: "Early Conflicts" (1637–1763); Struggles in the Northwest Territory" (1790–1815); "Relocation across the Mississippi" (1815–32); and "Wars of the West" (1860–98). At each of these you'll find a general overview with links to specific wars, battles, and personalities. These entries frequently include still other links that enable you to take your research further. For example, if you click on "Pontiac's Rebellion" under "Early Conflicts," you get a short description that takes you to "Causes" and "Course of the War" as well as a biography of Pontiac.

Don't worry if you don't know the date of the war you are researching. *Indian Wars* is part of the giant *Encyclopedia.com* site that contains the *Columbia Electronic Encyclopedia.* Just use the search function on the right side of the home page to find the specific term you need.

INDUSTRY, GROWTH OF

Best Search Engine: http://www.google.com/

Key Search Terms: Industrial Revolution + United States + history

Industrialization + history + United States

Modern History Sourcebook: The Industrial Revolution
http://www.fordham.edu/halsall/mod/modsbook2.html#indrev
middle school and up

The *Modern History Sourcebook* has a particularly useful section on the Industrial Revolution. To find it, scroll down to Part 5, near the bottom of the page.

The *Sourcebook's* specialty is its collection of original texts, but it also contains references to Web sites, such as one called *The Steam Engine Library* that contains wonderful information on the revolution in power.

The primary source material collected here is helpfully organized by topic. There's a section on the agricultural revolution and another on the revolution in the manufacture of textiles, for example. There's also a section called "Literary Response," which contains poems, essays, and excerpts from books that address some aspect of the Industrial Revolution.

The Fabulous Ruins of Detroit
http://detroityes.com/home.htm
middle school and up

When we think of industrialization in the United States, the automobile quickly comes to mind, and no one place in this country had more to do with the automobile than Detroit. In the early twentieth century, the development of massive industrial structures changed the face of Detroit and heralded a second industrial revolution. This awesome site will take you on a tour of these now abandoned automobile plants and company headquarters. Many of the pictures were taken during the destruction of the buildings, so you'll witness the detonation of the smoke stacks that once rose above a power plant and the crumbling of bricks as a factory folds in on itself.

The text that accompanies the photos highlights not only the historical significance of the structures, but also the current status of the buildings (some buildings survive, and people interested in preservation are seeking supporters to keep such buildings standing). In addition to the industrial ruins featured here, you can tour ruins of nineteenth century residences, ruins in downtown Detroit, and neighborhood ruins. There's also a section called "The City Rises," where you can see images of a resurgent Detroit. Lauded as a Yahoo Pick of the Year in 1998 and given four stars by *Encyclopedia Britannica*, this is a one-of-a-kind site.

Inside an American Factory: Films of the Westinghouse Works, 1904
http://lcweb2.loc.gov/ammem/papr/west/westhome.html
middle school and up

What was it like to work in the factories of Industrial Age America? This site takes you as close as you can get without a time machine. On this excellent site from the Library of Congress's *American Memory Project*, you can watch videos online that show various views of the Westinghouse Companies.

Before you lose yourself in the videos, read the history behind the project. To do so, click on "Westinghouse Works Collection." It's also essential that you get some background on this period. Scroll down the home page to the "Special Presentations" section and select "The Westinghouse World: The Companies, The People, and the Places." From here, you'll be able to access the history of the Westinghouse Works, scan a list of the company's major projects during this period, learn about working conditions in the factories, and read a biography of the company's founder, George Westinghouse. The "Timeline" (in "Special Presentations") gives a chronology of the company.

When you're ready to view the films, you can access the collection in three ways. The easiest is probably to scan the complete list of titles. Click on "List" from the top of the home page. From the index, all you have to do is click on the title that interests you. If you want to search for a specific film you can either "Search by Keyword" or "Browse the Subject Index." Both of these choices are also at the top of the home page.

INTEGRATION

Best Search Engine: http://www.google.com/
Key Search Terms: Integration + American history

The Columbia Encyclopedia: *Integration*
http://www.bartleby.com/65/in/integrat.html
middle school and up

This Web page contains an informative article on integration from the *Columbia Encyclopedia*. The article gives an overview of the efforts to break down discrimination barriers that separated Americans along racial lines from Reconstruction to the present. This is a plain vanilla site (it is pure text), but it is a good first stop for anyone interested in the topic. The page contains a few links that enable you to go deeper into certain aspects, such as Reconstruction and Jim Crow laws, of the topic. The page has many more links to biographical information about major figures of the Civil Rights era, such as Martin Luther King Jr. and Edward Brooke (the first African American elected to the U.S. Senate since Reconstruction).

Little Rock Central High 40th Anniversary
http://www.centralhigh57.org/
middle school and up

What happened after the Supreme Court handed down the *Brown v. Board of Education* decision that precipitated school integration? *Little Rock Central High 40th Anniversary* explores this question. By looking at the experience of Central High School in Little Rock, Arkansas, this site helps you understand the slow—and painful—battle that African Americans and the federal government waged to implement *Brown* and desegregate schools.

Little Rock Central High 40th Anniversary has a number of interesting sections. For a detailed chronology of the events at Central High before and after *Brown,* click on "1957–58 School Year." You can also read articles about the forced desegregation of Central High from the 1957 school newspaper. If you're curious about what happened to the nine students who were the first African American students to attend Central High, select "The Nine."

To get a better sense of what the desegregation of Central High was like, check out the photos and videos. There's a photo gallery of "The Nine" with President Bill Clinton celebrating the fortieth anniversary of the event. Better still are the two videos, one of "The Nine" entering Central High and the other of the first African American graduate of the school talking about his experiences on that first day.

IRAN-CONTRA AFFAIR

Best Search Engine: http://www.google.com/
Key Search Terms: Iran-Contra + history
                        Ronald Reagan + Iran-Contra
                        Oliver North + Iran-Contra
                        Boland Amendment + Iran-Contra

The Iran-Contra Affair: The Making of a Scandal, 1983–1988
http://38.202.78.21:80/icintro.htm
high school and up

This excellent Web site, which is part of the *Digital National Security Archives*, provides one of the best available overviews of the Iran-Contra affair. You won't be able to access the documents in the *Archives* unless you subscribe to the site. But the strength of this site isn't the documents (which you can find elsewhere on the Internet with a little hunting). It's the wonderful essay about the Iran-Contra affair.

To read this historical piece by Malcom Byrne and Peter Kornbluh, click on "Essay" from the menu at the top of the home page. "The Making of a Scandal" focuses on the actual events of Iran-Contra and tells you *what happened and why it did* in terms of American foreign policy. You'll be introduced to all the major players—Oliver North, Casper Weinberger, Edwin Meese, and Robert McFarlane. You'll also get a quick introduction to American foreign policy toward Iran and Central America. If you want to view photographs related to the Iran-Contra affair, select "Photo Archives" from the menu at the top of the home page.

Remember that this site doesn't really touch on the Senate hearings into the Iran-Contra affair (the ones that made Oliver North famous) or on the independent counsel's investigations. If you want to include information about those facets of the matter, supplement your research on this site with material from *Documents Related to the Iran-Contra Affair* or *Final Report of the Independent Counsel for the Iran-Contra Matters* (see the following entries).

Documents Related to the Iran-Contra Affair
http://www.webcom.com/pinknoiz/covert/irancontra.html
high school and up

There are hundreds of primary source documents related to the Iran-Contra affair, and sorting through them can be incredibly time-consuming and tedious. This site can help. *Documents Related to the Iran-Contra Affair* makes it easy to incorporate primary materials into your research on this crisis. Because it consists of several well-chosen documents that each illustrate a different facet of the Iran-Contra affair, this site is both informative and manageable.

To navigate *Documents Related to the Iran-Contra Affair* scroll down the home page, which contains an index of the selected documents with a brief description of each one. Just click on the one(s) that you need. Your choices range from excerpts from Central Intelligence Agency (CIA) training manuals to a summary of the independent counsel's report on the investigation.

Since this is a primary source site, don't count on it to give you much background information on the Iran-Contra affair. If you need that kind of material, use one of the more explanatory sites, such as *The Iran-Contra Affair: The Making of a Scandal.*

Final Report of the Independent Counsel for the Iran-Contra Matters
http://www.fas.org/irp/offdocs/walsh/
high school and up

This Web site makes available the ultimate source of information about the Iran-Contra affair—the 525 page report issued on Iran-Contra by the Independent Council's office. Before you panic at the thought of reading 525 pages, you should know that this site is neatly divided into easy-to-access sections. One of the great things about this site is that the *Final Report* is both a secondary and a primary source. You can learn a lot *about* the Iran-Contra affair by reading the report, and at the same time, the report is probably the most important document *of* the Iran-Contra affair.

Scroll down the home page to view the list of sections. You'll likely find "Part I (The Underlying Facts)" and "Part II (History of the Investigation)" quite helpful. Be sure to click on "Chronology of Key Public Developments" in Part II. This time line of Iran-Contra events is impressively detailed, and it'll be a great reference as you continue your research on other sites.

The rest of the *Final Report* is chock full of information. You can read about the government's cases against Oliver North, Casper Weinberger, and others. You'll also have access to the testimony of key figures such as Edwin Meese and George Bush Sr. The *Final Report* closes with sections on "Political Oversight and the Rule of Law" and "Concluding Observation."

JACKSONIAN AMERICA

Best Search Engine: http://www.google.com/
Key Search Terms: Jacksonian America
                     Jacksonian era
                     Jacksonian democracy

Democracy in America: deTocqueville
http://xroads.virginia.edu/~HYPER/DETOC/home.html
high school and up

In 1831 a young Frenchman, Alexis deTocqueville, traveled around the United States observing American culture and politics. These observations resulted in his *Democracy in America*, one of the most influential studies ever written on American life.

This first-rate site, developed by the American Studies program at the University of Virginia, reconstructs the America of 1831–32, using deTocqueville's study. Here you can read the complete text of his work and follow deTocqueville's itinerary, tracing his route on a map and reading his impressions of the cities he visited. But this site is not just about deTocqueville. It simply uses his study as a basis for a social history of the era. Here you can find essays on religion, race, and the role of American women as well as a series of maps illustrating the 1840 census. You can also learn about the individuals deTocqueville encountered and get a glimpse of the art of the period. There is also a section devoted to other European travelers of the time. This site has it all!

Democracy in America is really easy to use. Virtually everything is accessed from the home page, although some of the link titles are not very clear. To find the biographical material, click on "Representative Voices"; to find information on art, click on "The Hudson River," which discusses the Hudson River school of painters. "Inland Navigation" outlines the internal improvements that opened up the West and connected the growing nation. You can find a summary of deTocqueville's background and thoughts on American democracy in "European Perspectives on American Democracy," which also includes information on Francis Lieber, a German contemporary to deTocqueville who also wrote about America.

JAMESTOWN

Best Search Engine: http://www.google.com/

Key Search Terms: Jamestown Virginia + history

History of Jamestown
http://www.apva.org/history/index.html
middle school and up

The *History of Jamestown* tells the story of the first permanent British settlement in North America. Don't expect to be bored—Jamestown wasn't just any old town! It was the home of Pocahontas and Captain John Smith. Battle, disease, and death are prominent themes in the settlement's history. So sit back, forget what the Disney movie told you, and enter the world of America's past.

The home page contains a fairly detailed history of Jamestown, starting in 1606 when King James I of England granted the Virginia Company a charter to establish the settlement. Simply scroll down the screen to find the related topics. The text contains links to people, places, and events that you can follow for more information. Want to learn more about the Virginia Company? Simply click on the link to find additional material, pictures, and more. You'll also find links to lengthy pieces on Pocahontas, her father Powhatan, and Captain John Smith (the main characters from the Disney movie). For an even more in-depth history, check out one of the site's interesting online exhibits. Click on "Exhibits" from the menu on the left side of the home page. Select "National Geographic Exhibit" and then "The Story" to get a fuller history of the settlement. If you just want to read the biographies of the key figures in Jamestown's history, click on "The People" from the same menu in which you found "The Story."

Remember that Jamestown isn't inhabited anymore. But the place is in not empty. Archaeologists have been busy at the site for years, unearthing artifacts from early colonial American life. Even better, the friendly folks who created this site pass along all the archaeological discoveries to you! All you have to do is click on "Findings" from the menu on the left side of the home page. Then scroll down the screen and select one of the sites listed. You'll find annotated maps, descriptions of the buildings, and lots more.

In addition to getting an up close look at the excavations, you can view the artifacts themselves and read commentary on what these artifacts mean. To do so, click "Exhibits" from the main menu on the left side of the home page. Select the "National Geographic Exhibit," click on "Things," and then pick the items that interest you—tools, coins, armor, and dishes. They are all over 300 years old! The other online exhibit, "The Dale House Exhibit," does an even better job of interpreting the artifacts for you. You can read about the armor found at the site, learn about the trade between the settlers and the Native American tribes near them, and find out what these early colonists ate.

JAPANESE AMERICAN INTERNMENT

Best Search Engine: http://www.google.com/
Key Search Terms: Japanese American + internment

The Japanese-American Internment
http://www.geocities.com/Athens/8420/main.html
high school and up

The Japanese-American Internment is the most comprehensive collection of information on this topic on the Web. This plain but powerful site gives you in-depth information about one of the darkest episodes in

American history. One of its best features is that it uses contemporary reports, posters, and photographs to paint a chilling picture of the Japanese American experience in World War II. At the home page, click on "Pre-War Intelligence" to read the 1941 Munson Report that assesses the loyalty of Japanese Americans. Or click on "Poster" to see the orders that forced Japanese Americans from their homes. Links lead to more information on key places, such as Manzanar, and agencies, such as the War Relocation Authority. The site also contains a concise time line of important events in the Japanese American experience. Interspersed are entries describing events in Hitler's campaign against the Jews.

You can also find a glossary and a photo gallery as well as links to important documents and sites on the subject. The only downside to this site is that it lacks a search function, so the easiest way to access information is through the gallery or the time line.

JIM CROW LAWS

Best Search Engine:	http://www.google.com/
Key Search Terms:	Jim Crow laws + history
	Black codes + history
	Poll tax + Jim Crow

Jim Crow
http://www.africana.com/tt_026.htm
middle school and up

This Web page, which is part of the *Arfricana.com* site, isn't flashy, but it is an excellent history of the Jim Crow era in the American South. So if you want a quick lesson about Jim Crow laws, start here. The essay briefly covers a wide range of topics including the origin of the term *Jim Crow*, the post-Civil War *black codes*, the U.S. Supreme Court decision *Plessy v. Ferguson* (which enshrined the doctrine of separate-but-equal in U.S. law), types of Jim Crow laws, and the reasons for the breakdown of the Jim Crow system. To navigate the site, simply scroll down the home page. Click on "Next" at the bottom of the screen to read the second page.

Race and Place: An African American Community in the Jim Crow South
http://www.vcdh.virginia.edu/afam/cvilleenter.html
high school and up

This excellent Web site focuses on the community of Charlottesville, Virginia, during the era of Jim Crow laws. It tells the story of an African

American community fighting to claim its right to vote that had been guaranteed by the Fifteenth Amendment but denied under Jim Crow. It is a tale of oppression and also of heroic resistance.

After you've entered the site from the home page (click on "Enter"), you can easily access its three main sections. If you want to get a sense of the composition of the African American community in Charlottesville during this period of oppression, you can explore the city's 1910 census of families with at least one African American member. Just click on "Census" under the heading "Explore Our Databases." The site has a sophisticated search engine that lets you search the census by a person's name, gender, occupation, race, marital status, or position in the family. You can also explore Charlottesville's city directory and the directory of African American businesses in a similar way. You'll see those links right below the one for the census.

The site has another wonderful section that lets you look at primary documents related to voting rights during the Jim Crow era. Click on "Disenfranchisement and African American Resistance in Charlottesville: 1900–1925" (under the heading "Read about African American Life During the Era of Jim Crow"). There are also some fantastic interpretive articles in this section. Check out the "Timeline of State and Local Politics" for an overview. "Virginia Suffrage Legislation" lets you read the documents that disenfranchised African Americans—the state constitution of 1902 (you can read the passage requiring voters pay a poll tax) and the Walton Act (stipulating that voters must pass a literacy test). Access primary source documents by clicking on "Broadsides, Newsclippings, and Political Correspondence" where you'll find digital copies of fliers, newspaper articles, and letters.

For those of you who are more visually oriented, check out the site's tremendous Charlottesville African American community photograph collection. Click on "Holsinger Studio Collection" from the home page, followed by "Search the Digital Image Database" and "African American Photographs." You can then scroll through an index of all the photos, which include portraits of people and homes.

"Jim Crow" Laws
http://www.nps.gov/malu/documents/jim_crow_laws.htm
middle school and up

This site provides a quick overview of Jim Crow laws. The best part of the site is that it lets you read samplings of Jim Crow laws from states across the nation. Although it gives you just a taste of the primary source material, this site is perfect for younger students who aren't ready to plow through entire documents such as those on the *Race and Place* Web site. To navigate the site, simply scroll down the home page.

KOREAN WAR

Best Search Engine: http://www.history.searchbeat.com/
Key Search Terms: Korean War
                President Truman + Korean War
                General MacArthur + Korean War
                38th parallel + Korean War

Korean War
http://encarta.msn.com/index/conciseindex/1F/01FC9000.htm?z = 1&pg
    = 2&br = 1
middle school and up

You get a sense of why Korea is called the "Forgotten War" when you're looking for basic Web sites about it on the Internet. It's a challenge to find a site that provides an overview of the *whole* war—the build-up of tensions, the major battles, the goals of the war, the key figures, the outcome, and the significance. This *Encarta* article does an excellent job of conveying all this information to you. It's not a flashy site, and it doesn't make learning about the war very exciting. But the *Korean War* gets the job done.

When you've opened up the Web page, you can either read the entire article by scrolling down the screen, or you can pick the sections that interest you from the outline on the right side of the page. As you read the text, you'll see links to more information on related topics, such as Kim Il Sung, Dean Acheson, Mao Ze-dong, President Truman, the Truman Doctrine, and General MacArthur. The article covers two Web pages, so if you do want to read the entire piece, click on "Next" at the bottom of the first page when you're ready to move on.

Korean War Historical Documents
http://www.geocities.com/Pentagon/1953/
high school and up

Do you need primary documents from the Korean War? If you do, you'll love this well-organized clearinghouse of material. The site doesn't provide any explanatory information, so if you need some help interpreting the documents you find, supplement your research with a site like the *Korean War*.

Korean War Historical Documents is a snap to navigate. Just look around the home page to find the time period that interests you. The site organizes the documents into three sections: "Pre-Korean War," "Korean War (1950–1953)," and "1953–Present." All you have to do is click on the documents you want to view.

The Korean War Experience
http://mcel.pacificu.edu/as/students/stanley/home.html
middle school and up

Even though this Web site is disorganized, it provides some informative documents about the Korean War. What's great about *The Korean War Experience* is that it brings a number of terrific resources together for easy access. Scroll down the screen to locate the links to the material.

The "Oral Histories" are awesome—you can read what Korean War soldiers experienced in battle. These first-hand accounts are moving at times, funny at others. Just click on the ones you want to view. The "Maps" section is also good. For a searing look at the politics of race during war, follow the link to "When Black Is Burned," which discusses the treatment of African American soldiers during the Korean War. There's also a "Resources" section that recommends some other Web sites on the Korean War.

The weakness of the site is that no broad view of the war is provided. The "Introduction," for example, is fairly useless. Don't expect to find an overview of the war in it. If you need that type of background information, refer to the *Korean War*.

KU KLUX KLAN

Best Search Engine: http://www.google.com/
Key Search Terms: Ku Klux Klan + history

The Ku Klux Klan During Reconstruction
http://www.alabamamoments.alalinc.net/sec28.html
high school and up

This site, which was designed by the University of Alabama as part of its *Alabama Moments in American History* series, does an excellent job of explaining the rise of the Ku Klux Klan (KKK) during Reconstruction. The site is easy to navigate, presents complex material in an understandable way, and incorporates primary documents.

Finding your way around this site is no problem. At the bottom of the home page, you'll see its four main sections: "Quick Summary," "Details," "Primary Source," and "Bibliography." For a very brief overview of the Klan's reign of terror during Reconstruction, go to "Quick Summary," which presents material in bullet points. The "Details" section puts the compact information from the "Quick Summary" into a broader narrative about the Klan's activities during Reconstruction. For a first-hand account of the Klan's barbarity, go to the "Primary Source" section to read an excerpt from an 1868 newspaper. The "Bibliography" doesn't provide recommendations for further Internet research, but it is an excellent source for print material.

A Hundred Years of Terror
http://osprey.unf.edu/dept/equalop/oeop11.htm
high school and up

This Web site contains an excellent article from the Southern Poverty Law Center on the history of the Ku Klux Klan—the U.S. terrorist organization that unofficially enforced the principles of racial segregation. Although the Klan wasn't authorized to uphold Jim Crow laws (as the police were), the Klan's goal for Southern society was the same as that of the creators of Jim Crow laws—a fully segregated society in which African Americans were disenfranchised and totally marginalized.

A Hundred Years of Terror isn't a fancy Web page. All you do is scroll down the screen and read. Nevertheless, the article charts the history of the Klan and pays a lot of attention to the overlap between the Klan and Jim Crow laws.

LABOR

Best Search Engine: http://www.google.com/
Key Search Terms: American labor + history

Coal Mining in the Gilded Age and Progressive Era
http://www.history.ohio-state.edu/projects/Lessons_US/Gilded_Age/
     Coal_Mining/default.htm
middle school and up

This site takes you into the world of some of the less fortunate citizens of the Gilded Age—the coal miners. Since it lets you access both primary sources and articles describing the conditions in the coal mines, you'll get a full view of what life was like below ground in the mines of the late nineteenth and early twentieth centuries.

The site is really easy to navigate. You'll see an index of linked subjects on the home page. Choose the ones that interest you, and you're off! You might want to start with the secondary material that explains mining in general terms: "The Hazards of Coal Mining in the 19th Century"; "The Avondale Disaster"; "A View of Coal Mining in 1877";

"Machines and a Coal Miner's Work," and "The Work of a Coal Miner." The rest of the links in the index are to primary documents. Don't overlook these first-hand accounts, such as *The Life of a Coal Miner* (1902) or Stephen Crane's *In the Depths of a Coal Mine*, because they truly do make the subject come alive.

United Mine Workers of America
http://www.umwa.org/homepage.shtml
middle school and up

This site provides information about the history of organized labor in the American mining industry. Most of the material on the *United Mine Workers of America* (UMWA) Web page won't be related to your research. But the site does have one excellent section on the history of the UMWA.

To access the relevant material, click on "The UMWA has fought for workers' rights since 1890" from the home page. This takes you to an essay about the UMWA. From there, you can follow links within the text to read more about specific events. There are also links within the essay to biographical entries on important people in the history of the UMWA.

Women's Labor History
http://www.afscme.org/otherlnk/whlinks.htm
high school and up

The American Federation of State, County, and Municipal Employees maintains this great gateway to the history of women in labor. Here you can find links to general sites on the topic as well as links to information on the Women's Trade Union League, women in the International Workers of the World (IWW), and women in the textile and garment industries. There are also sections on Mary Harris "Mother" Jones who was a labor organizer in the nineteenth century, as well as to other famous women in labor history. You can even find a section on "Women's Labor Songs."

One of the most interesting links in the site is to NASA's *Female Frontiers: Continuity and Change in Her Work*. The site is a table that shows the percentage of women employed, the common types of employment for women, and the average earnings of women versus men from the 1890s through the 1990s. The table also includes a column on "Groundbreakers," a list of women who entered male-dominated fields.

The site is extremely easy to use. Information is located under six major heads. Just choose the head and scroll down to find what you need. The site does not have a search function, but it is not so extensive that scrolling becomes a problem.

Labor-Management Conflict in American History
http://www.history.ohio-state.edu/projects/laborconflict/
high school and up

If you need contemporary accounts of some of the most famous conflicts between labor and management during the Gilded Age and the Progressive Era, use this site. It covers the confrontations in the Pennsylvania coal region as well as the Homestead Steel strike of 1892 and the Chicago strike of 1905. The site is easy to use—just click on the incident you want from the list on the home page. The site does have a downside. In some cases you'll be connected to only one article. And don't use this site to research the Haymarket affair, which is listed. The link is to a contemporary photo only.

LEWIS AND CLARK EXPEDITION

Best Search Engine: http://www.google.com/
Key Search Terms: Meriwether Lewis + William Clark + history
                        Corps of Discovery + history
                        Lewis + Clark + Jefferson
                        Sacajawea + Lewis + Clark

Lewis and Clark: The Journey of the Corps of Discovery
http://www.pbs.org/lewisandclark/
middle school and up

Think of this site as one-stop shopping for your Lewis and Clark research. A companion to PBS's acclaimed documentary program on Lewis and Clark, *Lewis and Clark: The Journey of the Corps of Discovery* has everything you need on these two American explorers and their expedition. Make yourself comfortable—you could be here for a while.

Use the menu on the right side of the home page to navigate the site (the menu shifts to the left side on all of the other screens). To say that these sections have a good bit of information would be like saying that it's warm on the sun. "Inside the Corps" provides an abundance of background material on the expedition, lengthy biographies of each and every Corps member (including Lewis's dog), and an essay that explains the political and historical context in which the endeavor took place. And there's more. All told, the Corps encountered nearly 50 different Native American tribes, and from "The Native Americans" section, you can follow the links to essays about *all* of them.

"The Archive" contains searchable, chronological excerpts from the *Journal* of the Corps, an extensive time line of the trip (which actually extends to 1838 so that you can learn where, when, and how Clark died), links to other Internet sites about Lewis and Clark, a bibliography of print resources, and unedited interviews (in audio or text files) with the historians who appeared in the PBS documentary. The Archive also has a terrific map collection. You can view the original maps created by Clark as well as recent ones that show the route the Corps took. The "Living History" section lets you listen to six historians talk about various aspects of the Voyage of Discovery. And don't be afraid of going "Into the Unknown," where *you* get to lead the Corps.

Exploring the West from Monticello
"A Perspective in Maps from Columbus to Lewis and Clark"
http://www.lib.virginia.edu/exhibits/lewis_clark/home.html
high school and up

After having thoroughly explored *Lewis and Clark: The Journey of the Corps of Discovery*, you probably think you don't need any more information on Lewis and Clark. And (depending on your project) you could be right. But this site is worth a look anyway—especially if you like maps. *Exploring the West from Monticello* describes the map-making tradition that made the Lewis and Clark expedition possible.

The site is divided into eight essays that you can access from the menu on the home page. Not all of the material is *directly* relevant to the Lewis and Clark expedition, although it does reveal a lot about their world (one thing the PBS site doesn't directly cover). Make sure you read the essay "To the Western Ocean: Planning the Lewis and Clark Expedition," which puts the Lewis and Clark journey in the cool context of the 50 years of effort trying to cross the North American landmass to reach the Pacific. For links to other sites touching on topics addressed at this one (including the University of Georgia's nifty rare map collection), check out "Related Resources on the WWW."

LINCOLN ASSASSINATION

Best Search Engine: http://www.google.com/

Key Search Terms: Lincoln + assassination

Abraham Lincoln's Assassination
http://members.aol.com/RVSNorton/Lincoln.html
middle school and up

Looking for a comprehensive Web site that covers just about every aspect related to Lincoln's assassination? This one has it all—detailed biographies of John Wilkes Booth and his co-conspirators, a blow-by-blow account of the assassination, and the full text of Booth's diary. Created by a high school history teacher with over 25 years of experience, this Web site is your best bet to find information of any kind about Booth.

The site is comprised of three main sections: "Abraham Lincoln's Assassination," "Abraham Lincoln Research Site," and "Mary Todd Lincoln Site." The material about Booth is included in "Abraham Lincoln's Assassination." Click on the heading and dive into a world of conspiracies, murder, and political agendas. To get started, you might want to check out the "One Page Summary of the Lincoln Assassination," which provides an account of the fateful night in painstaking detail (you'll see this link from the home page). The essay has links to all sorts of related topics. Click on "Booth's Gun," to view a photograph of the weapon used to kill the president. Select "Ulysses S. Grant" to read a biography of the Civil War general whom Booth despised and also planned to assassinate.

For those of you interested in a biography of Booth, click on "The Life and Plot of John Wilkes Booth" from the home page. The long essay provides a thorough look at Booth's life—from his childhood to his death—and is enhanced with photographs, quotations from his letters, descriptions of his girlfriends, and a review of his acting career. The essay is well written, doing more than simply listing the details about Booth. You'll gain an understanding of why Booth planned the assassination and what his ultimate agenda was. Throughout the essay you'll see links to more information. For instance, you can access an account of Booth's activities during the day of the assassination and read Booth's diaries. You'll find an account of his capture (and death) by clicking on "Eyewitness to History" on the home page. Toward the bottom of the home page, you'll see other topics. For a profile of the man who shot Booth, choose "The Bizarre Soldier Who Killed John Wilkes Booth."

Several collaborators assisted Booth. To get a better understanding of Booth and his cohorts, read their biographies by selecting "The 1865 Conspiracy Trial" from the home page and scrolling until you see a list of their names. You can also read the transcript of the trial in which these conspirators were found guilty and sentenced to death. Look for the link to the transcripts in "The 1865 Conspiracy Trial."

If you're not satisfied with today's "authorized" version of the assassination, click on "Conspiracy Theories" from the home page for an overview of various theories about *what really happened*. If you think there are lots of crazy ideas about the Kennedy assassination, you'll be surprised by Americans' beliefs about Lincoln's death.

There is even more information about Booth, Lincoln, Mary Todd Lincoln, and the assassination on this site. Take the time to browse the subject headings on the home page. There are entire sections of photographs and other primary sources (including Lincoln's autopsy report). Whatever your interest in this topic, chances are you'll find information on this Web site.

Assassination of President Abraham Lincoln
http://memory.loc.gov/ammem/alhtml/alrtime.html
middle school and up

This Web site, which is part of the Library of Congress' *American Memory Project*, provides a basic introduction to the topic of Abraham Lincoln's assassination. While other sites, such as *Abraham Lincoln's Assassination*, may contain a lot more material, this Library of Congress site is perfect for learning the nuts and bolts of it. Click on "Introduction" at the top of the home page for a review of the events on the night of April 14, 1865. If you select "Timeline" from the home page index, you can access a handy, day-by-day chronology of the events that followed Lincoln's assassination. To make the time line come alive, the site provides links to documents and drawings. For instance, if you click on "President Lincoln Dies" on the time line, you see a digital copy of a newspaper published the day after the assassination. If you select "Tobacco Barn," you see a drawing that depicts Booth's capture in that barn in 1865. If you just want to look at the documents without the time line, go to "Gallery" (from the home page). You'll be able to view 25 unique exhibits, including illustrations of the assassination, Lincoln's funeral procession, and Booth's execution as well as copies of mourning cards from Lincoln's funeral and a digital reproduction of the U.S. War Department's wanted poster for Booth.

This Web site also offers more advanced researchers a unique feature. Click on "Abraham Lincoln Papers" at the bottom of the home page to access *American Memory Project's* collection of Lincoln's correspondence. This vast resource is a great place to check out detailed information about the man whom Booth murdered.

Ford's Theatre
http://www.nps.gov/foth/index2.htm
middle school and up

This Web site, which is operated by the National Parks Service, focuses on the location of Booth's triumph and the nation's tragedy—Ford's Theatre. This site features visual exhibits related to the night of the assassination at Ford's Theatre that are accompanied by interesting and easy-to-read essays. Use the menu on the left side of the screen to navigate the Web site. Start with the overview of the assassination on the home page. From there, you'll want to look at the exhibits. Click on "The Chair" to view the rocking chair that Lincoln sat in at the theater the night he died. Select "Booth's Escape" to examine a map of the murderer's escape route from the theater. "Booth's Life" provides a basic biography of Booth, but it does not have the detail that the *Assassination of President Abraham Lincoln* site does. "Chronology" takes you to a time line for Ford's Theatre, which includes photographs of the building draped in black after the assassination. You can access other related material such as the text of Lincoln's second inaugural address.

What makes this site unique are its exhibits. Although it lacks the sheer amount of information that the *Assassination of President Abraham Lincoln* offers, it does offer a clear account of the major topics related to Booth and the assassination.

The Death of John Wilkes Booth
http://www.ibiscom.com/booth.htm
high school and up

The *Assassination of President Abraham Lincoln* and *Abraham Lincoln's Assassination* both provide a lot of information about Booth's life and his assassination of Lincoln. This Web site concentrates on the events that took place after Booth shot the president. It includes a first-hand account by Lieutenant Edward Doherty who led the squad of cavalry that intercepted and eventually killed Booth.

The Death of John Wilkes Booth contains photographs and a map of Booth's flight south. Since the passage from Doherty describes Booth's death (and is a bit grisly), younger students should steer clear of this site. Although it lacks biographical information about Booth, you can certainly supplement this site with *Abraham Lincoln's Assassination*.

LOUISIANA PURCHASE

Best Search Engine:	http://www.google.com/
Key Search Terms:	Louisiana Purchase

The Treaty of the Louisiana Purchase
http://www.earlyamerica.com/earlyamerica/milestones/louisiana/index.
    html
middle school and up

Use this Web page to learn about one of Thomas Jefferson's important acts as president—acquiring the Louisiana Territory from France. The first part of this page, which is part of the *Early America* Web site, gives you a brief overview of the Louisiana Purchase. You'll learn how much land was acquired, how much it cost, the significance of the purchase, and how it contributed to Jefferson's legacy.

Scroll to the bottom of the page to access primary documents related to the Louisiana Purchase. You'll see links to the original treaty document, to a text version of the treaty, and to a 1790 map of the Louisiana Territory.

LUDLOW MASSACRE

Best Search Engine: http://www.google.com/
Key Search Terms: Ludlow massacre
                       United Mine Workers + America + history
                       Mother Jones + mining + history

Looking Back: The Ludlow Strike and Massacre of 1914
http://www.proactivist.com/photojournal/ludlow.html
middle school and up

The Ludlow massacre is one of the saddest episodes in American labor history. Innocent men, women, and children were murdered when miners went on strike against dangerous working conditions and low pay at their Colorado mine and the private mining company summoned the National Guard to quell their legitimate protest. This site tells the story—through pictures, eyewitness accounts, and an excellent essay by historian Howard Zinn. If you're only going to check out one site on the Ludlow massacre, make sure it's this one.

Looking Back is easy to navigate. Scroll down the page to read the essay and view the moving photographs of the miners and their families and supporters. As you read Zinn's piece, you'll come across some primary material. For instance, you'll find a long excerpt from the speech Mary Harris "Mother" Jones made to rally the striking miners at Ludlow. The essay is on two pages, so be sure to click on "Continue" at the bottom of the first.

Another excellent aspect of this site is that, unlike many Internet resources about the Ludlow massacre, this one explores the consequences of the tragedy—particularly its impact on the broader labor movement.

We're Coming, Colorado
http://www.fortunecity.com/tinpan/parton/2/werecomi.html
middle school and up

This site gives a good accounting of the Ludlow massacre. Although slightly disorganized, it provides plenty of material on this tragic assault on working men and women. *We're Coming, Colorado* is not as comprehensive as *Looking Back,* but it does have a cool twist—it incorporates songs from the early labor movement, including one by Woody Guthrie commemorating the Ludlow massacre, to help tell its story. Each page you access automatically plays a different labor song, many of which are about the Ludlow massacre. Listening to this music helps you realize the powerful effect of the massacre on labor consciousness in America.

The home page covers the background of the massacre and reprints the lyrics from a song that honored the victims of the brutality. You can read what labor leader Marry Harris "Mother" Jones said about it by clicking on the link to "Ludlow." On the same page as the Mother Jones excerpt, you can also check out the lyrics to Woody Guthrie's song about the Ludlow massacre.

Scroll to the bottom of the page to access the main menu and click on "Louis Tikas, Ludlow Martyr" to read about the people who were killed in the massacre. The page also contains a poem praising the fallen Tikas. Select "Our Cause Is Marching On" for an overview of the terrible labor conditions during this period.

MANHATTAN PROJECT

Best Search Engine:	http://www.google.com/
Key Search Terms:	Manhattan Project
	Manhattan + atomic

The History and Ethics Behind the Manhattan Project
http://mohican.me.utexas.edu/~uer/manhattan/
high school and up

As its title suggests, this Web site focuses on the Manhattan Project, the code name for the U.S. effort during World War II to produce an atomic bomb. It provides short biographies of the key people behind the Manhattan project, an overview of the scientific discoveries that resulted from the project, a discussion of the atomic bomb design, and a perspective on the Trinity Test (the first test of an atomic bomb). Additionally, the site contains a section on the ethical issues raised by using the bomb, including arguments for and against the United States' decision to drop the atomic bomb on Japan.

The History and Ethics Behind the Manhattan Project is easy to navigate. It is basically one long essay, which you can either read straight through or choose the parts that interest you from the index on the home page. Perhaps the best part of this Web site is its straightforward discussion about the science behind the atom bomb. This is one of the few places on the Internet that you'll find a basic description of complicated processes such as fusion and fission. Most scientific terms are in hypertext. Click on the ones you don't understand to access the glossary. There are also diagrams, charts, and photographs to help explain concepts.

MANIFEST DESTINY

Best Search Engine: http://www.google.com/
Key Search Terms: Manifest Destiny + history
                     Westward expansion + U.S. history

USA: Index on Manifest Destiny
http://odur.let.rug.nl/~usa/E/manifest/manifxx.htm
high school and up

Getting a grip on what the concept of Manifest Destiny is all about can be a tough task. The term is very broad and can refer to several different dimensions of U.S. westward expansion in the nineteenth and twentieth centuries. You're not going to find one Web site that will answer every question about Manifest Destiny, but this one does a good job of laying out the fundamentals. It concentrates on the *idea* of Manifest Destiny—how the concept was formulated, why it caught on, how it was used to drive U.S. expansion, and the results of the migration westward.

The site is organized with a handy index on the home page. If you want to read the whole essay, start with the first item and keep hitting "Next" at the bottom of every screen. If you want to be more selective, you can also pick and choose from among the sections that interest you. One helpful feature of this site is that it has many links to more information on related topics, including The Monroe Doctrine, Lewis and Clark, and the Mexican-American War, among many others.

Be forewarned that this is not a glamorous site. There are no pictures, photographs, or interactive features. But despite its dull appearance, it does convey a lot of useful information.

The U.S.-Mexican War
http://www.pbs.org/kera/usmexicanwar/dialogues/prelude/manifest/d2heng.
   html
high school and up

This page, which is part of PBS's great site on the Mexican-American War (see entry) contains a superb essay on Manifest Destiny, one of the causes of this war. There are no frills here—no links or graphics—but you'll come away with a good background on Manifest Destiny and particularly on the influence Great Britain had in the development of the concept.

John L. O'Sullivan on Manifest Destiny
http://www.mtholyoke.edu/acad/intrel/osulliva.htm
high school and up

Where did the term *manifest destiny* come from? What exactly did it mean when it was first used? This simple site answers these questions. *John O'Sullivan on Manifest Destiny* contains the article in which that phrase was coined. All you have to do is scroll down the screen to read the complete text. So if you're a looking for a primary source about Manifest Destiny, don't ignore this site.

MARBURY V. MADISON

Best Search Engine: http://www.google.com/
Key Search Terms: Marbury + Madison

Marbury v. Madison (*1803*)
http://www.jmu.edu/madison/marbury/index.htm
middle school and up

There is no provision in the Constitution giving the U.S. Supreme Court the power to declare laws unconstitutional. So how did the court get it? This Web site tells you.

The Supreme Court established what is known as its "doctrine of judicial review" in 1803 when it heard the case of *Marbury v. Madison.* This site tells you all about this historic landmark case. For an overview of the case, click on "Explanation and Background" from the menu on the home page. For a more detailed look at William Marbury (and why he was suing James Madison, the secretary of state), read "Marbury's Travail." (Click on the title from the home page to access it). If you'd like to read a detailed perspective on John Marshall and the impact of this case, select "John Marshall—Definer of a Nation" from the home page. For biographies of the key people in this case, click on their names under "Note on the Players" on the home page.

MARSHALL PLAN

Best Search Engine: http://www.google.com/
Key Search Terms: Marshall Plan

For European Recovery: The Fiftieth Anniversary of the Marshall Plan
http://lcweb.loc.gov/exhibits/marshall/marsintr.html
middle school and up

This Library of Congress Web page focuses on the implementation and consequences of the Marshall Plan. This plan, formulated by Secretary of State George Marshall, was a U.S.-sponsored program designed to stabilize the economies of 17 European countries and, thereby, prevent them from turning to communism in response to the poverty, unemployment, and upheaval of the post-World War II period. The Marshall Plan was the centerpiece of the American Cold War strategy in Europe during the late 1940s and early 1950s.

For European Recovery is an excellent Web site. You'll find an easy-to-follow time line, a blow-by-blow description of the Marshall Plan, and lots of primary source documents. For a quick overview of the Marshall Plan, click on "Introduction" from the table of contents on the home page. For a detailed chronology of the events that took place in Europe and the United States, select "Key Dates" from the table of contents.

The bulk of this Web site is devoted to describing the Marshall Plan. You'll find a number of subject headings under "Key Dates" in the table of contents. You can either click on the specific topics that interest you or read them all to get the big picture. When you click on a heading, you are brought to a brief essay that gives you the rundown on what happened. Almost all of these essays contain links to primary source material. For instance under "Marshall Announces His Plan," you can read a digital copy of the 1947 *Washington Post* article that outlined Marshall's program right after he first formulated it.

You'll find other interesting primary source documents as well. For example, you can view digital copies of books published about the Marshall Plan. Click on their titles (*The Marshall Plan and the Future of U.S.-European Relations*, *How to Do Business under the Marshall Plan*, or *The Marshall Plan and You*) from the table of contents on the home page. If you're after photographs, click on "Album: The Marshall Plan at the

Midmark" from the table of contents. Then click on the title of the photograph that interests you.

The one major downside is that *For European Recovery* has no search function. This means you must pick through the individual subject essays to find the documents you need.

MASSACHUSETTS BAY COLONY

Best Search Engine: http://www.google.com/

Key Search Terms: Massachusetts Bay Colony + history

                                  Puritans + history + Massachusetts

Massachusetts Bay Colony
http://members.aol.com/ntgen/hrtg/mass.html
middle school and up

This Web site is a good place to start your research on the Massachusetts Bay Colony. It gives you the basic history of the colony, including who the key people involved in its founding were and their reasons for coming to America. It also discusses the growth of the colony and its conflicts with the British crown. The major downside to this site is that it's dull. There are no maps, illustrations, or interactive features to liven up your reading.

You can navigate this site in two ways. Either scroll down the home page to read the whole thing or pick the topics that interest you from the index at the top of the page. "The Beginnings of the Colony" looks at the settlement of Massachusetts, and "Immigration to New England Diminished after 1640" looks at the colony's growth. For more general material on the Puritans go to "The Puritan Background in England" section and follow the link. *Massachusetts Bay Colony* also provides extensive recommendations for other Internet resources.

Original Documents
http://www.winthropsociety.org/document.htm
high school and up

This Web page, which is part of the John Winthrop Society's site, has one of the largest collections of Massachusetts Bay Colony documents on the Internet. The page doesn't provide help with interpreting these documents, though. Use *Massachusetts Bay Colony* to put the material into a historical framework.

To access the documents, scroll down the *Original Documents* index. The materials are all directly related to the Massachusetts Bay Colony and were written between 1622 and 1641. If you want to read the Massachusetts Bay Charter (which is the most commonly cited primary source about the Colony), select the "Constitution of the Governor and the Massachusetts Bay Colony."

MAYFLOWER COMPACT

Best Search Engine: http://www.google.com/
Key Search Terms: Mayflower + history
                       Mayflower + Plymouth + history

The Mayflower *Web Pages*
http://members.aol.com/calebj/mayflower.html
middle school and up

If you're only planning to visit one Web site about this topic, make sure this is it! This site has just about everything you'll need, including the text of the Mayflower Compact. Better still, it's a snap to navigate. Some big Web sites are disorganized and make you constantly click back and forth between screens. Not this one. All you have to do is scroll down the "Table of Contents" on the left side of the screen. The pages you select pop up on the right side. You won't have to spend a lot of time hunting around either because the table of contents is detailed enough that you know what you'll get when you select an item.

Do you need passenger lists of the people aboard the *Mayflower?* No problem—this Web site has them, along with photoscans of William Bradford's original passenger list and genealogical charts for every person on the ship. Maybe you're looking for information about the ship itself? Again, this site has you covered. You'll find a history of the vessel, an essay on its crew, and a description of its voyage to America. What about primary source material? This site has the Internet's largest collection of original documents on this subject. There's the Mayflower Compact and the "Peace Treaty with the Massasoit." There's a complete library of full text version of Pilgrim writings, including "Mourt's Relation: A Journal of the Pilgrims at Plymouth," "Of Plymouth Plantation" (William Bradford's history of the colony), copies of the colonists' letters, and contemporary accounts of Plymouth written by the Pilgrims.

With all this primary material, does the site overlook general historical background? No way. Just look in the "Historical Information" section for essays on all sorts of topics, such as the Pilgrims' religious beliefs, common *Mayflower* myths, and Native Americans in the region. There's even a section of lists that contains a ton of quirky details (like a list

of all the passengers who died in the first winter, or a list of Revolutionary War soldiers who were descendants of *Mayflower* families).

McCARTHYISM

Best Search Engine: http://www.google.com/
Key Search Terms: Joseph McCarthy + U.S. + history
                      House Un-American Activities + McCarthy

McCarthyism
http://www.spartacus.schoolnet.co.uk/USAmccarthyism.htm
middle school and up

If you want a solid overview of the McCarthy era with lots of links
to other resources, look no further. This Web site does a terrific job of
explaining the McCarthy era. It begins its coverage in 1940 when Congress passed the Alien Registration Act and concludes with McCarthy's
public downfall in 1954. In between, it provides a thorough history of
McCarthyism with links to just about every conceivable related topic.
Although this site conveys a lot of complex material, it does so in a
clear and concise style.

It's also easy to navigate the site—all you have to do is scroll down
the home page. As you go, you'll see numerous links to people, organizations, and events that are connected somehow with McCarthyism.
There are links to J. Parnell Thomas, the Hollywood 10, the Rosenbergs,
and the American Communist Party, to name just a few.

Senator Joseph McCarthy—A Multimedia Celebration
http://www.webcorp.com/mccarthy/mccarthypage.htm
middle school and up

This site is a terrific place to learn about the McCarthy era—the
period during the 1950s when Senator Joe McCarthy hunted down supposed Communists as the head of the House Un–American Activities
Committee.

What makes this site interesting is that you can listen to audio clips
of McCarthy denouncing so-called Communists. You'll get a sense of
how McCarthy manipulated people's fear and prejudices to institute the
reign of political persecution now known as McCarthyism. You'll find
out how Communists were imagined in the collective American mind.

After you've listened to several of McCarthy's speeches, do check out
the audio clip of his downfall. The very first audio clip listed on the site
is the one delivered by the Counsel for the Army before a live national
television audience. ("At long last, have you no sense of decency?")

The one major downside to *Senator Joseph McCarthy—A Multimedia Celebration* is that it contains no interpretive articles or essays for you to read. Also the site contains no biographical material about this senator from Wisconsin. Nevertheless, the various audio clips are invaluable in developing an understanding of the history of anti-Communism in America.

The Fight for America: Senator Joe McCarthy
http://www.sirius.com/~mcjester/writings/cjb/joemccarthy.html
middle school and up

This site does an excellent job of laying out the important events in McCarthy's life. The essay is especially strong in its analysis of how McCarthy created a sense of the threat of Communists in government and then used that threat to advance his own political career.

You can read either the entire biography by simply scrolling down the home page or choose the sections that interest you from the linked table of contents at the top of the page. The one glaring absence on this site is any visual material. It's unfortunate that amid all of the biographical information, there's not a single picture of McCarthy.

MEXICAN-AMERICAN WAR

Best Search Engine: http://cybersleuth-kids.com/
Key Search Terms: Mexican-American War
                      Texas + history

The U.S.-Mexican War: A Concise History
http://www.dmwv.org/mexwar/concise.htm
middle school and up

This site is a terrific place to learn about the Mexican-American War. It's written clearly, is well-organized, and contains tons of information about the war. *The U.S.-Mexican War: A Concise History* is especially strong in laying out the background information about the war and giving an overview of all the important events. It also links to many primary documents, illustrations, and maps to supplement its interpretation.

To read about the war, use the menu on the left side of the home page. It's neatly divided into sections, so you can focus your reading easily. "Introduction" and "Countdown to War" give background material and go over the causes of the war. "Soldiers and Soldados" is a fascinating section that discusses the people on both sides who fought the war. "Northern Campaign," "New Mexico Occupied," "California Conquered," and "War in Central Mexico" go over the war itself. "The Peace" is about the Treaty of Guadalupe Hidalgo. Within the text, look for links to colored illustrations of major battle scenes.

For those of you looking for primary source materials, use the other menu on the home page (at the top of the screen). Check out the drawings and photographs in the "Archives." There are, not surprisingly, plenty of documents in the "Documents" section, including speeches, legislation, treaties, first-hand accounts of battles, and letters. Use the "Maps" section of the home page to find several contemporary maps of specific battle sites.

The U.S.-Mexican War (1846–1848)
http://www.pbs.org/kera/usmexicanwar/mainframe.html
middle school and up

The *U.S.-Mexican War: A Concise History* does a terrific job of explaining the causes, events, and consequences of the Mexican-American War. *The U.S.-Mexican War (1846–1848)* approaches the topic in a totally different way. This PBS site isn't quite as direct as the other *The U.S.-Mexican War* site, but it is more interesting. You'll probably want to go to the other one first to get all the basic history. Then use this site to get a more varied look at the Mexican-American war. One added bonus of the PBS site is that it's quite a treat to view. It has great graphics and a cool format and is genuinely fun to use.

The heart of the PBS site is its section of "Dialogues," which are individual essays in which scholars talk about specific aspects of the Mexican-American War. While it's a bit harder to focus your reading with this format, it's fantastic to get different perspectives on the war. Once you've selected "Dialogues" from the menu at the top of the home page, you can choose the scholarly discussion you want (look at the menu that pops up on the left side of the screen). There are three main areas in the "Dialogues" section: "Prelude to War"; "War: 1846–1848"; and "Legacy." You'll find more specific topics in each of these broad categories. For instance, in the "Preludes to War" category, you can read about Manifest Destiny, James Polk, Santa Ana, and divisions within Mexico. What's particularly nifty about these "Dialogues" is that a bunch of historians—from both Mexico and the United States—write about each topic. So you get five different perspectives on James Polk, for example.

The site has other helpful resources such as a detailed multipage time line. You can access it from the menu at the top of the home page. Pick the year you want to view from the left side of the "Timeline" page. To find other Internet sites on various aspects of the war, look at the "Resources" section from the main menu. It recommends a lot of Web sites by topic. Another part of this site that could be useful in your research is the site's "Discussion" section on set topics. Although it no longer takes new postings, you can still read what people had to say in response to thought-provoking questions on the Mexican-American War. Click on "Discussion" from the main menu to sample it.

Documents Relating to U.S. Foreign Policy
http://www.mtholyoke.edu/acad/intrel/pre1898.htm
high school and up

Need primary source material on the Mexican-American War that you can't find at the *U.S.-Mexican War* site? Try this exhaustive collection. Even though *Documents Relating to U.S. Foreign Policy* is somewhat disorganized, it has many documents that are all just a click away.

The home page contains an index of all the documents available on this site, starting with the "Mayflower Compact" of 1620. Luckily, the index is arranged chronologically, so all you have to do is scroll down. Unfortunately, the documents relating to the Mexican-American War are not clearly labeled (unlike those, say, for the War of 1812). So just keep your eyes peeled. Roughly speaking, the documents connected to the Mexican-American War start with John O'Sullivan's Manifest Destiny article of 1839. Continue scrolling and you'll find dozens of diverse listings, such as the Joint Resolution of the U.S. Congress to annex the Republic of Texas, the proclamation from the Mexican president denouncing this resolution, first-hand accounts of individual battles in the Mexican-American War, and Army dispatches (including ones from future president Zachary Taylor and General McClellan). Click on the ones you want to read, but remember that this site doesn't provide any help interpreting these documents. Use *The U.S.-Mexican War: A Concise History* or *The U.S.-Mexican War (1846–1848)* for reference.

MONROE DOCTRINE

Best Search Engine: http://www.yahoo.com/
Key Search Terms: Monroe Doctrine + history
                               Monroe Doctrine + Latin America + history

The Monroe Doctrine (1823)
http://usinfo.state.gov/usa/infosa/facts/democrac/50.htm
high school and up

Use this Web site, part of the large site maintained by the U.S. State Department, to read the text of the Monroe Doctrine as well as an article putting it in historical context. The site also includes some suggestions for further reading. The site is very simple—just scroll the narrative and the text of the document.

The Roosevelt Corollary to the Monroe Doctrine
http://www.uiowa.edu/~c030162/Common/Handouts/POTUS/TRoos.
   html
high school and up

In 1902, President Theodore Roosevelt announced an official broadening of U.S. policy in Latin America. This Web page allows you to read his modification of the Monroe Doctrine, which is known as the Roosevelt Corollary to the Monroe Doctrine. The site provides some background on the Roosevelt Corollary. To read the primary document, scroll down the home page.

MONTGOMERY BUS BOYCOTT

Best Search Engine: http://www.google.com/

Key Search Terms: Montgomery boycott

The Montgomery Bus Boycott Page
http://socsci.colorado.edu/%7Ejonesem/montgomery.html
middle school and up

If you're studying the Montgomery Bus boycott, you'll love this site! *The Montgomery Bus Boycott Page* is a clearinghouse of information on the boycott. All you have to do is click on the links to access the best of the Internet on this topic.

Scroll down the home page to view the index of links available. There are links to several detailed articles about the boycott, an essay that focuses on Rosa Parks, a ready-to-use lesson plan on the subject (with photographs and other material), and an online exhibit about the boycott from the National Civil Rights Museum.

MOON LANDING

Best Search Engine: http://www.google.com/

Key Search Terms: Apollo 11 + history

                      U.S. + space + history

Project Apollo
http://science.ksc.nasa.gov/history/apollo/apollo.html
middle school and up

The *Project Apollo* Web site takes you out of this world! This terrific Web site is the best place to begin your research on Apollo 11. You'll find detailed information about the mission and its crew. There are hundreds of photos from the first moon landing and audio files of the taped transmissions between the Apollo 11 crew and the National Aeronautics and Space Administration (NASA). There's even NASA's 1969 press report about the mission.

From the home page, scroll down to the "Manned Missions" heading and click on "Apollo 11." Keep scrolling down the page to find a wealth of information. Under the "Milestones" heading, there's a list of key technological advances that preceded Apollo 11's launch. In the "Launch" section, you can read detailed information about the launch itself in the words of the crew. "Mission Highlights" provides similar first-hand accounts, including Neil Armstrong's recollection of "coaxing the American flag" to stand on the moon.

To access the photographs, video clips, and audio recordings, scroll to the bottom of the page, where you'll find the link "Click here for more information about Apollo 11" that automatically takes you to another menu. Click on "Apollo 11 Image Directory" for hundreds of photographs—of the crew, of takeoff, of Armstrong descending the ladder to walk on the moon's surface, of the mission control center celebrating Apollo 11's successful launch. If you click on "Apollo Sounds" you can hear audio clips, such as the sound of the ship splashing down in the water. "Apollo 11 Movies" provides video clips. To gain an understanding of the mission's significance at that time, click on "Apollo 11 Press-kit" to read the 250-page report that NASA gave to the media in 1969.

Keep in mind that this Web site can also give you an overview of the American space program beyond Apollo 11. Go to "Apollo Flight Summary" from the home page for a quick history of the various Apollo missions and their crews. Scroll down to the "Unmanned Missions and Manned Missions" headings to find links to the specific flights that interest you—ranging from the Saturn 1 Test Program to Apollo 17.

Apollo 11: Where Were You?
http://www.msnbc.com/news/289739.asp
middle school and up

Although this Web site, which is the product of MSNBC News, is not as well organized as NASA's site, it does provide some good material on Apollo 11 that you won't find anywhere else. The home page is interesting from the perspective of social history. You can read accounts from all sorts of people—famous and not—about how Apollo 11 impacted them. This allows you to understand the significance of the Apollo 11 mission on Americans' sense of themselves and their country. Without this down-to-earth perspective, you may have trouble getting your brain around why people saw the mission as "a giant leap for mankind."

For detailed information about the history of the U.S. space program, scroll down the screen. Click on "Space Transporter" to get a sense of what space flight feels like. You can access MSNBC's surround videos of control centers, space shuttles, space stations, and landing sites. All you have to do is click on the topic that interests you, sit back, and let the adventure begin. If you keep scrolling down the home page, you'll find "Heaven and Earth" where you can learn about the political and social events that took place during space milestones.

The best section for all of you Apollo 11 buffs is located toward the bottom of the home page. You'll find a list of topics under the blue "Apollo 11" banner. Click on "Voyage of the Millennium" and then "July, 1969" to view images, such as Buzz Aldrin standing next to the American flag on the moon, of the historic mission. Under "Apollo 11 Remembered" select "Buzz Aldrin Plans the Next Leap" to read an interview with him. Throughout the interview, you can select audio clips and hear Aldrin speaking. You'll find a similar article about Neil Armstrong under the "Apollo 11 Remembered" banner. Don't miss the video clip of President Kennedy encouraging Congress to support his efforts to land a man on the moon. If you want to test your knowledge of Apollo 11, take MSNBC's handy interactive "Apollo Quiz." For more general information about space history, including contemporary topics, click on "Space History" and "Space News" under "Apollo 11 Remembered."

1969: The Moon Landing
http://news.bbc.co.uk/hi/english/special_report/1999/07/99/
   the_moon_landing/newsid_396000/396037.stm
middle school and up

This incredible site was created by the British Broadcasting Company (BBC). It is easy to navigate, informative, and provides a wealth of information without drowning you in every specific fact about Apollo 11. The site consists of a series of articles written by Dr. David Whitehouse, BBC News's Online Science Editor. You'll find multimedia material on every aspect of the Apollo 11 mission.

Follow the links down the center of the home page. If you're trying to understand the background of the mission, click on "The Space Race," which charts the events that caused the United States to focus on a moon landing. Under this topic you'll find audio clips and a lengthy essay. If you select "The Eagle Has Landed" from the home page, you can read about the Apollo mission before Apollo 11 as well as a description of Apollo 11 itself. You can listen to audio clips from the previous mission and watch a video clip of Apollo 11 touching down on the moon's surface. You can also read the transcript of an interview with Apollo 11 astronaut Buzz Aldrin. Click on "Buzz Aldrin" (which is under "The Eagle Has Landed" link on the home page). For a detailed portrait of the moon landing, click on "Walking on the Moon" from the home page. You'll be able to access video and audio clips and read a play-by-play account of the astronauts' activities on the moon.

For an entirely different perspective, select "The Story from Mission Control" (under "Walking on the Moon") to learn what it was like to direct the mission from earth. The "Legacy of Apollo" section recounts the events that took place after Apollo 11 and why the United States lost interest in moon missions after the success of Apollo 11. Click on "Revealing the Moon's Secrets" to learn about the scientific discoveries that came from the triumphant mission. Finally, scroll down to the "Multimedia" section to find audio or video clips to help your research. One of the neatest features here is the "Newspaper Front Pages." You can read the front pages of various British papers the day Apollo 11 landed on the moon.

MOUNTAIN MEN AND FUR TRADERS

Best Search Engine: http://www.google.com/
Key Search Terms: Mountain men + history
                              Mountain men + west

Mountain Men and the Fur Trade
http://www.xmission.com/~drudy/amm.html
high school and up

This Web page tells the story of the mountain men—mainly fur trappers and traders—who made the West their home both before and after the Lewis and Clark expedition came through. The site tells its story through historical essays, primary documents, artifacts, and artwork. The site is a snap to navigate. Simply scroll down the home page and select the section(s) that interest you.

The best section is the "Library." It contains a diverse collection of documents about the mountain men, ranging from their first-hand accounts (including diaries and memoirs) to contemporary second-hand tales of heroic figures, such as Washington Irving's *Adventures of Captain Bonneville*. The "Archive" section contains business records of the fur trade, and the "Gallery" has portraits of mountain men and their artifacts.

NATIVISM

Best Search Engine: http://www.google.com/

Key Search Terms: nativism + United States + history

Cycles of Nativism in U.S. History
http://www.immigrationforum.org/pubs/articles/cyclesofnativism2001.htm
middle school and up

As much as Americans like to mythologize our great melting pot, the truth is that not everyone welcomes immigrants into the country. This Web site provides an overview of the history of anti-immigration sentiment—or nativism—in the United States.

To navigate the site, simply scroll down the page. It is arranged chronologically, starting with the Alien and Sedition Acts of 1798 and closing with the 1990s. In between, you'll read about the Know-Nothing Party, the Chinese Exclusion Act of 1882, the Palmer Raids, and other low points in American history.

At the bottom of the screen, you'll find links to other pages that are part of the National Immigration Forum site. Most of these links deal with contemporary issues and so probably won't be directly relevant to your research on Ellis Island. But do not overlook *Immigration Facts*. Once you've selected it, click on "Chronology" to view a detailed time line of changes in immigration and naturalization law.

NEW DEAL

Best Search Engine: http://www.google.com/

Key Search Terms: New Deal + history

                       Franklin Roosevelt + New Deal

                       Great Depression + history

New Deal Network: A Guide to the Great Depression
http://newdeal.feri.org/
middle school and up

This site is a fantastic place to find documents and photographs related to the New Deal. The *New Deal Network* also does a great job covering various aspects of the Great Depression and the New Deal. Its only drawback is that it doesn't have a basic overview of the history of the New Deal. So *don't* use this Web site if you're only looking for secondary source material describing what the New Deal was. Visit an encyclopedia site like gi.Grolier.com (see the New Deal Web site in the following section) or the Great Depression section of the *1930s* site (discussed later in this chapter) first and then use the *New Deal Network* to get a fuller picture of the era. That said, this site does have a "Timeline" about New Deal and Depression events.

The site is organized into two main categories—"Research and Study" and "Features"—both of which you can access from the same main menu on the home page. The "Research and Study" section allows you to look for specific documents and photographs in the *New Deal Network's* gigantic online collections. If you need primary texts, select "Documents" from the main menu. You then have over seven hundred newspaper and magazine articles, speeches, letters, and other texts at your fingertips. You can search the collection by subject, date, author, or publisher/collection. So, if you're looking for President Roosevelt's speeches, search by author, find his name in the author index, and select the speeches you want to read. The "Photo Gallery" works similarly. Select it from the main menu and then click on a subject heading from an index (you can search the photographs only by subject).

The "Features" section has online exhibits of Depression- and New Deal-era topics. They contain documents, photographs, and essays written by historians. Because they are about fairly narrow subjects, the "Features" probably won't be the most helpful part of this site if you're trying to find material on a specific subject (unless you're lucky enough to have picked a topic that's the same as a feature!). Nevertheless, the "Features" are interesting, and they help you get a feel for the New Deal. Some of the topics are "Student Activism in the 1930s," "African-Americans in the Civilian Conservation Corps," and "Dear Mrs. Roosevelt" (letters to the first lady from poor children requesting assistance of some kind).

And there's more! The "Classroom" section (in the main menu) provides "Lesson Plans," a "Discovery Guide," a "Student Showcase" of online New Deal history projects by students, and "Additional Resources." Don't overlook the "Timeline" that covers 1933 and 1934. It conveys the important political, economic, and social events that took place then. Some of the entries in the "Timeline" have links to particular events. You can access the "Timeline" in the menu at the very top of the page once you select "Classroom."

New Deal
http://gi.grolier.com/presidents/ea/side/newdeal.html
middle school and up

If you need a quick overview of the New Deal, this Web site is for you. As part of the *Grolier Encyclopedia's* excellent online series *The American Presidency*, the page also offers easy access to a summary of New Deal policies and program.

To read about the New Deal, just scroll down the page. The essay covers the two phases of the New Deal, the various relief and recovery programs that comprised the New Deal, and an analysis of the opposition to Roosevelt's proposals. It concludes with an evaluation of the New Deal's legacy.

There are very few links in the essay, but the one to Franklin D. Roosevelt leads you to a biography that puts the New Deal in the context of Roosevelt's political life. The links to the Democratic Party and Congress lead you to general overviews. They do not focus on the role of these institutions in the New Deal.

NEW DEMOCRATS

Best Search Engine:	http://www.google.com/
Key Search Terms:	New Democrats
	Democratic Leadership Council

New Democrats Online
http://www.ndol.org/
high school and up

You'll find this Web site very helpful if you want to learn about the Democratic Party of the late twentieth and early twenty-first century, particularly about the Democrats during the administration of Bill Clinton. At the heart of the New Democrat movement was the Democratic Leadership Council (DLC), an organization founded by Al From and once chaired by Clinton. Many of the programs and policies Clinton pursued while in office—such as welfare reform and balancing the federal budget—had been promoted by the DLC as a way to help Democrats get credit for things that previously been thought of as "Republican" issues. *New Democrats Online* explains these positions. For an overview of the New Democrat position, click on "The Third Way" from the menu on the left side of the home page. To read about New Democrats in the news, click on "Press Center" in the same menu. Farther down the home page, you'll find a discussion of New Democrat policies on an issue-by-issue basis. Click on the one that interests you; the topics range from "Technology and the New Economy" to "Trade and Global Markets" to "Health Care."

1980s

Best Search Engine: http://www.google.com/
Key Search Terms: 1980s + social history

American Cultural History: 1980–89
http://www.nhmccd.edu/contracts/lrc/kc/decade80.html
high school and up

Use this site, part of Kingwood College's *Twentieth Century Decades*, for a great overview of key events and trends in the 1980s. The information in this site is on American society and culture. There are sections on "Art and Architecture," "Books and Literature," "Fashions and Fads," "Education," "Music and Media," and "Theater, Film, and Television." There's also a section on "Events and Technology," which highlights key events in science. Each section links you to key people and events in the topic area. You can learn about Stephen King and Tom Clancy in "Books and Literature," MTV in "Music and Media," and the Challenger disaster in "Events and Technology."

Unfortunately, this site has a big downside. Unlike the "Events" sections in other parts of *Twentieth Century Decades*, the 1980s section has very little useful political information. The "Events and Technology" section leads you to links on Presidents Ronald Reagan and George Bush Sr. that are either dead or useless. But do explore this site for culture. It's fascinating.

1950s

Best Search Engine: http://www.google.com/
Key Search Terms: 1950s + social history

American Cultural History: 1950–59
http://www.nhmccd.edu/contracts/lrc/kc/decade50.html
high school and up

This section Kingwood College's *Twentieth Century Decades* is a great source for researching the social and cultural history of the decade.

There are sections on "Art and Architecture," "Books and Literature," "Fashions and Fads," "Education," "Music," "Television," "Theater, Film, and Radio," and "Sports." There's also a section on "Events and Technology," which highlights the major social and political trends and connects to biographies of the decade's most important figures. Each section links you to key people and events in the topic area. You can learn about *I Love Lucy* in "Television," the All-American Girls Professional Baseball League in "Sports," and integration in "Education." This is an absolutely fascinating site with hundreds of links to more information. You can spend hours here.

Unfortunately, this site has a downside. The link to "Music" is dead. You'll have to scroll down the text to find the information, but there's a lot here if you are patient.

1940s

Best Search Engine: http://www.google.com/
Key Search Terms: 1940s + social history

American Cultural History: 1940–49
http://www.nhmccd.edu/contracts/lrc/kc/decade40.html
high school and up

Here's another part of Kingwood College's *Twentieth Century Decades*, which provides a decade-by-decade overview of key events and trends in U.S. history. The site does contain information on political developments, but the vast majority of information is on American society and culture. There are sections on "Art and Architecture," Books and Literature" "Fashion and Fads," "Music and Radio," and "Theater, Film, and Television." Significant political developments are discussed in "Historic Events." Each section links you to key people and events in the topic area. You can learn about the jitterbug, Abbott and Costello, and frozen dinners as well as the Marshall Plan and the beginning of the Cold War. The text is primarily an outline that connects you to hundreds of links. You'll have to do some clicking to get detailed information on your topic, but it's well worth the effort. This is a great site.

1990s

Best Search Engine: http://www.google.com/
Key Search Terms: 1990s + social history

American Cultural History: 1990–99
http://www.nhmccd.edu/contracts/lrc/kc/decade90.html
high school and up

Use this site, part of Kingwood College's *Twentieth Century Decades*, for a great overview of key events and trends in the 1990s. Although the site does contain information on political developments, the vast majority of information is on American society and culture. There are sections on "Art and Architecture," "Bestsellers," "Fashions and Fads," "Education," "Music," "People and Personalities," "Theater and Film," and "Television." There are also sections on "Events" that highlights the major social and political trends and on "Historical Documents" that gives an overview of key legislation. Each section links you to key people and events in the topic area. You can learn about hip-hop in "Fads and Fashion," welfare reform in "Historical Documents," and the Oklahoma City bombing in "Events." This site contains hundreds of links that connect you to vast amounts of material.

1970s

Best Search Engine: http://www.google.com/

Key Search Terms: 1970s + social history

American Cultural History: 1970–79
http://www.nhmccd.edu/contracts/lrc/kc/decade70.html
high school and up

This site, part of Kingwood College's *Twentieth Century Decades*, is a gold mine of information on American social and cultural history in the 1970s. There are sections on "Art and Architecture," "Books and Literature," "Fashions and Fads," "Education," "Music," "Theater, Film, and Television," and "Technology." There's also a section on "Events and People," which highlights the major social and political trends and connects to biographies of the decade's most important figures. However, the strength of the site is social rather than political history. Each section links you to key people and events in the topic area. You can learn about hyperrealism from "Art and Architecture," get 1970s crime statistics from "Events and People," or find out what a pet rock is from "Fad and Fashion." There are hundreds of links in this site.

Unfortunately, this site has a downside. Some of the links to the major sections are not active. Click on "Events and People" or "Technology" and you get nothing. You'll have to scroll down the text to find the information, but there's a lot here if you are patient.

1960s

Best Search Engine: http://www.google.com/
Key Search Terms: 1960s + social history

American Cultural History: 1960–69
http://www.nhmccd.edu/contracts/lrc/kc/decade60.html
high school and up

Use this part of Kingwood College's *Twentieth Century Decades* if you are researching the social history of the 1960s. There are sections on "Art and Architecture," "Theater, Film, and Radio and Television," Books and Literature," "Fashion and Fads," "Education," and "Music." You can get a cursory overview of key political developments in "Events and Technology," but political history is not the focus of this site. Each section links you to key people and events in the topic area. You can learn about Andy Warhol in "Art and Architecture," *The Feminine Mystique* in "Books and Literature," and the growth of the consumer movement in "Events and Technology." The text connects you to hundreds of links from which you can get detailed information on your topic. This site is fascinating. You'll find you can spend hours here.

1930s

Best Search Engine: http://www.google.com
Key Search Terms: 1930s + social history

The 1930s
http://xroads.virginia.edu/%7E1930s/front.html
middle school and up

This Web site covers the cultural aspects of the New Deal era—and with a lot of style. It's a terrific site that can take you hours to explore. It has essays about interesting topics, excerpts from radio shows of the 1930s, film clips, and old magazines to read. It's also a highly interactive site. No sitting back and scrolling down the screen here. You'll be clicking, listening, watching, reading, learning, and having fun.

The site, which is part of the University of Virginia's American Studies project, is divided into four main sections: "On Film"; "In Print"; "On Display"; and "On the Air." You can access the sections from the main menu at the top of the home page (after you've entered the site). "On Film" covers cinema-related topics from the 1930s. In this section, click on "Projects" for special exhibits that include "The Talkie and the Tramp" (about Charlie Chaplin), "Mammy Dearest" (about depictions of African Americans in films of this period), and "Reaping the Golden Harvest" (about the television and radio public relations campaign by the New Deal to keep people aware of its programs). In the "Archives" section of "On Film," you can read about the popular movies of the 1930s. Although the site contains links to clips of the films, this function was *not* working when the site was reviewed.

"In Print" discusses a lot of different issues loosely related to the printed word. The newspaper that pops up when you select "In Print" is your menu for this section. Click on the "articles" that grab you. You'll see sections on William Faulkner, comics, *Fortune* magazine, gender and sexuality in *Vanity Fair,* and the Great Depression. The section on the Great Depression is incredibly cool—and (as an added bonus) related to the New Deal. You'll see the link to it near the bottom of the newspaper page. It covers the entire spectrum of the Great Depression and the New Deal, offering the background information on the New Deal that is lacking in the *New Deal Network* site. The Great Depression section even has clips of Roosevelt making speeches about the New Deal.

"On Display" also has several multimedia exhibits about the artistic and architectural trends of the decade as well as a time line that lists these achievements. The exhibits include the Hoover Dam, the Chrysler building, the New York World's Fair, Chicago's Century of Progress, and Dumbarton Oaks.

Lastly, "On the Air" examines radio in the 1930s. There's an audio archive of excerpts from radio shows of this period as well as a "Projects" section that looks at several issues in depth. The "Projects" cover diverse topics. "A Gullible Nation? A Closer Look at the Night of Panic" explores the mass hysteria caused by the broadcast of Orson Welles's *The War of the Worlds* when many people believed that Martians were actually invading the nation. "This Land Is Your Land" is a study of rural music during the Great Depression.

The 1930s makes available a wealth of multimedia material, presenting this information in a creative and engaging way. You should be aware, though, that this site contains the equivalent of about 30 typical Internet sites. Try to be selective in your browsing (or else set aside part of a rainy afternoon to enjoy it).

1920s

Best Search Engine: http://www.google.com/
Key Search Terms: Jazz Age + history
                        1920s + U.S. + history
                        Lost generation + U.S. + history

The 1920s
http://www.louisville.edu/~kprayb01/1920s.html
middle school and up

This Web site is one of the most comprehensive sites on this decade that you'll find. It's packed full of information that covers every aspect—political, cultural, economic, and social—of the period in the United States and in Europe.

The 1920s is divided into three very large sections: " '20s Timeline"; "People and Trends"; and "A Remarkable Decade." You'll see the links to each section on the home page. For a chronology of the Jazz Age, go to the "Timeline." Be warned, though, that this is a time line on steroids! You pick the year that interests you, and the link tells you *everything* that happened, sometimes day at a time.

"People and Trends" is the heart of the site. It has six sections of its own: "The Arts"; "News and Politics"; "Science and Humanities"; "Business and Industry"; "Society and Fads"; and "Sports." "The Arts" deals with the culture of the Jazz Age. From an index you pick the topic, ranging from "Architecture" to "Theater." The amount of information in each of these subject sections is mind-boggling. Select "Literature," for example, and you access a detailed list of the "Writers of the 1920s" (with links to pages with biographical material on each of them). "Literary Trends," "Movements," and "Fads" discuss the Algonquin Round Table, the Bloomsbury Group, and the Harlem Renaissance (and provide links to additional sites on each of them). "Magazines," "Book Clubs," and "Publishing Empires" deal with William Randolph Hearst and the Book-of-the-Month Club. And these are just in the "Literature" section of "The Arts" section of "People and Trends." Get the idea?

"People and Trends" also covers "News and Politics." Here the section on "U.S. History" is especially good, looking at the period from almost every conceivable angle—the political leadership, labor movements, Prohibition, and lots more. "Science and Humanities," "Business and Industry," and "Sports" (three of the other sections) are all worth a look as well. And don't skip "Society and Fads," which presents the popular culture of the Jazz Age.

The third main section of this site is "A Remarkable Decade." Probably the weakest section, it consists of two interpretive essays on the decade that take opposite perspectives: "The Roaring Twenties" and "The Boring Twenties?"

You probably sense that you could get lost easily on this site. You're right. Luckily, its creator added a keyword search function that helps you locate specific information. To access this feature, scroll down the home page until you hit the heading "This Site Is Large." Below this there's a link called "Navigation and Other Tips." Click on it and then on "Keywords Page."

Chances are this site is the most useful one on the Jazz Age that you'll encounter. Unfortunately, it's not the most fun, and it really doesn't make the period come alive. There are limited photographs and illustrations and no audio clips. Although it tells you everything you need to know, you just don't get a full sense of the Jazz Age from it. Don't worry, though. Plenty of other Web sites (such as *The Jazz Age Page* below) evoke the period more fully, and you can use *The 1920s* in conjunction with them.

The Jazz Age Page
http://www.btinternet.com/~dreklind/Jazzhomemac.htm
middle school and up

This light-hearted site makes researching the Jazz Age fun. You probably won't be surprised that 1920s jazz is the focus of the site. But that doesn't mean that *The Jazz Age Page* covers only music. Rather, it means that the site tells the story of the Jazz Age using jazz. For example, it has a section on the Stock Market Crash of 1929. You can read a couple of essays about the crash and its place in history. Even better, though, you can listen to a Jazz Age song about the crash—"I'm in the Market for You."

The Jazz Age Page is easy to navigate. From the home page, you can access three "Special Features" sections on defining events of the period. In addition to the "Crash of 1929," there's "The St. Valentine's Day Massacre" and "Coolidge Welcomes Lindbergh." Each of these sections contains essays about the events, illustrations and drawings from the period, and a Jazz Age song about the event.

Scroll down the home page a little more for the other parts of the site. Are you interested in reading biographies of important Jazz Age artists? If so, click on "Biographies." If music is your thing, you'll love the "Sound Room" and the "Sound Room Docks" where you can listen to audio clips from the period.

Don't assume this site is comprehensive, though. It's not, nor does it claim to be. What it does do is give you a slice of Jazz Age culture and history, presented in a unique and charming way. *The Jazz Age Page's* use of jazz is especially effective. After all, they named the period after its music, right? Supplement this Web site with material from *The 1920s* (discussed above) for a complete look at the Jazz Age.

The Jazz Age: Flapper Culture and Style
http://www.pandorasbox.com/flapper.html
middle school and up

Women occupied a central role in the Jazz Age. This site focuses on the cutting-edge women of the period, known as flappers, who redefined social roles and women's fashion. It contains photographs, illustrations, and quick looks at Dorothy Parker, Louise Brooks, Anita Loos, and Zelda Fitzgerald. The site's other terrific feature is its links to primary source material, written during the Jazz Age, by or about flappers. Click on these links to read the 1922 "Flapper's Appeal to Parents" or the "Flapper Jane" article that appeared in a 1925 issue of *The New Republic*. You'll also find a Dorothy Parker poem entitled "The Flapper" as well as "Does Jazz Put Sin in Syncopation?"—a 1921 *Ladies Home Journal* article.

The major downside to this site is that it's fairly disorganized. So it's a good thing that it's not nearly as large as *The 1920s*. To navigate, scroll down the home page, and keep your eyes peeled for the links to primary sources.

OREGON TRAIL

Best Search Engine: http://www.google.com/
Key Search Terms: Oregon Trail + history

The Oregon Trail
http://www.isu.edu/~trinmich/Oregontrail.html
middle school and up

The Oregon Trail is clever, informative, and engaging. Instead of hitting you over the head with long essays, it uses shorter pieces about various aspects of the massive migration west. The result is that this site is easy to navigate and fun. Even better, it incorporates different kinds of material to help tell its story. You'll find full-text versions of diaries, memoirs, and guidebooks about the Oregon Trail and the two thousand-mile journey across the North American landmass. You're also just a click away from interactive maps and panoramic photographs of key sites along the trail. If you get tired of reading, you can stop and listen to recordings of historians discussing an array of topics. There's also plenty of background material, such as biographies of the major explorers and quirky anecdotes about life on the trail.

The best way to navigate the site is to use the main menu at the top of the home page. It's divided into four main sections (not including the commercial part where you can buy merchandise). Select "All about the Trail," and you'll find an index of many short essays about the history of the trail, the journey, and the lives of the people who made the trip along it. These essays are labeled by topic, so you shouldn't have problems finding what you want, whether that's something about the Native Americans and the Oregon Trail or about what people packed to take with them. In these essays, you'll see links to follow to hear the historians talk about the topics. And there are also plenty of photographs and other visual aids.

The other main sections in the site are also terrific. "Historic Sites" contains an interactive map. Just pick the state and location to read about important places on the Oregon Trail. If you want to check out the panoramic photographs, scroll down below the main menu and click on "Super Panoramas" in the middle of the home page. The "Fantastic Facts" section will liven things up a bit. Like "All about the Trail," it has an index of articles. The ones in "Fantastic Facts" tell outrageous (but true) vignettes about the trip along the Oregon Trail. You can read about the "$100 Glass of Water" and "A Very Strange Honeymoon" among others.

The site saves the best for last. The "Trail Archive" section has virtual shelves bulging with full-text versions of historical documents about the trail, including diaries, memoirs, and period books. If you want to look for a specific document or topic use the site's handy search feature. Otherwise, just have a great time browsing.

PEARL HARBOR

Best Search Engine: http://www.google.com/
Key Search Terms: Pearl Harbor + history
                        Pearl Harbor attack

Pearl Harbor: Remembered
http://www.execpc.com/~dschaaf/mainmenu.html
middle school and up

World War II had been raging in Europe for over two years without the United States getting involved; but in December of 1941, President

Roosevelt declared war on Germany and Japan. What happened? Two words—Pearl Harbor. On December 7, 1941, Japan launched a massive surprise attack on a U.S. naval base in Hawaii called Pearl Harbor. This site, dedicated to the casualties and the survivors of the attack, is your ticket to understanding what happened on that fateful day.

The site is easy to get around. The home page displays links to the site's various sections. Unless you're particularly interested in the military nuts and bolts of the Japanese assault (in which case you'll really love this site), you'll probably want to limit your research to just a few sections, especially "An Overview of the Attack" and "Timeline of Events." The real strength of this site, though, lies in its collection of first-hand accounts of what it was like to be at Pearl Harbor when the Japanese attacked. To find these, click on "Survivors' Remembrances" from the home page.

PENTAGON PAPERS

Best Search Engine: http://www.google.com/

Key Search Terms: Pentagon Papers

                                       Pentagon Papers case

The Pentagon Papers: Secrets, Lies and Audiotape
http://www.gwu.edu/~nsarchiv/NSAEBB/NSAEBB48/supreme.html
high school and up

The Pentagon Papers was a classified study of United States' involvement in Vietnam that former Defense Department aide Daniel Ellsberg leaked to the *New York Times*. The Nixon Administration attempted to block publication of the document on the grounds of national security and ultimately took the case to the Supreme Court, which ruled against the Administration. You can read the documents in this unprecedented clash between freedom of the press and national security on this Web site, maintained by the National Security Archive at George Washington University. Here you'll find a short introduction to the case as well as court documents and decisions on it. You'll also be able to access audio and transcripts of conversations President Richard Nixon had with his aides about the case as well as audio and transcripts of the arguments before the Supreme Court. Everything is easily accessible from the home page. The site isn't glitzy, but hearing the conversations and arguments makes you feel part of history.

The Pentagon Papers
http://www.mtholyoke.edu/acad/intrel/pentagon/pent1.html
high school and up

If you want to read the Pentagon Papers, use this site. It doesn't include the complete text, which is quite long; but it does give you the highlights and is a good place to get general background on the involvement of the United States in Southeast Asia in the 25 years following World War II.

Conversations with History
http://globetrotter.berkeley.edu/people/Ellsberg/elsberg98-0.html
high school and up

To learn more about Daniel Ellsberg's involvement in Vietnam and the Pentagon Papers, turn to this interview conducted by the Institute of International Studies at the University of California at Berkeley. Ellsberg discusses not only his career and involvement in the Pentagon Paper incident, but also the ethical issues surrounding his actions.

PERSIAN GULF WAR

Best Search Engine: http://www.google.com/
Key Search Terms: Gulf War + history
                        Gulf War + documents

Frontline: The Gulf War
http://www.pbs.org/wgbh/pages/frontline/gulf/index.html
middle school and up

This amazing Web site combines basic factual information about the Gulf War with interviews of those involved, special radio broadcasts about the war, first-hand accounts of battles, reports on Gulf War syndrome, and a detailed analysis of the weapons and technology used in the war. It is an engaging, informative, well-organized Internet resource that will likely prove invaluable to your research on the Gulf War.

Navigating this large site is no problem. From the home page, you'll see links to all the major sections. The basic information is at the menu on the bottom of the page. Follow the links to access maps, a chronology of the war, and a thorough look at the weapons and technology utilized during it.

Although you'll find this material helpful, it's this site's other sections that make it so special. Look for the links in the center of the page. Click on "Oral History" and you'll be able to read extensive interviews

with the major players of the Gulf War including Colin Powell, Dick
Cheney, Margaret Thatcher, Norman Schwartzkopf, and many others.
This section also includes interviews with Iraqi officials as well as historians, so you get a well-rounded view of the war. The site doesn't stop
there, though. How can you discuss a war without hearing from the
people who actually fought in it? *Frontline: The Gulf War* lets you hear
the stories from the women and men who put their lives on the line in
the Persian Gulf. Click on "War Stories" from the home page to listen
to or read these accounts. Another terrific feature is the "Voices in the
Storm" section. Click on this to listen to (or read) four 15-minute-long,
award-winning radio reports from the BBC on the Gulf War.

Don't overlook the site's special feature on "Gulf War Syndrome,"
which you can access from the home page. As it does throughout its
sections, *Frontline: The Gulf War* covers Gulf War syndrome by letting
you listen to a number of different voices and perspectives. "Analyzing
the Major Theories" gives you a synopsis of the different theories on
what causes Gulf War syndrome. "Five Interviews" are lengthy interviews with physicians, members of Congress, and the head of the Presidential Advisory Committee on Gulf War Syndrome. The "Veterans"
section lets soldiers, with and without the illness, talk about their experiences of it. You'll also find a section on the events at Kamisiyah and
an analysis on the media's performance covering Gulf War syndrome.

Desert-Storm.com
http://www.desert-storm.com/
middle school and up

This site isn't of the caliber of the *Frontline* one, but it does provide
some valuable information that is either lacking or difficult to find on
the larger *Frontline* site. What *Desert-Storm.com* does well is to simplify
some of the material so that you can grasp it quickly. Some of the
information, such as the number of troops deployed and casualties suffered, is presented in easy-to-read tables. The site also has an excellent
photo archive as well as an excerpt from an Iraqi soldier's war diary.
These visual images make a stunning companion to *Frontline's* interviews
and first-hand accounts.

Desert-Storm.com is a snap to navigate. Just use the menu on the left
side of the home page. For the most part, the headings are self-
explanatory. Click on the ones that interest you. The "Chronology" and
"Nations Involved" sections form a good informational backbone for
your research. "Units Deployed" gives a quick overview on which American military units were sent to the Persian Gulf and where they served.

The photo archives are in the "Image Gallery," and the Iraqi soldier's diary and interview can be found by clicking on "The Soldiers."

There is some overlap between *Desert-Storm.com* and the *Frontline* site. For example, both have material on the weapons used. However, the *Frontline* section on this topic is much better. If you go there first, you can just skip "The Machines" section on *Desert-Storm.com*.

PLESSY V. FERGUSON

Best Search Engine: http://www.google.com/

Key Search Terms: Plessy v Ferguson

Plessy v. Ferguson
http://www.africana.com/Articles/tt_325.htm
middle school and up

Use this Web site to learn about the 1896 U.S. Supreme Court decision in *Plessy v. Ferguson.* This landmark decision essentially allowed states to continue to enforce Jim Crow laws in the South, holding that so long as services of "equal" quality were available to both races, there was no constitutional problem with enforced segregation. The site offers a plain vanilla essay on the case from *Encarta Africana.* There are no bells and whistles or links to other articles here, but the essay really helps you put the landmark case in historical context.

Plessy v. Ferguson
http://civnet.org/resoures/teach/basic/part6/33.htm
middle school and up

If you want to read portions of Supreme Court opinions in the case, go to this site. It gives you excerpts from the majority opinion and Justice John Marshall Harlan's eloquent dissent, in which he wrote, "Our Constitution is color blind."

PLYMOUTH

Best Search Engine: http://www.google.com/

Key Search Terms: Plymouth + history

Plimoth Plantation

Plimoth on the Web
http://www.plimoth.org/index.html
middle school and up

This site lets you see the Plymouth Colony (as it was reconstructed) on a great virtual tour. *Plimoth on the Web*, which is run by the Plimoth Plantation Historical Site, also has some general material about the colony and its early inhabitants.

If you want to take the virtual tour, follow the link for it from the menu going down the left side of the home page. The site's other exhibits (under "Plimoth Plantation" in the menu) aren't worth visiting in cyberspace. Basically they just give a synopsis of what you'd see if you were at the actual museum. But if you want to read about the history of the colony without leaving the site, go to the online library. There's an overview of the colony as well as an essay on the Wampanoag Indians.

Pittsburgh Kids Online
http://www.pghkids.com/112398.html
middle school

As you probably already know, the settlement at Plymouth wouldn't have succeeded if it weren't for the Native Americans who taught the Pilgrims what to grow. One Native American was particularly important to the Pilgrims' survival. This Web site tells his story in a style that is perfect for younger students. More advanced students will probably find this site a little too basic for their research needs.

To read a biography of Tisquantum—or Squanto as the colonists called him—click on "Thanks, Squanto!" from the home page. The piece lays out what's known about Tisquantum's life and the role he played in saving the Plymouth colonists. There's also an article on the history of Thanksgiving.

PRESIDENTIAL HISTORY

Best Search Engine: http://www.google.com/
Key Search Terms: U.S. presidents + history

The American Presidents
http://www.pbs.org/wgbh/amex/presidents/nf/record/reagan/reagansnap.
   html
middle school and up

This is a truly wonderful, easily navigable site based on the PBS series *The American President.* Here you'll find very detailed biographies of each of the presidents from George Washington to Bill Clinton as well as links to other Web resources; essays by historians, journalists, and teachers; primary documents; and a glossary. To access the material just scroll down the home page.

To find a particular biography just lick on "Presidential Biographies" and select the specific president. All the biographies have a similar structure, making it easy to compare and contrast presidents and trace historical themes. Biographical sections include "Life before the Presidency," "Campaigns and Elections," Domestic Affairs," "Foreign Affairs," "Impact and Legacy," and a lot more. There are also quotes that reveal the presidential character as well as links to Web sites on the particular president. If you need a quick summary of a president's life, just click on "Brief Biography." There you'll find a table giving facts such as birth and death dates, political party, domestic and foreign policy highlights as well as a not-so-brief overview of his life. You can also compare presidents by clicking on a biographical section, such as "Domestic Affairs," and then choosing the presidents you want to investigate.

One minor flaw in the site is that on very rare occasions some of the presidents are missing some of the biographical sections. For example, there is no "Impact and Legacy" for Thomas Jefferson! Nevertheless, this is a really great site.

Presidents of the United States
http://www.ipl.org/ref/POTUS
middle school and up

If you just need a quick fact about a president, try this site. It doesn't have detailed biographies, but it gives you a great who's-who-type entry on each president. Here you can look down a list and find out what other government positions he held, who his vice president was, who was in his cabinet, and even what his presidential salary was. Each entry also has a bulleted list of notable events during his administration, but you'll have to go to the PBS site for details. This site has an impressive list of Internet biographies for each president as well as a list of other Internet resources including historical documents associated with the president. There is also a fun "Points of Interest" section of interesting facts. Did you know that President James Polk hosted the first annual Thanksgiving dinner at the White House?

PROHIBITION

Best Search Engine:	http://www.google.com/
Key Search Terms:	Prohibition + history + U.S.
	Temperance + history + U.S.

Women's Christian Temperance Union + history

Anti-Saloon League + history

Temperance and Prohibition
http://prohibition.history.ohio-state.edu/Contents.htm
middle school and up

Do you need a comprehensive overview of the history of Prohibition in the United States? This is the place. *Temperance and Prohibition* looks at this topic from a number of different perspectives and also has a variety of primary texts. The site is pretty easy to navigate and is loaded with photographs, political contemporary cartoons, and old-time saloon music to make your time on the site more enjoyable.

From the home page, select "Table of Contents," which lists the topics of the sections on this site. *Temperance and Prohibition* combines thorough essays about the history of Prohibition with primary source material from the people who fought for and against Prohibition. Just scroll down the "Table of Contents" and click on the headings that interest you. Watch out, though. The list isn't organized in any way, so you'll need to scan it carefully to be sure that you don't miss anything.

If it's secondary sources you're after and you want to learn *about* Prohibition, you'll be glad to discover that this site has some excellent essays on the topic. For background information, read "Why Was There Prohibition," "Prohibition and the Growth of the Brewing Industry," and "American Prohibition in the 1920s." There's even some terrific explanatory material about the organizations and people that lobbied hard for Prohibition. To find it, just click on the sections titled "Women's Crusade of 1873–1874," "Frances Willard," and "The Anti-Saloon League" from the table of contents.

Temperance and Prohibition also incorporates a number of primary documents to help you taste the flavor of the era. In the "Frances Willard" section, you'll find a speech by that leader of the Women's Christian Temperance Union (WCTU) as well as the last interview she gave before her death. Click on "Saloons" to read contemporary accounts of saloons in different cities. You can also check out a 1914 speech by Richard Hobson (an Alabama Congressman) favoring Prohibition and a 1908 essay by Percy Andrae vehemently opposing it. Don't overlook the cartoons from the Prohibition Party or the campaign poster from the Ohio Dry Campaign of 1918 either.

When you've finished exploring the sections in the "Table of Contents," there's not much else to spend time on here except for the links to recommended Web sites. Click on "Links to Other Sites" from the home page to access these.

Women's Christian Temperance Union
http://www.wctu.org/index.html
middle school and up

If you want more information on the part that women played in enacting the Eighteenth Amendment (1919) banning alcohol, check out this Web site. Most people probably don't know that the WCTU still exists and that it still advocates abstaining from alcohol. Although most of their Web site isn't relevant to your research, it does have an excellent section on the history of the WCTU, complete with profiles and photographs of the key women of the WCTU.

To find the material you need, click on "History" from the menu on the left side of the WCTU's home page. Once you do, you'll find another menu that lists the different parts of the history of the WCTU. Click on the subjects that interest you. The section on the "1873 Women's Crusade" charts the growth of the WCTU from a small group of women in Fredonia, New York, to a national organization with a lot of clout. The sections on the "Early WCTU" and "Frances Willard" also provide good historical background as well as photographs.

Because the WCTU maintains this Web site, it does not give you a balanced look at the total failure of Prohibition. It also doesn't cover the other groups that fought for Prohibition, such as the Anti-Saloon League. Despite these shortcomings, the WCTU site is still a good source of material on the history of Prohibition.

The Anti-Saloon League: 1833–1933
http://www.wpl.lib.oh.us/AntiSaloon/
middle school and up

This Web site focuses on the different groups that fought to implement Prohibition. It has the best coverage of the Anti-Saloon League, providing a detailed history of the organization and an extensive collection of primary material that was used by the Anti-Saloon League to advocate its cause. This site is also valuable because, unlike the WCTU's Web site, the *Anti-Saloon League* looks at why Prohibition's didn't work.

The easiest way to get around this site is to click on the sections that interest you from the main menu on the site's home page. The "History" section examines the background of both the Anti-Saloon League and the wider movement for Prohibition. The "Leaders" section has fairly lengthy biographies of the key figures in the Anti-Saloon League. Don't miss the "Printed Materials" section that includes copies of the fliers, periodicals, cartoons, songs, and dramas that the Anti-Saloon League circulated. There's even some information about the League's *Encyclo-*

pedia. In the main menu you'll also find "Classroom Activities" and a "Museum" with a small digital collection.

And there's more. Click on "Related Organizations" for information on other pro-Prohibition groups of the era, including the Lincoln-Lee Legion, the Scientific Temperance Federation, the World League against Alcoholism, and the Prohibition Party. Although the WCTU is also listed here, *Anti-Saloon League* doesn't really give any history of the organization; it offers only a photograph.

RECONSTRUCTION

Best Search Engine:	http://www.google.com/
Key Search Terms:	Reconstruction + history
	Andrew Johnson + reconstruction

Spartacus Encyclopedia: *Slavery*
http://www.spartacus.schoolnet.co.uk/USAslavery.htm
middle school and up

This site is a great place to get background information on a slew of topics related to Reconstruction. As the title suggests, this site looks at the period mainly through the lens of slavery, but it provides a firm footing for conducting further research about the entire Reconstruction period. *Spartacus Encyclopedia: Slavery* could use some pictures or other nontext features to liven it up, though.

Navigation is simple. Just scroll down the page to the "Events and Issues" section and you'll find links to brief essays on Reconstruction-era subjects like "Reconstruction Acts," "Radical Republicans," "Black Codes," "Ku Klux Klan," "Freedman's Bureau," and the "13th and 14th Amendments," among others. Just click on the ones that interest you. If you click on "Black Codes," for example, you'll be able to read a brief description of what these Codes were and how they related to the national Reconstruction effort. At the end of the essay you'll find one of this site's best features—excerpts from Reconstruction-era figures who wrote about the subject. Similar excerpts appear at the end of many— but not all—of the essays. It's sometimes hard to tell exactly why a particular piece was selected for inclusion, but they make for interesting reading in any event. There are also links within most of the essays to related topics that are mentioned in them.

These internal links could prove particularly helpful since the site seems beset by occasional technical difficulties. When this review was written, for example, the link to "Radical Republicans" from the "Events and Issues" heading was broken. However, this material was still accessible from a "Radical Republicans" link in the "Black Codes" essay. Which is a good thing, since the "Radical Republicans" page has a ton of useful material, including a detailed essay, links to information about many key personalities of the period, and some great primary source excerpts.

Reconstructing the South: Documents
http://itw.sewanee.edu/reconstruction/html/documents.html
middle school and up

This site is *the* place to visit if you need primary documents related to Reconstruction in the South. While some sites do a good job of providing access to the legislation of Reconstruction, this site covers the period from many different angles. There are diary entries and letters, speeches delivered for and against Reconstruction, the text of Supreme Court decisions and federal laws about Reconstruction, and copies of contracts binding former slaves to their former masters as indentured servants.

Scroll down the home page to navigate the site. The documents are organized according to type. All you have to do is click on the ones you want to read. If you're looking for documents about the legislative history of Reconstruction, check out the sections on "Congressional Investigations and Testimonies," "Legislation and Civil Decrees," and "U.S. Supreme Court Decisions." For insight into what people of the time thought about Reconstruction and the Civil War, read documents in the sections on "Diary Entries," "Personal Correspondence," and "Journalism and Memoir." The texts in "Party Platforms, Pronouncements, and Proposals" shed some light on the Ku Klux Klan and other anti-Reconstruction organizations. To get a feel for how Reconstruction issues were debated in public discourse, don't overlook the "Speeches."

As with many sites oriented toward primary sources, though, *Reconstructing the South: Documents* doesn't explain the texts it contains. If you need help placing the documents in their historical context, consult a Web site such as *Spartacus Encyclopedia: Slavery.*

RED SCARE

Best Search Engine: http://www.google.com/
Key Search Terms: Red scare

The Red Scare
http://www.spartacus.schoolnet.co.uk/USAredscare.htm
middle school and up

How did U.S. government officials react to the possibility of Communism taking root in America? This Web site answers that question. In the process it tells you a lot about the early history of Communism in the United States. *The Red Scare* is easy to navigate and has many links for you to follow to learn more about important American Communists and their enemies in the U.S. government.

The Red Scare focuses on a narrow period of American history—from 1917 to 1920. The Russian Revolution had successfully overthrown the czarist regime in Russia in 1917 when President Woodrow Wilson appointed A. Wilson Palmer as his attorney general. Palmer was convinced that Communists were plotting to overthrow the United States, so he carried out a series of measures that violated people's civil rights (and were, in fact, patently illegal). *The Red Scare* gives you all the details of official Washington's first reaction to Communism.

Follow the links within the text to learn more about suspected Communists, including Emma Goldman, Alexander Berkman, and Mollie Steimer. There are also brief overviews of International Workers of the World (IWW), Herbert Hoover, the Espionage Act of 1917, and the Sedition Act of 1918.

RELIGION

Best Search Engine: http://www.google.com/
Key Search Terms: U.S. history + religion
                                 U.S. religious history

Religion and the Founding of the American Republic
http://lcweb.loc.gov/exhibits/religion/religion.html

This site, part of the Library of Congress's online *Exhibitions*, explores the role religion played in the founding of the American colonies, in the shaping of early American life and politics, and in forming the American Republic. Over 200 books, manuscripts, letters, prints, paintings, and pieces of music are at the heart of the site, but the accompanying text gives you an excellent overview of the place of religion in early America.

This site covers a wide range of topics from the religious persecutions that brought people to the colonies to the Great Awakening to the growth of deism and the role religion played in the American Revolution. There's information on church architecture and art as well as sacred music. The documents to which the site links are fascinating. You can read Jonathan Edward's "Sinners in the Hands of an Angry God" or Tom Paine's *The Age of Reason,* denounced as the atheist's bible.

The only real downside to this site is that there is no search function. You have to choose a section at the home page and then scroll down the text to find the material you want.

REVOLUTIONARY ERA

Best Search Engine: http://www.google.com/

Key Search Terms: American Revolution + history

American Revolution + documents

Liberty! The American Revolution
http://www.pbs.org/ktca/liberty
middle school and up

This companion site to the PBS series *Liberty!* is a great starting point for anyone researching the Revolutionary era, the period between the end of the French and Indian War in 1763 and the adoption of the Bill of Rights in 1791.

To get a good overview of the period just go to "Chronicle of the Revolution." This takes you to a menu of six key dates around which the site organizes the historical narrative. Clicking on "April 1774," for example, takes you to the section on the roots of the conflict where you learn about the causes of the Revolution. Clicking on "Philadelphia, 1791" leads you to a discussion of the battle for the ratification of the Constitution and the adoption of the Bill of Rights.

One of the great features of this site is the links to related topics that enable you to expand your research in key areas. From "April 1774," for example, you can click on "Native Americans" to learn about their role in the Revolution or on "Diversity" to get an overview of the ethnic make up of the colonies. From "Chronicles of the Revolution" you can also access a simple time line. This section helps you with the chronology of the period, but it does not contain all the key events mentioned in the text. Therefore, to get a good overview of the period, use the six key dates. The site also contains a bibliography as well as a great list of links to other Internet resources.

The Revolutionary War: A Journey Towards Freedom
http://library.thinkquest.org/10966/
middle school and up

If you need quick information on the Revolutionary era, you can try this site that includes primary documents, biographical sketches, and essays on major Revolutionary battles.

To navigate *A Journey Towards Freedom,* use the menu on the left side of the home page. Click on "Infopedia" to access historical material. You'll see links there to "Major Battles," "Historical Documents Collection," and " Historical Figures Collection."

The site has a couple of other neat features as well. If you have questions or comments, you can explore the site's online bulletin board. Click on "Forum" from the main menu to reach it. Younger students will appreciate the interactive features of the site's games. Go to the "Fun Zone" from the main menu. If you play "The Flames of Rebellion," you can command the colonial or British forces in this strategy and war game. The "British Are Coming" game is directly related to the Battle of Lexington and Concord. You have to guide Paul Revere on his famous ride to Lexington and Concord; if you don't answer questions correctly, the British will beat him there.

This is not a comprehensive site, but it is easy to navigate and includes the basics. For more in-depth information you must look elsewhere.

The American Colonist's Library: A Treasury of Primary Documents
http://personal.pitnet.net/primarysources/
high school and up

This is a must for anyone needing primary documents on the era. See **Colonial America** for full description.

REVOLUTIONARY WAR

Best Search Engine:	http://www.google.com/
Key Search Terms:	Revolutionary War
	Revolutionary War + battles
	American Revolution + documents

Revolutionary War Battles
http://www.wpi.edu/Academics/Depts/MilSci/BTSI/Lexcon/
middle school and up

This site, developed by the Department of Military Science at Worchester Polytechnic Institute, is an excellent resource on the military aspects of the Revolutionary War. *Revolutionary War Battles* focuses on four battles—Lexington and Concord, Breed's Hill/Bunker Hill, Saratoga, and Monmouth—but uses them to present broader information about military campaigns during the war. Here you find discussions of tactics, terrain, communication, leadership, and the psychological factors of combat as well as background on the action. The site also contains maps, charts, and biographical information about the key figures in the battle.

Navigating the site is a snap. Scroll down the home page to reach the different sections. The site starts with an excellent brief overview of the battle, putting it in historical context. Beneath this history is an "Overview of Events Precipitating the Battle." Click on the links to learn more about the French and Indian War, Washington's failed New York campaign of 1776, and others. The next section, "Key Events Prior to Start of Action," contains a helpful chart that lays out what both the British and Americans were doing on each day leading up to and including the battle. In the "Definition of Subject Matter" section, you can access a map of the battle and information about the key British and American people involved. There are also links to find out about the British and American units deployed.

This is a great site for the military buff as well as for anyone researching the Revolutionary War.

Virtual Marching Tour of the American Revolution
http://www.ushistory.org/march/index.html
middle school and up

This Web site will put you in the shoes of a soldier in the American Revolution. It uses interactive maps, songs, and games of the Revolution and informative essays to take you back in time. Most of the Web site is devoted to the battles fought by the Continental Army. From the home page, look for "The Road to Valley Forge" heading. Beneath it are listed your campaign stops as a Revolutionary soldier. You can follow along with the Continental Army—from "Landing at Head of Elk" to "Winter at Valley Forge." Each stop is a multipage adventure. Read the essay to learn about the strategies and tactics of each side. You'll find highlighted names and terms within the text that you can click on if you want to learn more. The text is nicely interspersed with maps, quotations, colorful descriptions, and pictures. You'll see links to "Play a Tune" at the left side of your screen. Click on these to listen to Revolutionary War songs.

The Web site has other great features. From the home page, click on "Timeline" on the left side for an incredibly detailed overview of the events of the American Revolution. Click on "People" to read over 20 biographies of participants in the war. Most of these are the stories of everyday soldiers, like Jacob Latch, who served in the Continental Army at the age of 17. Click on "Games" on the left side of the home page and you can play "Rebus," a popular eighteenth-century game as well as "Who Is It?" to test your knowledge of the Revolution.

Keep in mind that this Web site is still growing. As it is now, you could spend a couple of hours on it finding material. The most detailed information is about the war (specifically its battles), so don't expect to find much of the political and social data that the *American Revolution Home Page* contains (see **Boston Tea Party**).

Journal of Richard Williams
http://members.aol.com/GuardsSite/JournalofRichardWilliams.html
middle school and up

You might wonder what it was like to *be involved* in a Revolutionary War battle. This site lets you know. It contains passages from the journal of Richard Williams, a British lieutenant who fought in the Battle of Lexington and Concord and recorded a description of the battle. Reading his account really makes the event come alive. It's also an excellent primary source if you are looking for material for a paper.

The site isn't fancy; there are no interactive features or illustrations. But all you have to do is scroll down the screen to read Williams's writing. The first excerpt is about Boston; the second recounts the Battle of Lexington and Concord; the third is about the Battle of Charlestown. There is no secondary source material on this site, though. If you need to review the facts, use *The Revolutionary War: A Journey Towards Freedom* (see **Revolutionary Era**) or the *Revolutionary War Battles* sites.

The War for American Independence
http://home.ptd.net/~revwar/index.html
middle school and up

This Web site is the best place on the Internet to find primary source material related to the American Revolution. If you're interested in reading newspaper accounts of battles, speeches delivered by an anonymous soldier, or touring a virtual museum of Revolutionary War artifacts, then set aside some time to tour this excellent Web site. All links to documents are from the home page. Just click on a heading and you will be transported back in time! You can read an advertisement from a 1778 newspaper that offers a reward for the capture of deserters. Click on the "Connecticut Gazette" to read the first published account of a battle (1781). You can access a letter written by a soldier, the text of speeches given by George Washington, and a biography of one of Washington's most trusted commanders. Click on "Virtual Museum" to browse through a collection of artifacts such as a receipt for bounty money, an example of colonial currency, and a receipt for transporting the baggage of the French army. This is a terrific Web site, especially for those of you looking for first-hand accounts of the war; but do keep in mind that it provides only primary sources. You won't find descriptions or analysis of events here like you will on the other Web sites.

Diplomacy of the American Revolution
http://www.state.gov/www/about_state/history/time1.html
middle school and up

This Web page, put up by the U.S. State Department, focuses on one important aspect of the American Revolution—the diplomacy. The site is organized into seven categories, five of which deal with the earliest American diplomats. Click on the topic that interests you to read a short essay.

You can explore Benjamin Franklin's attempts to gain French support for the colonial uprising or John Jay's work in Madrid to get Spain to officially recognize the United States. The other categories include "John Adams in Holland," "Francis Dana in Russia," "Robert Livingston," "French Assistance to the American Cause," and the "Treaty of Paris." At the bottom of the page you can connect to the "Timeline of Diplomatic History" home page, which has summaries of U.S. diplomatic policy in other eras. Click here if you want to read about the "Diplomacy of the New Republic (1784–1800)."

What is great about this Web site is that it addresses a specific—and often overlooked—element of the American Revolution. However, the entries are brief and might require that you look for additional information elsewhere.

ROSENBERG TRIAL

Best Search Engine: http://www.google.com/
Key Search Terms: Ethel Rosenberg
                        Julius Rosenberg
                        Rosenberg trial

The Trial of Ethel and Julius Rosenberg
http://www.law.umkc.edu/faculty/projects/ftrials/rosenb/ROSENB.HTM
middle school and up

This Web site tells the story of Ethel and Julius Rosenberg who were accused and convicted of being part of a Soviet spy ring and were executed in 1953. This tale helps you understand many of the elements—

McCarthyism, Communism, the Cold War, fear and paranoia—that came together in the United States in the 1950s. So as you read about the husband and wife who were two of America's most notorious Communists, you'll learn about the broader history of Communism in America.

To read the narrative of the Rosenberg case, start with the text on the home page and then click on "Continue." You can access biographies of the major players within the text. From the menu on the left side of the home page, you can choose to view a number of other interesting sections. "Diagram of a Spy Ring" lays out the Rosenbergs' alleged associates. There are "Trial Transcript Excerpts" and the statement of the judge who sentenced the Rosenbergs to death (this speech reveals a lot about American attitudes towards Communism). "Images" is a photo archive, and "Stories of Love and Longing" discusses the Rosenbergs relationship.

The Rosenbergs: A Case of Love, Espionage, Deceit, and Betrayal
http://www.crimelibrary.com/rosen/rosenmain.htm
high school and up

This Web site provides a comprehensive look at the Rosenberg case. In the process, it conveys a lot about Cold War-era America, especially about the fear of Communism and the general sense of insecurity that allowed McCarthy to run rampant for four years.

The site presents the material in an innovative way. It is constructed like a play to emphasize the drama of the events. The Rosenberg story is divided into five acts: "Trail of the Crimes"; "Julius and Ethel"; "Trial"; "Sentencing"; and "Appeal." Each act begins with "the cast of characters" and the "scene." Don't worry, though, each act also includes an excellent historical essay bolstered with photographs, excerpts from primary texts, and a lot of details. To navigate the site, use the command links at the bottom of each page.

ST. VALENTINE'S DAY MASSACRE

Best Search Engine: http://www.google.com/
Key Search Terms: Valentine + massacre

St. Valentine's Day Massacre
http://www.btinternet.com/~dreklind/threetwo/valentine.htm
high school and up

Fans of movies like *The Godfather* or *The Untouchables* will be interested in reading about the St. Valentine's Day Massacre on this Web page that is part of the excellent site *The Jazz Age Page*. The story of the St. Valentine's Day massacre is more like a movie script about the Mafia than a history lesson about Prohibition. Nevertheless, this tale of intrigue, violence, and Al Capone is *all* about Prohibition in Chicago—or rather, all about the *failure* of Prohibition there.

To read the essay, simply scroll down the page. Be sure not to miss the "Song Break" in the middle of the page that lets you listen to a digital recording of a 1928 song about the massacre. The essay explains the significance of the St. Valentine's Day massacre, especially in relation to Prohibition. If you want to learn about the Jazz Age culture in which Prohibition and the massacre took place, click on the link to the *Jazz Age Page* at the bottom of the screen.

SALEM WITCHCRAFT TRIALS

Best Search Engine: http://www.google.com/

Key Search Terms: Salem + trials

Salem + witchcraft

Salem Witchcraft Hysteria
http://www.nationalgeographic.com/features/97/salem/
middle school and up

This dramatic and fun Web site lets you walk in a witch's shoes. You play the part of an accused witch during the Salem trials of 1692. Instead of just reading about the trials, you go through the actual experiences—the time in the dark jail, the trials, and the hangings. Learning has never been as enjoyable—or as intense—as this Web site makes it! All the material used in the site, including the quotations, is accurate and taken from historical archives.

Salem Witch Hysteria is easy to use. Simply follow the on-screen prompts. Make sure to read the "Prologue," which gives you the history of the events leading up to the trials. When you're done with the "Prologue," click on "Experience the Trials." You assume the role of a New England merchant who is fingered as a witch by three young Salem girls. You make the choice of whether or not to confess to being a witch. Your journey into the dark side of Puritan America is made all the more real by the numerous photographs and illustrations. Throughout this virtual drama, you'll also find links to more information about the key players, such as Ann Putnam, Samuel Parris, and Cotton Mather. When you've finished, take the time to read the "Epilogue," which explains how the trials wound down. You have to go to the pull-down menu (which is available on every screen) and select "Epilogue" in order to access it. From the "Epilogue" you can post questions or comments on the site's "Forum" and even send a virtual postcard from Salem to a friend.

SCOPES TRIAL

Best Search Engine:	http://uk.yahoo.com/
Key Search Terms:	Scopes trial
	Monkey trial

Famous Trials in US History: Tennessee vs John Scopes
http://www.law.umkc.edu/faculty/projects/ftrials/scopes/scopes.htm
middle school and up

Whatever info you need about the Scopes "monkey" trial and its participants, this site is absolutely THE best place to find it. The introductory text alone—well-written and comprehensive as it is—gives a clear and detailed view of the events. But you can get a lot more in-depth information than just that on this site.

Your choices are listed in the boxes running down the left side of the page. Why not start at the beginning—with the link to the text of the Tennessee statute that set the whole historic trial in motion? Then you can have a look at the biographies of the trial participants (the biography of defense attorney Clarence Darrow is particularly worth reading), many of whom were as high profile as the case itself. In addition to actual excerpts from the trial, you can follow the "Observer's Account" link to read the impressions of one woman who was present at the trial. The controversy over teaching evolution in schools didn't end when the trial did, so if you want to find out what's happened with it since then—all the way up through the Kansas school board fight in 1999—follow the "Evolution Controversy" link to that text.

And just in case you don't find everything you need right here, this site is even kind enough to present you with a link to . . . other related links! You'll find that option toward the bottom of the home page.

The Scopes 'Monkey Trial': July 10–25, 1925
http://www.dimensional.com/~randl/scopes.htm

This site might not have the most information, but it definitely has the best presentation. Pictures of the trial participants (yes, even including a monkey) are interspersed with images of actual newspaper clippings from the 1925 coverage of the trial. As you scroll down the page, be sure to read the transcript of the interchange between the two lawyers, Darrow and William Jennings Bryan, when Darrow called on Bryan to take the stand. The substance of the exchange deals with whether the teachings of the Bible should be interpreted literally. Farther down, you get a glimpse of how European nations viewed the famous "monkey trial" in the United States.

William Jennings Bryan, the Scopes Trial, and Inherit the Wind
http://www.bryan.edu/scopes/inherit.htm
middle school and up

It's not flashy, but this site is a very good place to get a sense of one of the main figures in the trial, prosecution attorney William Jennings Bryan. You'll find a lot more information here than a simple rundown on Bryan's role as an attorney at the Scopes trial, though. This site gives a concise overview of his life and the strongly held convictions that led him to take up the cause of creationism in the courtroom. As you scroll down the page, you'll see paragraphs on Bryan's personal life, the political offices he held, his religious beliefs, his lasting accomplishments, and of course, Bryan's role in the Scopes trial. If you get nearly all the way down the site, you'll notice a numbered list. Check this out to read corrections of misconceptions that have sprung up surrounding Bryan and the trial. Here's a particularly interesting one: Bryan wasn't, in fact, opposed to the teaching of evolution in schools. He simply wished it to be taught as a theory, alongside other theories like creationism.

SCOTTSBORO BOYS

Best Search Engine: http://www.google.com/
Key Search Terms: Scottsboro boys
                        Scottsboro trial

Famous American Trials: "The Scottsboro Boys" Trial 1931–1937
http://www.law.umkc.edu/faculty/projects/Ftrials/scottsboro/scottsb.htm
high school and up

This site is an excellent source of information on the famous trial of nine black teenagers unjustly sentenced to death for raping two white women in 1931. The trial fanned racial and political divisions in the country and ultimately led to Supreme Court rulings that became the first step in creating the right of defendants to have lawyers in state cases and in declaring racial discrimination in jury selection unconstitutional. The site has everything you need to understand the case—all accessible from the home page. To access a time line of events, just click on "Chronology." "Biographies" will lead you to information on the key players in the drama including Judge James E. Horton, who set aside the death penalty for one of the defendants despite popular pressure.

For a detailed narrative of the trial, click on "A Trial Account," which not only describes the incident and subsequent trials but also links you to key players as well as to more information on testimony. If you need the actual appellate decisions, just click on the box with that name at the home page. This is not a very fancy site, but you'll get everything you need on the incident here.

Scottsboro: An American Tragedy
http://www.pbs.org/wgbh/amex/scottsboro/
high school and up

If you don't need an in-depth treatment of the case, go to this Web site that is a little easier to navigate than *Famous American Trials*. Here the story is told in a detailed time line with links to key players. You can also access biographies directly through "People & Events" at the home page.

One of the great features of this site is "Voices," found at the bottom of the home page. Click here for a summary of why this case is so important and to read the opinions of contemporaries on the various sides of the issue.

SECESSION

Best Search Engine:	http://www.google.com/
Key Search Terms:	Secession + U.S. history
	Secession + Civil War

Chronology of the Secession Crisis
http://members.aol.com/jfepperson/secesh.html
middle school and up

Here's a simple site that presents the chronology of events that lead to South Carolina's firing on Fort Sumter in April 1861, the event that precipitated the Civil War. *Chronology* is a first-stop source for outlining the story or checking a date and event. You will have to go elsewhere to gain an understanding of the politics of the crisis. Nevertheless, it's a good source for key documents. The site includes the text of Abraham Lincoln's Cooper Union address in which he presents his views on slavery, the platforms of the parties contesting the 1860 election, the text of the Crittenden Compromise that was one of the last ditch efforts to prevent secession, and the "Cornerstone speech" delivered by Confederate Vice President Alexander Stephens extolling the Confederate constitution. Each document is prefaced by a short introduction.

SECTIONAL CONFLICT

Best Search Engine: http://www.google.com/
Key Search Terms: "Civil War" + causes

The Time of the Lincolns
http://www.pbs.org/wgbh/amex/lincolns/index.html
high school and up

This is a great place for learning about the prominent issues that faced the United States in the years before the Civil War. In this site, which is a companion to a PBS series on Abraham and Mary Todd Lincoln, you can learn about slavery and the abolition movement, the emerging women's movement, the growing political divisions over slavery, and the changing American economy that deepened the divisions between the industrial North and the agricultural South. The site has a really great "Political Party Timeline," which summarizes each party's stand on key issues for the presidential elections from 1836 through 1864.

Each of the main sections of the site is subdivided into three topics, most of which contain links to primary documents and interviews. For example from "A Women's World," "Antebellum Women's Rights" presents biographies of Susan B. Anthony, Elizabeth Cady Stanton, and Sojourner Truth as well as writings by women activists and an interview with a historian who is a specialist on antebellum women's rights. Because the site centers on the Lincolns, you will also find information about the Civil War, but there really isn't enough here to use for research on this topic.

SENECA FALLS CONVENTION

Best Search Engine: http://www.google.com/
Key Search Terms: Seneca Falls convention

Women's Rights: 1848 to the Present
http://usinfo.state.gov/usa/womrts/
high school and up

In July 1848, a group of women and men met in upstate New York to raise the issue of women's rights. In preparation they issued a Declaration of Rights and Sentiments outlining women's issues and demands. Many historians consider this meeting to have been the beginning of the women's rights movement. To learn more about the convention and to read the Declaration, which is modeled after the Declaration of Independence, go to this site that traces the history of the women's rights struggle. Here you can find an overview of the Seneca Falls convention, the text of the Declaration of Rights and Sentiments, and a short history of the women's rights movement. You will also find a few short biographies of prominent women's rights reformers as well as valuable links to other sites.

The site is extremely easy to use. Just choose what you want from the home page. The links to "Official Texts, Speeches, and Remarks" and "Articles, Books, and Reports" offer only very limited late twentieth-century material that you will not find helpful in your historical research.

Although you will be using this site to trace the events surrounding the Seneca Falls convention, remember to look at the Declaration as an important document in American social history. It gives you a succinct statement of the position of women in mid-nineteenth century America.

SEPTEMBER 11 TERRORIST ATTACKS

Best Search Engine: http://www.google.com/
Key Search Terms: 9/11 terrorist attack
                       September 11 + terrorism
                       Osama bin Laden + terrorism
                       World Trade Center + terrorism

America's War Against Terrorism
http://www.lib.umich.edu/govdocs/usterror.html
high school and up

This Web site from the University of Michigan's Documents Center is your best bet for a one-stop resource on the September 11 terrorist attacks. An exceptionally thorough and reliable research tool, it is a comprehensive index of what happened that day as well as of what was going on in the world of terrorism before September 11 and since. You won't find original material here, but you will find links to the best resources for research on this topic, and they are organized in a logical, easy-to-use format.

The following sections comprise *America's War Against Terrorism*: "September 11th Attack"; "Counterterrorism"; "Post-September 11 Attacks"; "Previous Attacks"; "Other Countries"; "Background Research"; and "Related Web Pages." Each section contains numerous links. The "September 11th Attack" section is by far the largest, with links to the following topics: "Afghanistan"; "Airlines"; "Al-Qaeda"; "Anthrax" "Antiterrorism Law"; "Antiwar Activism"; "APEC"; "Archives"; "Bremer Commission"; "Children"; "Chronologies"; "Comprehensive Sources"; "Counterterrorism Measures"; and much, much more. The list even includes a link for "Volunteer Opportunities."

The link for "Afghanistan," for example, turned up dozens of sites with a wide array of information—everything from the United States Army's 1986 country study on Afghanistan to an ABC News site on the Taliban to a list of academic links on the history, language, and politics of the country. Other topics covered in depth were women, famine, and mercenary fighters.

How Stuff Works: September 11, 2001
http://www.howstuffworks.com/sept-eleven.htm
middle school and up

If you're pressed for time and just need to get some basic information, skip the previous site and go straight to this one. You won't be able to dig deep here, but sometimes you don't want the temptation of hundreds of intriguing links to distract you from a simple mission.

Although this is a commercial site, with all the annoying flashing windows and distracting ads that entails, you'll find answers to basic questions about the September 11 terrorist attacks, such as "What Exactly Happened When?"; "Who Did It?"; and "Why Did the WTC Towers Collapse?". The answers are brief but useful, and some offer links to other pages on the site, such as a page on Osama bin Laden and another one on terrorism in general.

SLAVE NARRATIVES

Best Search Engine: http://www.google.com/
Key Search Terms: Slave narratives

Excerpts from Slave Narratives
http://vi.uh.edu/pages/mintz/primary.htm
middle school and up

This Web site, created by a professor at the University of Houston, allows you to read excerpts of first-hand accounts of what it was like *being* enslaved. As you read these narratives, you won't be able to distance yourself from the subject. The voices of the silenced and the forgotten tell their own stories, which makes this material come alive.

The site is divided into eleven sections: "Enslavement"; "The Middle Passage"; "Arrival"; "Conditions of Life"; "Childhood"; "Family"; "Religion"; "Punishment"; "Resistance"; "Flight"; and "Emancipation." Each section contains excerpts from slave narratives about the particular topic. Simply scroll down the screen to find each section, and then click on the narratives you want to read.

This site is an excellent resource if you want to learn about slavery. You can read Charles Bell's description of the working conditions of slaves on a Louisiana cotton plantation or Lunsford Lane's recollection of the childhood moment when he first recognized the meaning of slavery. Another link, "Olaudah Equiano, an 11-year-old Ibo from Nigeria remembers his kidnapping into slavery," lets you enter into the mind of a young boy who was captured in Africa.

North American Slave Narratives
http://docsouth.unc.edu/neh/neh.html
high school and up

If you are conducting extensive research on slave narratives, this is the site for you. It is part of the ambitious *Documenting the South* project being developed by the University of North Carolina at Chapel Hill. When completed, *North American Slave Narratives* will contain the complete text of almost 200 slave biographies, autobiographies, and fictionalized slave narratives.

The site is very easy to use. You can search the material either alphabetically by author or chronologically. Just click on "Alphabetical Bibliography" or "Chronological Bibliography" at the home page. You can also read an essay explaining the importance of slave narratives by clicking on "An Introduction to the Slave Narrative."

This site is an extraordinary resource, but it is not for you if you want to search slave narratives thematically because there is no topical index. If this is what you want, use *Excerpts from Slave Narratives* described above. However, if you need a complete collection of narratives, this site should be your first stop.

SLAVE REBELLIONS

Best Search Engine: http://www.google.com/
Key Search Terms: Slave rebellions
                              Slave revolts

Black Resistance: Slavery in the United States
http://www.afroam.org/history/slavery/index.html
middle school and up

Black Resistance presents the on-going struggle of slaves to free *themselves* and to resist the oppression they encountered on a nearly-constant basis. Once you enter this site, you can choose from links that will tell you about how the slaves got to America in the first place ("Africa to America"), the different ways many of them responded to being enslaved ("There Were No Docile Slaves"), the ways female slaves sought to resist their oppressors ("Women Resist"), and a rundown of major slave uprisings ("Chronology of Revolts"). Each of these sections really brings its topic to life by incorporating pictures and first-hand accounts from slaves. This site is a great way to get an understanding of slavery from the slaves' perspective—an often overlooked aspect of the history of this period.

SLAVERY

Best Search Engine:	http://www.google.com/
Key Search Terms:	Slavery + U.S. history
	Slavery + American history
	Black slavery

Africans in America
http://www.pbs.org/wgbh/aia/home.html
middle school and up

This Web site, the companion to the PBS series, chronicles slavery in the United States from the beginning of the slave trade to the end of the Civil War. It is a terrific online resource for general information, documents, essays, illustrations, and historical commentary on slavery in the United States.

Africans in America is divided into four main sections based on historical periods: "The Terrible Transformation" (1450–1750); "Revolution" (1750–1805); "Brotherly Love" (1791–1831); and "Judgment Day" (1831–65). Each main section contains a narrative and a resource bank of images, documents, stories, biographies, and modern commentaries associated with the specific period. Each also has a teacher's guide.

To get to the narrative, just scroll down the home page and select the period you want. Then select "Narrative." (Do not use the period designations at the top of the home page. Although they are active, it will take you longer to get to the material you want.) As you read the text, you'll discover one of the site's best features—its links to all sorts of related topics. For example, from the "Fugitive Slaves and Northern Racism" section of the "Judgment Day" essay, you can find information about Frederick Douglass and Harriet Tubman. You can even find both a biography and an excerpt from an autobiography of the less well-known Harriet Jacobs, a slave who successfully escaped to freedom in the North (click on "Incidents in the Life of a Slave Girl" for this one). You'll also find an excerpt from the influential abolitionist book *Uncle Tom's Cabin* and a long article on the relationship of the Fugitive Slave Law of 1850 to the acceptance of the Compromise of 1850.

If you don't need the narrative overview, go directly to the resource bank that connects you directly to the biographies, essays, and documents for the period. The only drawback to the resource bank is that it is organized according to the narrative outline, so if you don't access the resources through the narrative, you may have to scroll through a lot of material. You can also access documents, essays, and biographies through the resource bank index. The index divides the resources into "People and Events," "Historical Documents," and "Modern Voices." But there are problems with going through the index. People and documents are a little difficult to find because the material is organized chronologically. "Modern Voices," essays by some prominent modern historians, is organized alphabetically by the historian's name, which is frustrating. Bottom line: The best ways to access this material are through the main section narratives or the search feature.

Aboard a Slave Ship, 1829
http://www.ibiscom.com/slaveship.htm
high school and up

While *Africans in America* gives you an excellent overview of slavery, this site focuses on one aspect of the slave's experience—the appalling conditions Africans faced during the transatlantic crossing. This very simple site, part of the larger *Eye Witness* site, lets you read the account of the Reverend Robert Walsh, who served aboard a ship assigned to intercept slavers off the African coast. His report of conditions he observed on a slave ship is chilling.

SOCIAL MOVEMENTS

Best Search Engine:	http://www.google.com/
Key Search Terms:	"19th century" + "social movements" + U.S.
	"19th century" + "reform movements" + U.S.

Women and Social Movements in the United States, 1776–1940
http://womhist.binghamton.edu/
high school and up

Women played an important part in founding and developing a wide variety of American social movements, from antilynching campaigns, to factory reform, to antiwar crusades. And, of course, they led the movement for women's suffrage. This excellent, easy-to-use site enables you to research the impact of women through a combination of background material and primary documents.

Women and Social Movements is organized by topics, called Projects. Each Project presents a research question such as "The 1912 Lawrence Strike: How Did Immigrant Workers Struggle to Achieve an American Standard of Living?"; an introduction; links to 20 to 30 documents and images; a bibliography; and related links. The site includes 30 topics and over 600 documents, many of which can be found nowhere else. Getting around is easy. To find the Projects, just click on "Documents" at the home page. From there you can browse by subject or date, or you can view a Project list by using the pull-down menu at the bottom of the page.

SPACE PROGRAM

Best Search Engine: http://www.google.com/
Key Search Terms: Space program + U.S. history
                        NASA + history

NASA Historical Archive
http://science.ksc.nasa.gov/history/l
middle school and up

The U.S. space program is about far more than the moon landing or the space station. To learn about its history, turn to this terrific site. It has it all—narrative, time lines, primary sources, and loads of out-of-this-world photographs. You can read the act that created the National Aeronautics and Space Administration (NASA) in 1958, access a history of rocketry, or research space launches.

The site is very easy to use. If you are interested in manned missions, click on the program you want from the main menu. You'll be connected both to a program overview that describes the goals, spacecraft, and flights in the series and to very detailed information about specific missions. Each mission entry gives the name of the crew and backup crew, launch date and time, mission objectives, mission highlights, and milestones achieved, if any.

If you want information on unmanned activities, click on "Astronautics History." There you'll find links to information on important lunar and planetary probes as well as to key documents in the history of space policy. Click on "Chronology of Aeronautics and Astronautics" and you can get special chronologies on lunar and planetary exploration and highlights of the first human space flights. From here you can also access a transcript of the *Challenger* operation in the minutes before the 1984 disaster. The site also includes "This Month in Space History." There's so much here that you can spend hours at this site!

SPANISH-AMERICAN WAR

Best Search Engine: http://www.google.com/
Key Search Terms: Spanish-American War + history

Imperialism + U.S. history

Rough Riders + Spanish-American War

USS Maine + Spanish-American War

The Spanish-American War
http://www.smplanet.com/imperialism/remember.html
middle school and up

This Web site is a treat for those of you searching the Internet for information on the Spanish-American War. This site is easy on the eyes, with lots of photographs, graphics, and a clean design. It's also comprehensive and looks at the war from a number of different angles.

Part of what makes this site so enjoyable is that it's arranged both chronologically *and* thematically. Instead of just tossing out a ton of facts about the often-complicated Spanish-American War, it sticks to the major themes of the war—the sinking of the USS *Maine*, yellow journalism, the war with the Philippines, the Rough Riders, and post-war expansionism. There's no table of contents, but just scroll down the pages, and you'll hit each of topics (some of them are given clever titles, but you should be able to sort out what you need easily enough). At the bottom of each page, click "next page."

Just because this site is easy to follow and breaks the war down into bite-sized conceptual chunks doesn't mean that it doesn't provide a lot of specific material. Look to the left side of each page to access dozen of links for more information. For instance, on the section on the "USS *Maine*," you can select "Cuba Libre" for an essay about the Cuban insurgency movement before and after the sinking of the *Maine*. You'll also find an interactive map of Cuba, photographs of U.S. military men associated with the *Maine*, samples of political cartoons about the disaster, a stereoscopic view of the destroyed ship, and several other photographs of the wreckage. Check out the "Chronology of the War" in the section on the Philippines, where you'll also find "Philippine History 101," several maps of the Philippines, and a chronology of events leading up to the Philippine-American War.

There are actually too many links to list, which touches on the site's one main drawback. There's no search engine that allows you to search for a particular document. But since the site is so easy to maneuver, this shortcoming isn't really that big a deal. Also keep in mind that the site's sweep is not just limited to the Spanish-American War. Instead, it keeps on going through history. But you can stop when you get to the page on the Boxer Rebellion in China.

The Spanish-American War Centennial Web Site
http://www.spanam.simplenet.com/
middle school and up

This Web site provides tons of good historical information on the war and its impact on the United States. Click on "Spanish American War Chronology" from the home page for a detailed time line of events related to the war. Click on "Some General Information" for other useful facts. Under this heading, for example, you'll find two different viewpoints on the war—one from an American perspective, the other from a Spanish perspective. You'll also be able to read about the experiences of the "Average American Soldier" in this war.

This Web site also has a long essay on how the Spanish-American War fit into U.S. foreign policy in the nineteenth century. To find it, click on "Some General Information" from the home page, and then on "American Foreign Policy in the Late 19th Century: Some Philosophical Underpinnings." But don't expect too much material other than this essay on the broader subject of the Age of Imperialism. This Web site is for those of you focusing more closely on the Spanish-American War.

The Spanish-American War in Motion Pictures
http://memory.loc.gov/ammem/sawhtml/sawhome.html
high school and up

This stunning web site from the Library of Congress's *American Memory Project* looks at the Spanish-American War through a specific lens— the camera's. Set aside some time to explore this site thoroughly. *The Spanish-American War in Motion Pictures* is the kind of site that makes you feel warm and fuzzy about the Internet. It's also a terrific resource for your research!

The Spanish-American War was the first "media war" in world history. The motion picture camera had been invented recently, and adventurous journalists brought the newfangled technology to Cuba and the Philippines to record the war's events for eager viewers back home. This site lets you watch the same footage that they did. Simply click on "The Motion Picture Camera Goes to War" in the center of the home page.

What you'll get is a narrative about the Spanish-American War that combines text with film clips. The presentation is divided into six sections: "War Begins"; "Cuba"; "War Ends"; "Philippine Revolution"; "Homecoming"; and "War Drama." As you work your way through the text, just click on the films you want to see. It's absolutely fascinating to sit at your computer and watch footage of the sinking of the USS *Maine* or U.S. troops landing in Cuba. Equally interesting are the "re-enactments" of key events that were made during the same period. Check out the re-enactment of "Rough Rider Skirmishes" in the "Cuba" section.

If you have the time and the inclination, you can also access the *American Memory Project's* digital archives to search for film footage of specific events and/or locations in the Spanish-American War. At the top of the home page, you'll see the links to search by keyword, an alphabetical title list, and a topical title list. You can also scan the subject index of the Spanish-American War footage.

Don't think that just because you've watched the film clips that you've exhausted this site. Be sure to explore the special presentation—"The War of 1898: The Spanish-American War." This online exhibit is a treasure that provides primary and secondary material about the war along with time lines and pictorial displays. Like all other Library of Congress sites, it's organized and very easy to navigate.

Start your journey at the "War of 1898" presentation by reading the excellent overview of the war that uses primary documents to describe the significant events. Click on "Overview Essay" under the "World of 1898" heading on the home page of the "Motion Picture Camera Goes to War." For a quick summary of the war, select "Chronology" (right above the "Overview Essay" link). Pick a country in this time line to get a detailed list of important happenings.

When you've gone over the basics, dive into the rest of the presentation by clicking on the title from the "Motion Picture Camera Goes to War" home page. Scroll down until you reach the "Special Presentations" heading, and then select the country you want to focus on—

Cuba, the Philippines, Puerto Rico, or Spain. Each of these sections then refers you to selected literature and photographs that deal with the Spanish-American War.

The Spanish-American War
http://www.pbs.org/crucible/frames/_journalism.html
middle school and up

Part of what made the Spanish-American War so unique was the role the media played in promoting the war. This PBS site examines the all-out war for headlines that was waged between the media moguls William Randolph Hearst and Joseph Pulitzer.

Scroll down the home page for a short and sweet explanation of yellow journalism and the impact it had on the American policy in the Spanish-American War. On the left side of the screen, you'll see links that take you to biographies of William Randolph Hearst and Joseph Pulitzer. In the same menu, you'll find links that let you look at some political cartoons about the war as well as some of the outrageous newspaper headlines from the period.

STAMP ACT

Best Search Engine: http://cybersleuth-kids.com/
Key Search Terms: Stamp Act + American Revolution

Sugar Act and Stamp Act
http://www.stjohnsprep.org/htdocs/sjp_tec/projects/internet/sact.htm
middle school and up

This straightforward Web site explains the basic significance of the Stamp Act in simple terms. Younger students will particularly appreciate this site. Just scroll down the screen to read the overview. As you go, you'll notice that key terms, events, and people are in hypertext. Follow these links to learn more about the topics, which include a quick look at the French and Indian War, a biography of British Prime Minister George Grenville, an essay about the Stamp Act Congress, and a piece on the Townshend Duties (which were passed at the same time that the Stamp Act was repealed).

Older students will probably need more detail than this site gives, although the *Sugar Act and Stamp Act* makes a good starting point. The site could definitely use a makeover, though. There are no graphics, pictures, maps, or illustrations to supplement the text.

Declaration of Rights of the Stamp Act Congress
http://www.constitution.org/bcp/dor_sac.htm
high school and up

Would you like to know how the American colonists felt about the Stamp Act—in their own words? *Declaration of Rights of the Stamp Act Congress* is the place! As its name indicates, this site reproduces the Declaration of Rights issued by the Stamp Act Congress—a 1765 meeting of representatives from 9 of the original 13 colonies—in response to the Stamp Act. Not only did the Stamp Act Congress help engineer the repeal of the hated Stamp Act, but it also helped lay the foundation for the American Revolution.

To read the Stamp Act Congress's resolution, simply scroll down the page. This site contains *only* the primary text (not even a picture), so use another resource, such as *Sugar Act and Stamp Act* for background information about the Stamp Act.

The American Revolution Home Page
http://www.americanrevwar.homestead.com/files/INDEX2.HTM
middle school and up

Tap into this Web site's vast resources to examine the historical context of the Stamp Act. See **Boston Tea Party** for full description.

SUPREME COURT DECISIONS

Best Search Engine:	http://www.google.com/
Key Search Terms:	Supreme Court + decisions
	Supreme Court + cases
	Supreme Court + opinions

Supreme Court Hallmarks
http://library.thinkquest.org/11572/cc/index.html
high school and up

If you need a quick, layperson's summary of some of the most important Supreme Court decisions, this is the site for you. Here you can find thumbnail descriptions and short summaries of 21 decisions, from *Marbury v. Madison* in 1803 to the *Bakke* decision in 1978. The site is rather plain vanilla. It has no links to other information, and it does have some downsides. It only goes to 1978, and the cases are arranged chronologically. So if you don't know the approximate date of the case you want, you have to scroll.

Selected Historic Decisions of the U.S. Supreme Court
http://supct.law.cornell.edu/supct/cases/historic.html
high school and up

Sponsored by the Legal Information Institute and Cornell University, this Web site gives you access to over 600 of the Court's most important decisions from its inception to the present. You can access cases from the main page either by clicking on "Topic" or "Party Name," (that is, the name of the case). If you use "Party Name," the site also connects you to a list of recent U.S. court of appeals decisions and Supreme Court opinions citing the case in which you are interested.

The site also enables you to research the opinions of individual justices. Just click on "Opinion Author" to get a list of all Supreme Court justices. Clicking on a linked name retrieves all opinions by that justice (including dissenting and concurring opinions) involving cases included in the collection. The list of justices also includes links to brief biographies.

This site is not just historical. Go to the home page and you'll be able to view the Court's most recent decisions as well.

SWEATSHOPS

Best Search Engine: http://www.google.com/

Key Search Terms: Sweatshops + U.S. history

Between a Rock and a Hard Place
http://americanhistory.si.edu/sweatshops/
high school and up

This site, prepared by the Smithsonian National Museum of American History, provides a virtual exhibition that traces the history of sweatshops and their laborers using images and extensive captions.

To access the material, click on the image on the title page. This opens the "Exhibition." Skip the floor plan and scroll to the bottom of the page where you find links to "Introduction" and "History" that present the information you want. "Introduction" gives you a quick overview of the problem. If you click on the text in the lower picture, a definition of *sweatshop* is brought up. Then go to "History" to trace the growth and change in sweatshops from 1820 to the present.

One of the most fascinating aspects of this site is the "Fashion Food Chain," which presents the present-day issue of clothes production in foreign countries, often made by cheap labor. Click on various elements in the text of the picture to get a table that outlines the advantages and disadvantages of domestic and offshore production and a list of the top 15 apparel exporters to the United States.

TENEMENTS

Best Search Engine: http://www.google.com/
Key Search Terms: Tenements + U.S. history

Lower East Side Tenement Museum
http://www.wnet.org/tenement/
middle school and up

Lower East Side Tenement Museum looks at immigrant life through the lens of one building—97 Orchard Street, a tenement where some ten thousand people lived from 1870 through 1915. The site is a terrific resource that allows you to take a virtual tour of this New York City tenement building. You can view rooms furnished as they were during the Industrial Revolution and get a sense of how people lived. Better yet, you can read a fascinating history about tenement life during the late nineteenth and early twentieth centuries.

Start your online journey back in time with the "History" section, which is the last item in the menu on the home page. This section provides an overview of the tenement building, describing when it was built, who owned it, what changes were made to it over time, and what sorts of rents were charged. It also gives the history of tenement life as a whole in New York City as well as some background on the series of laws that were passed to try to raise the standard of living for workers. You can scroll down the "History" page or pick the topics that interest you from the menu at the top.

Then go back to the home page and explore the "Urban Log Cabin" section. You'll see two photographs of 97 Orchard Street—one taken in 1870, the other in 1915. Click on a room in one of the pictures to view a diorama of it (complete with furniture and people). Each diorama is accompanied by a description of the residents who are on display. In these narratives you'll learn where the families are from, what they do for a living, what's going on in the diorama, and what these people's future prospects are. The narratives are taken from the actual tenants who lived at 97 Orchard. As you read about the different families that called the tenement home, you'll learn about the changing demographics of America's working poor between 1870 and 1915.

The "Excavation" section lets you take part in a virtual excavation of the building. (The building had been sealed from 1935 to 1987. The actual excavation took place in 1993.) One exhibit allows you to peel off 13 layers of wallpaper from the walls of 97 Orchard. In the other, you look under old floorboards to find lost objects (that were found during the excavation), such as a Yiddish newspaper ad for a palm reader and a box of Russian cigarettes from 1907. "VR Tenement" is probably the coolest section. Using a controllable panoramic movie, you can take virtual tours of two tenement rooms from two different periods.

On the Lower East Side: Observations of Life in Lower Manhattan at the Turn of the Century
http://tenant.net/Community/LES/contents.html
high school and up

On the Lower East Side offers a collection of primary sources by contemporary social reformers describing the living and working conditions in the slums of New York City's Lower East Side at the end of the nineteenth century and the beginning of the twentieth century. It's an excellent way to learn about the horrible conditions in which immigrants lived and the efforts of reformers to improve those conditions. It also gives you a very interesting glimpse into how reformers viewed various ethnic groups and immigrants in general.

The site contains excerpts from 17 articles by reformers. Here you can read Jacob Riis on "The Jews of New York" or Mary Van Kleeck on "Child Labor in New York City Tenements." You'll also be able to study attempts at housing reform, vitally important to Progressive reformers who thought that tenement housing was the chief source of urban social ills. To reach the material just scroll down the list on the home page. The site also contains an appendix of statistical data on the foreign population in New York City collected in 1901.

How the Other Half Lives
http://yale.edu/amstud/inforev/riis/title.html
high school and up

If you want to read the book that galvanized the Progressive movement for housing reform, go to this site. Here you'll find the text of Jacob Riis's 1890 work, which describes conditions in New York City's Lower East Side in the late nineteenth century. The work contains Riis's photos of slum life, which graphically illustrate the appalling conditions under which immigrants lived.

TENNESSEE VALLEY AUTHORITY

Best Search Engine: http://www.google.com/
Key Search Terms: Tennessee Valley Authority + history
                        New Deal + history
                        Rural Electrification Project + history

A Short History of the TVA. From the New Deal to a New Century
http://www.tva.gov/abouttva/history.htm
middle school up

This Web page paints the history of the Tennessee Valley Authority (TVA) in broad strokes from its founding in 1933 to the present. It's the perfect place to start your research! The page also contains photographs of the TVA at various points in its history as well as the full text of the Tennessee Valley Authority Act that authorized the project in 1933.

Just scroll down the screen to find everything. You'll see the link to the Tennessee Valley Authority Act embedded in the text near the top of the page. Keep moving down the page to view the photographs. Although this page is comprehensive, it doesn't give a lot of specific details about the TVA. Instead, it concentrates on laying out the major projects and events related to the TVA that took place in each decade.

Since this page is part of the TVA's site, you can easily access a wealth of information about current TVA projects if you're interested. Just click on the "TVA" icon at the top left corner of the history page.

TRAIL OF TEARS

Best Search Engine: http://www.google.com/
Key Search Terms: Trail of Tears
                        Cherokee

Trail of Tears
http://rosecity.net/tears/retrace.html
middle school and up

The Trail of Tears, the forced removal of the Cherokee Indians from their homes in Georgia, North Carolina, and Tennessee in 1838, was one of the darkest episodes in American history. You can learn the details of this event by going to this easy-to-use site. Scroll down the home page to get a detailed chronology of the relocation, statistics on some parts of the removal, and stories from along the trail. The only necessary elements missing from the site are a map of the trail and links to other resources, but this site is a good place to start your research.

Trail of Tears
http://ngeorgia.com/history/trailoftearsmap.html
high school and up

While the previous site concentrates on the events of the removal, this site gives you the background to put it into historical context. To understand what prompted the removal, scroll down the home page and click on "Trail of Tears." The essay provides links to important elements in the story including a history of the Cherokee and biographies of Cherokee leaders such as Major Ridge, who supported the removal, and John Ross, who opposed it. If you want to learn more about the history of the forts built to house the Cherokee before the removal, click on "Cherokee Removal Forts." There you'll get a list of the forts by county. Although some entries give you general overviews of the county, you can learn a lot about the interaction of settlers and Indians in the years before removal. The only downside to this site is that it focuses only on Georgia.

TRANSCONTINENTAL RAILROAD

Best Search Engine: http://www.google.com/

Key Search Terms: Transcontinental railroad + U.S. history

Steel Rails and Iron Horses
http://www.blm.gov/education/railroads/railroad.html
middle school and up

The completion of the transcontinental railroad had a huge effect on westward expansion. The railroad made the West more accessible. People from the east coast and from Europe flocked to the open land of the American West. This Web site, which was created by the Bureau of Land Management's Environmental Education Project, relates this history of the transcontinental railroad.

Steel Rails and Iron Horses is made up of several long historical essays on different topics related to the railroad. The writing gets dull at times; but for the most part, the site does a great job of exploring the history of the railroad from different angles. Each piece contains photographs that help make reading more interesting.

You move straight through the site by selecting "Introduction" from the home page and then clicking on "More" at the bottom of each screen. Or you can just pick the essays that interest you from the index on the home page. Since a chunk of this site is devoted to articles about scientific advances in railroad-related technology, it makes sense to be selective. The only essays that are directly relevant to the history of westward expansion are the "Introduction," "America Embraces the Railroad," and "Transcontinental Railroad," but there is a section that tells you how to build your own steam engine!

TRIANGLE FACTORY FIRE

Best Search Engine: http://www.google.com/

Key Search Terms: Triangle shirtwaist

                      Triangle factory fire

The Triangle Factory Fire
http://www.ilr/cornell.edu/trianglefire
high school and up

Here's a first-rate site on one of the most tragic incidents in American labor history—the deaths of almost 150 young women in a sweatshop at the beginning of the twentieth century. Maintained by Cornell University, the site recounts the story of the fire and also provides information on contemporary labor conditions so that you can put the incident in a broader historical context. You'll also learn about the investigations and reforms that the fire generated.

One of the real pluses of this site is the resource section, which contains first-hand descriptions of labor conditions, newspaper accounts of the fire, and excerpts from the transcripts of the government investigation that followed the incident. You'll also be able to listen to oral histories and view photos and illustrations. The site also contains a list of victims, a bibliography, links to related sites, and—a real plus—tips for writing a high school paper on the fire. This is a really great site. You'll want to spend a lot of time here.

TRUMAN DOCTRINE

Best Search Engine: http://www.google.com/

Key Search Terms: Truman Doctrine + history

                      Harry Truman + foreign policy + history

Truman + containment

Dean Acheson + Truman Policy

Project Whistlestop: A Student Guide to Our Web Resources
http://www.whistlestop.org/coordinate_alias/lessonstuff/student_guide.htm
middle school and up

This Web site is a great place to start your research into the Truman Doctrine and President Harry Truman. A partner site to the more complicated *Harry S. Truman Library and Museum* and the *Truman Digital Archive*, *Project Whistlestop* has collected the best information from these two broader sites and arranged it in an index according to topic. Just click on the documents you want to view, and *Project Whistlestop* fetches them for you.

To begin your research on the Truman Doctrine, go to the "Truman's Major Decisions (Document Collection)" link under the "Truman's Decisions" heading and click on it. You'll be taken to a screen that has links to all of Truman's important policy decisions, such as the Marshall Plan, desegregating the army, and recognizing the state of Israel. Once you click on "Truman Doctrine," you'll be taken to the "Truman Doctrine Study File" page, which consists of nine digital folders stuffed with primary documents about the Truman Doctrine.

"The Truman Doctrine Study File" mimics the organization of the paper version of the collection. Unfortunately, the paper collection isn't really organized at all. To find material, you have to browse through all of the folders. Simply click on the folder number that interests you to find an index of the items in it (with direct links to each document). It's worth the work, though, because of the wealth of material you can find. Do you want to read the Truman Doctrine itself, the address Truman gave recommending assistance to Greece and Turkey, or the congressional act that authorized the assistance? They're all in folder five. Other folders contain memos from the CIA to Truman about Turkey, State Department notices, telegrams about Greece's needs, letters between Truman and Eleanor Roosevelt concerning the post-World War II relief effort, and much, much more.

And you're not done yet. To get some background information on the Truman Doctrine, check out the lesson plan on the "Truman Doctrine Study File" page. Scroll down the screen below the folders and select "The Truman Doctrine (Truman Library Lesson)." Ignore the sample class activities that are described in this online presentation, but do read the sections listed in the menu at the top of the screen. The "Introduction" gives background information about the Truman Doctrine.

There are two sections on the conditions in Greece and Turkey that will explain the urgency behind the implementation of the Truman Doctrine. There's even a map analysis and a vocabulary section that defines some of the terms you come across in the text of the Truman Doctrine.

UNDERGROUND RAILROAD

Best Search Engine:　　http://www.google.com/
Key Search Terms:　　Underground Railroad + history
　　　　　　　　　　　　Fugitive slaves + history
　　　　　　　　　　　　Slavery + history + U.S.

The Underground Railroad
http://www.nationalgeographic.com/features/99/railroad/index.html
middle school and up

This highly interactive site lets you walk a mile—or several hundred—in the shoes of an escaped slave following the Underground Railroad to freedom in Canada. Created by *National Geographic Online*, it combines text with images and background audio to make an online experience that feels real. But a word of caution. This is really not a reference site. On this Web site, *you* are a slave. *You* have to decide whether or not you want to try to escape, whether or not you want to stop at a particular safe house on the Underground Railroad, and whether or not you want to make a final push for the Canadian border. And *you* have to deal with the consequences of these decisions. History doesn't seem quite so remote on this site.

The best part of this site is "The Journey," which takes you on a frightening page-by-page trip from your enslavement in Maryland to the free soil of Canada. Along the way, you get directions from Harriet Tubman, learn how to recognize a safe house, stop in different American cities, meet abolitionists Thomas Garrett and William Still, sleep in the woods with the sound of baying dogs in your ears, and figure out how to cross Lake Erie in the winter. You hear yourself singing Gospel songs as you trudge along. All you have to do is follow the prompts on each screen (and make those key decisions about certain situations). At least you don't have to worry about finding "The Journey"—you're automatically taken to it once you enter the site.

The Underground Railroad has some other interesting sections that are both educational and fun. To find these sections, use the pull-down menu that's at the top of every screen. Select "Routes to Freedom" to see a map that details your trek north. The route you take on this site is the same one on which Tubman sent real fugitives. For a chronology of events related to slavery from 1500 to 1900, choose the "Timeline" from the pull-down menu. Both students and teachers will enjoy "For Kids" and "Classroom Ideas," which have some terrific suggestions for additional activities to help you learn about the Underground Railroad. Select "Faces of Freedom" to learn about key people in the abolitionist movement. The biographical information on these folks is so scant that it's hardly useful, but you do get to look at a portrait of each of them. Plus, you can look them up on another site to learn more.

The Underground Railroad
http://www.historychannel.com/exhibits/undergroundrr/index.htm
middle school and up

If what you're after is a straightforward synopsis of the Underground Railroad, then this *History Channel* online exhibit is for you! It doesn't give you the virtual reality of the National Geographic site or that site's level of detail. But it does give you an informative and engaging history of the Underground Railroad, a section of biographies of key abolitionists, and links to Web sites about locations on the Underground Railroad. The text is interspersed with photographs, maps, and quotations. It's also easy to navigate and well-organized.

You can access the site's various sections either from the main menu on the home page or from a menu box at the bottom of each of the main section pages (this is more obvious than it might sound). Click on "The Story" for the history of the Underground Railroad. The essay hits the major events of the period and their connection to the Underground Railroad. Go to "The People" for biographies of Underground Railroad conductors and abolitionists. In addition to one on Tubman, you'll find biographies of William Lloyd Garrison, Frederick Douglass, John Brown, Lucretia Mott, the Grimké sisters, and Harriet Beecher Stowe in this section. These bios are more helpful than the one on the National Geographic site, and they also have useful links to topics related to the people they talk about at the end. Select "The Places" for links to Web sites connected to the Underground Railroad or the abolitionist movement, such as the Johnson House (an Underground Railroad station) and Frederick Douglass's home.

Another great feature of this Web site is that it lets you to access other essays about slavery. Click on "Slavery in America" from the menu at the bottom of any page, and you are taken to an index of related topics, ranging from the abolitionist movement to the "Dred Scott Case" to the "Fugitive Slave Law." Also, don't miss the "Recommended Web Site" section. You'll see the link to it in the same menu as "Slavery in America."

Buxton: Celebrating the Underground Railroad and Early Black Settlement in Canada
http://www.ciaccess.com/~jdnewby/museum.htm
middle school

If you took the virtual journey of an escaped slave on the National Geographic *Underground Railroad* site, chances are you made it to Canada and freedom. This is typically where the happy stories about the Underground Railroad end—in Canada. But what happened to the former American slaves in Canada? What were their lives like? This Web site does what so many others don't! It finishes the story of the Underground Railroad and provides you with a history of a community of escaped slaves in Canada.

The site incorporates a number of different materials to give a full view of life in the settlement of Buxton (also called Elgin). Once you enter the site, you'll find photographs, letters, biographies, and essays about aspects of the place, such as the faith community and farming. The easiest way to navigate the site is to use the menu on the left side of the home page. Only two of the sections in the menu provide material for the online researcher: "Background" and "History." The "Background" essay consists of a written snapshot of Buxton/Elgin. It's a good place to start, but that's about it.

For more detailed information, go to the "History" section. When you select it, a new menu pops up on the left side of the screen. Take time to explore the different entries. Each item in the menu takes you to an essay about an aspect of Buxton/Elgin that is supplemented with historical documents, such as excerpts from letters and photographs. Several of these essays are particularly good. Be sure to check out "Black Kent's History," which includes a detailed time line of events, profiles of Buxton/Elgin residents before the American Civil War, and material about the racism that the former slaves encountered in Canada. "Threshing Time" looks at agriculture in the Buxton/Elgin area. You'll be able to read excerpts from letters written by former slaves to families and friends back home that talk about the joys of their own land. Also be sure to read the "Women of Buxton" section, which contains biographical information about several women who made it to Buxton/Elgin via the Underground Railroad.

VIETNAM WAR

Best Search Engine: http://www.google.com/

Key Search Terms: Vietnam War + history

Lyndon Baines Johnson + Vietnam War

Richard Nixon + Vietnam War

Vietnam War Internet Project
http://www.lbjlib.utexas.edu/shwv/shwvhome.html
middle school and up

There is a mind-boggling amount of information on the Vietnam War available on the Internet. Your research will quickly show that the problem isn't finding lots of facts—it's sorting through them! A good starting place for a general overview is the *Vietnam War Internet Project*.

This hugely comprehensive site covers most any aspect of the war that you might want to find information on. The site tries to tell the truth of the war from the perspective of both those who fought in it and those who resisted it. The page-long introduction merely tells you this, so you can probably just scroll to the bottom of the page to see the site's main offerings.

The resources are plentiful. The top link, the general "Resources" list, covers every aspect of the war, however remotely related. In the list of links, arranged alphabetically by topic, everything from specific army divisions that participated, to their offensives, to the resistance viewpoint and the perspective of the People's Army of Vietnam is covered.

After "Resources," you will see that the main menu also has sections on "Images" from the war, "Articles," "Documents," "Military Unit Home Pages," "Memoirs and Personal Narrative Accounts," as well as suggested further reading.

Since the site has not been updated recently, its one drawback is that some links amidst this huge array no longer work. But it still more than enough material for you research.

The American Experience: Vietnam Online
http://www.pbs.org/wgbh/amex/vietnam/
middle school and up

This is another terrific general resource site. If you don't mind that the color scheme makes reading the information on screen difficult, *The American Experience: Vietnam Online* has a lot of good information on the war, and the site menu on the left of the page makes it very easy to access. If you need a time line of the war, you can follow that link.

Each point on the time line links you to further information on the event it describes.

If keeping track of all the historical figures involved in the Vietnam conflict gets confusing, this site is your best bet for help sorting out Henry Kissinger from John F. Kennedy and everyone else. Head straight for the "Who's Who" link to find a list of names of all the major personalities in the war. These are the important figures not just from the United States, but also from Cambodia and North and South Vietnam. Clicking on any name brings up a photo of that person, along with a quick overview of his role in history.

You can also learn about one of the important issues in the aftermath of the Vietnam conflict: prisoners of war and persons missing in action (POW/MIA). To read this material, click "In the Trenches" from the main menu and then "The MIA Issue" on the next page.

Battlefield: Vietnam
http://www.pbs.org/battlefieldvietnam/
middle school and up

Battlefield: Vietnam takes a comprehensive look at the Vietnam War as a whole. As an added bonus, this site is a real treat to use. It is well-organized and loaded with photographs. There's even a multimedia interactive retrospective for you to enjoy.

For an easy-to-digest chronology of the key events of the Vietnam War, check out the "Battlefield: Timeline" section (one of the six links in the main menu on the home page). This multipage time line hits the highlights (and lowlights) of the Vietnam War with documentary photographs. For a more detailed look at the war, go to "A Brief History" from the home page.

The other four sections focus on military aspects of the Vietnam War. Although they're not directly related to the Gulf of Tonkin incident, they're certainly interesting and help convey the tenor of the times. The multimedia retrospective on the 1968 Battle of Khe Sanh is especially interesting. Don't overlook the "Web Resources" section that provides links to other informative sites. The other PBS site, *Vietnam: A Television History*, is particularly good.

Vietnam on About.com
http://americanhistory.about.com/homework/americanhistory/msub48.htm
high school and up

This is another good place to find lots of links on a variety of war-related topics. The *About.com* site, with its simple and effective organization, is great for locating resources and information on particular events that happened during the war. For instance, if you're looking for information specifically about the My Lai massacre, one of the worst American war atrocities, the top link on the page takes you to a thorough and objective article on that topic. The subject matter is difficult, but the article is recommended if you are investigating this U.S. campaign that exterminated between 175 and 504 civilian Vietnamese elderly men, children, and women, or looking into the outcome and aftermath of that event.

The History Place—The Vietnam War
http://www.historyplace.com/unitedstates/vietnam/
middle school and up

The beauty of this site is the simplicity of its organization—look here if you need a nearly day-by-day time line of the war's happenings. The home page, with its four chronological sections, divides the war into the following periods: "Seeds of Conflict (1945–1960)," "America Commits (1961–1964)," "The Jungle War (1965–1968)," and "The Bitter End (1969–1975)." Choose a link, and you'll get a page with an even more in-depth chronology of events.

You can also navigate based on specific topics of interest. Across the bottom of the home page are links covering the "Tet Offensive," the "Kent State Massacre," "Dien Bien Phu," the "Pentagon Papers," "Peace," and more. Because they are cross-referenced to the chronologies, you can use these links to jump straight to the dates with entries relevant to these topics. Some entries also provide links to further info on the subjects they cover.

The Rise and Fall of the Anti-Vietnam War Movement in the United States
http://chss.montclair.edu/english/furr/Vietnam/riseandfall.html
high school and up

There are countless sites about the Vietnam War, but few mention a simultaneous conflict that was taking place much closer to home: the war resistance movement. It's surprisingly difficult to find Web sites that really look at this movement that took place in the United States while conflict raged in Vietnam. In case you're looking for such information, this long article on the topic should be comprehensive enough to cover your needs. First the article looks at the origins of the movement and its ties to anti-imperialist and antiracist sentiment. It then investigates the forms of resistance, from campus protests to large demonstrations, and the organizations behind the agitation. The important year 1968 gets close coverage as does the institutional response to the protest events of that year. The article concludes by examining what was gained or, perhaps, lost as a result of the movement.

VIRGINIA AND KENTUCKY RESOLUTIONS

Virginia Report of 1799–1800, Touching on the Alien and Sedition Laws, Together with the Virginia Resolutions of December 21, 1798
http://www.constitution.org/rf/vr.htm
high school and up

See **Alien and Sedition Acts** for description.

WAR OF 1812

Best Search Engine: http://www.google.com/
Key Search Terms: War of 1812 + history

Treaty of Ghent + War of 1812

James Madison + War of 1812

War Hawks + War of 1812

Reliving History: The War of 1812 in North America
http://library.thinkquest.org/22916/index.html
middle school and up

If you're only going to visit one Web site on the War of 1812, this is it! Of course the site is so big and contains so much good material that you'll probably be here for a while. But that's okay because this terrific site is not just informative—it's fun. *Reliving History: The War of 1812 in North America* is so chock full of pictures, music, and cool graphics, you might not notice that you're learning.

This site is even easy to use. From the home page, you're given the choice of clicking on "Introduction" or "Main Menu" as your gateway to the site. You'll probably first want to check out the "Introduction," which briefly places the War of 1812 in the context of North American history. After you've read this, you can go directly to the "Main Menu," which details all of the resources this site offers. The main menu is divided into three general sections—"Explore History," "Expand Your Knowledge," and "Exchange Information"—each with several parts.

Most of what you're going to want is in the "Explore History" section. Each of its five parts—"Causes," "Timeline," "Battles," "People," and "Aftermath"—has tons of great information. Be sure to look at all of them. "Causes," for example, consists of an essay (accompanied by a music clip and a pair of excellent illustrations) that picks up at the end of the Revolutionary War and lays out the events that led up to the War of 1812. The site is so well-designed that you can click directly from one topic to another (even across the broader categories) without having to go back through the main menu.

Be sure to hit "Expand Your Knowledge" as well. This section contains an extensive collection of maps related to the war (just click on "Atlas"), a "Quiz" to see how closely you've been paying attention, and a guided tour of the site (this feature wasn't working when this review was written). But that's not all! The "Exchange Information" section allows you to join a discussion group about the War of 1812 (click on "Forum") and to enter feedback directly onto this site (click "Feedback"). There's also a helpful section with links to other Internet sites on the War of 1812 and its key figures. Just click on "Links" to find them. To top it all off, the site even has an alphabetized index. So if you know what you're looking for and don't want to browse, you can click on "Search" from the main menu. The indexed terms are all in hypertext, so you can just click on the ones that interest you. How much better can it get?

The War of 1812
http://www.gatewayno.com/History/War1812.html
middle school and up

Just looking for the basic facts on the War of 1812? This site is the place. Plus it's incredibly easy to use—all you have to do is scroll down the screen. The well-written and easy-to-understand essay helps you grasp the factors that led to the war, how the war was fought, and how it came to an end. *The War of 1812* isn't much to look at and its coverage of the Treaty of Ghent that ended the war is too skimpy to be really helpful, but the site makes a good starting point for your research.

The War of 1812 Web Site
http://www.militaryheritage.com/1812.htm
high school and up

If you want to know what the War of 1812 was like for the men fighting in it, then this is your site. Keep in mind that *The War of 1812 Web Site* has no background information to help you put the war in context or to explain the political and economic issues involved. You'll need to use a site like *Reliving History: War of 1812* for that. Also, this site is maintained by a Canadian with decidedly British sympathies, so most of what you'll find will look at the war experience from the perspective of the British troops. But most of the material here is truly fascinating. There are also a couple quizzes you can take to test your knowledge of the war, and a list of links to other War of 1812-related Web sites. A word of caution—this site has a tendency to try to sell you things, which can get a bit annoying.

Of the 11 topics you can link to from the home page, the only one that is likely to be relevant to your research is "Articles." As the name suggests, this section contains a slew of articles on various aspects of soldiers' lives during the war. They're divided into useful categories. You can choose from those listed under headings "Army Life," "Battles," "Biographies," "Forts," "General," and "Naval." Some of the articles go into ridiculous levels of detail (would you ever want to know what British Army beds and bedding were like during the war?), but others are great and will really help bring the war alive for you.

Once you've exhausted "Articles," you'll probably want to head for "Links" or "Quiz" or just move on to another site. Although the section called "British Regiments" sounds promising, it only has an absurdly detailed chart listing when and where various British regiments engaged in the war. (Though it will tell you the color scheme of their distinguishing regimental uniforms.)

WAR POWERS RESOLUTION

Best Search Engine:	http://www.google.com/
Key Search Terms:	War Powers Resolution + history
	War Powers Act + history
	Richard Nixon + War Powers Resolution + history
	Bill Clinton + War Powers Resolution + history

War Powers Resolution
http://school.discovery.com/homeworkhelp/worldbook/atozhistory/w/
    591570.html
middle school and up

Part of *Discoveryschool.com's* "A-to-Z History" section, this page contains an easy-to-understand capsule history of the War Powers Resolution (also known as the War Powers Act).

Since this site only contains the essay, navigation is a piece of cake. As you work your way through it, you'll learn what the resolution did, why it was passed, and how it has affected the conduct of foreign policy since its enactment. This site doesn't give you a whole lot of detail, but it makes a great starting point for your research.

The Historical Battle Over Dispatching American Troops
http://www.ripon.edu/Faculty/ShankmanK/130/Leahy.html
middle school and up

This site, which simply contains an article that ran in *USA Today* in July, 1999, provides excellent and comprehensive background information on the War Powers Resolution, and takes a look at the way the Resolution has been invoked and avoided since its enactment. Just scroll down the page to read the lengthy piece. The site is drab—only two little pictures break up the unnecessarily small text—but the essay is written in a straightforward fashion that makes this complicated topic easier to understand.

War Powers Resolution
http://www.yale.edu/lawweb/avalon/warpower.htm
high school and up

If you're going to study the War Powers Resolution, you probably need to read the resolution. That's what this site is for. Part of Yale University's massive Avalon Project, this site has the entire text of the 1973 law—no frills, no muss, no fuss, just a whole lot of legalese. Since there's no contextual information to be found here, you'll probably want to get some background on the resolution from a site like *Discoveryschool.com's* or *The Historical Battle Over Dispatching American Troops* before you tackle this site.

WATERGATE

Best Search Engine:	http://www.google.com/
Key Search Terms:	Richard Nixon + Watergate
	Richard Nixon + impeachment
	Watergate + impeachment
	Woodward + Bernstein + Watergate

The History Place: Presidential Impeachment Proceedings—Nixon
http://www.historyplace.com/unitedstates/impeachments/nixon.htm
middle school and up

The 1972 Watergate break-in ultimately led to President Richard Nixon's resignation from office. Amid all of the debates, hype, and hoopla surrounding Nixon's presidency, finding a brief and understandable explanation of what happened that June night and how exactly it led to the downfall of a president can be difficult. This site can help.

This isn't a complicated site, and it doesn't go into a tremendous amount of detail. But it's a great place to get your feet under you as you start your research. The site consists of an essay that provides a *very* brief introduction to Nixon's political career. Then it takes you through the events surrounding the break-in and how what the White House originally called "a third-rate burglary attempt" snowballed into a scandal bad enough to force Nixon from office. As an added bonus, the site includes the full articles of impeachment drawn up against Nixon (he resigned before Congress could vote on those articles) as well as a couple of audio links where you can hear Nixon's words (including his famous "I am not a crook" remark) in his own voice. And be sure to click on the essay's hypertext—there are some great pictures of some of the key players in the Watergate scandal.

> *Watergate 25*
> http://www.washingtonpost.com/wp-srv/national/longterm/watergate/
> middle school and up

While *The History Place* site will give you a brief overview of the Watergate affair, this site—constructed by the *Washington Post* to commemorate the 25th anniversary of the break-in—goes into almost overwhelming detail. But there's not a better place on the Internet to find *everything* you need on this topic.

The site is divided into six main sections, two of which are likely to be the ones you'll use most: "Watergate Chronology" and "Key Players." Because so many links connect these two sections, probably your best bet is just to start with the chronology and follow the hypertext to the various key players as you read about them. The chronology section also lets you access one of the site's best features—links to top *Washington Post* stories that ran as the scandal was unfolding. (You can also search for these stories directly from a box on the home page.) If you're looking to explore the broader consequences of the Watergate scandal, you might want to check out "The Reforms" section as well, which looks at the adoption of all kinds of governmental ethics rules in the wake of Watergate.

WEST, THE

Best Search Engine: http://www.google.com/

Key Search Terms: American West + history

> *New Perspectives on the West*
> http:/www.pbs.org/weta/thewest/
> high school and up

New Perspectives on the West, a companion to PBS's documentary film, *The West,* is a great place to begin your research on the history of the western United States. Here you can find an interactive biographical dictionary, a chronology of key events, and information on key historic sites. You'll be able to read a biography of explorer Alvar Nuñez Cabeza de Vaca, look at a map of Texas cattle trails, or follow the growth of western railroads. What's really great about this site is that it covers history from prehistoric times through 1917, so you get a lot of information about the Spanish influence in the West. (Unfortunately, it has little on Native Americans.) The time line even includes key dates from other areas of the United States, like the founding of Jamestown, Virginia, that enable you to put the history of the American West into broader historical context.

New Perspectives is very easy to use. Just choose from "People," "Places," or "Events" to find what you need. To learn about a particular state, go to "Places" and then click on the state on the map. You are directed to information on cities, towns, settlements, trails, natural features, and historical conflicts. If you are looking for primary material go to "Resources" and click on "Archives." From there you can retrieve memoirs, journals, diaries, letters, and other documents. The site also includes links to other resources as well as a quiz on the history of the American West.

New Perspectives does have a downside, however. It has no search function, so you have to follow the menus to find what you want. But it is so fascinating that you won't mind the extra effort.

The American West: A Celebration of the Human Spirit
http://americanwest.com/
high school and up

The American West is a great site for researching the Old West, the West during the mid- and late-nineteenth century. It contains an enormous amount of information on Native Americans, cowboys, pioneers, explorers, outlaws, towns, and forts. Need a history of western expansion, a map of the Pony Express route, or a biography of Doc Holliday? It's here. Each of the links leads to a world of information on a topic. Click on "Santa Fe Trail" under "Frontier Trails," for example, and you get a history of the trail, pictures, and a list of resources.

The American West is also a good source of information on Native Americans. Links lead you to biographies of key leaders, short histories of important events, and resources on historical and contemporary topics.

The site is comparatively easy to use, although the organization does not reveal the vast amount of information included in the site. Material is organized under major categories that contain short descriptions. Just scroll to the area you want. There is a new section on nineteenth century biographies and technology that doesn't fit here. Just ignore it. Instead, enjoy a ramble through this wonderful site.

WHISKEY REBELLION

Best Search Engine: http://www.google.com/
Key Search Terms: Whiskey Rebellion

Whiskey Rebellion
http://www.whiskeyrebellion.org/INDEX.HTM
middle school and up

The Whiskey Rebellion in 1794 was an uprising of Pennsylvania farmers against the federally imposed whiskey tax. Among other things, it gave the new U.S. government its first opportunity to assert federal authority over a state government.

From the home page, scroll down until you see the "Schedule of Events" heading. Click on "Summary of the Whiskey Insurrection" beneath the heading to read a long essay about the Whiskey Rebellion. You'll learn about the underlying causes, the key people involved, and the significance of the uprising. There are links to follow for more information on people and related events, such as Shay's Rebellion, General Neville, and George Washington. At the bottom of the screen, you'll see a link to a "Timeline," which gives a quick chronological sketch of the Whiskey Rebellion.

WILLIAMSBURG

Best Search Engine: http://www.google.com/
Key Search Terms: Williamsburg + history
                     Colonial Williamsburg

Historical Almanack
http://www.history.org/almanack.htm
middle school and up

The *Historical Almanack* explores the people, places, and events of colonial Williamsburg, Virginia. Because of the level of detail it provides, *Historical Almanack* can make colonial life come alive. You'll learn what people wore and ate, where they lived, shopped, and prayed, and what political issues mobilized them. You can find out all about the residents of Williamsburg, from the highest to the lowest. You'll also find biographies of famous residents, such as George Washington and Patrick Henry, as well as of those of the forgotten—slaves, children, and women. The best part is that this Web site is so well put together and so full of cool information that learning about a long-ago period seems like fun, not work.

Historical Almanack consists of four main sections that you can access from the home page: "Meet the People"; See the Places"; "Colonial Dateline"; and "Experience Colonial Life." If you want to learn about the lives of colonial Americans, start with "Meet the People" where you can read about African Americans, colonial children, families, and the town's founders. The information about African Americans is especially interesting. In addition to a brief essay on what life was like for the enslaved Africans, you'll find primary source material and biographies of individual African Americans. You can read "Lord Dunmore's Proclamation," a document advocating the emancipation of slaves, as well as advertisements placed by slave owners trying to track down runaway slaves. If you want to browse the biographies of Williamsburg residents, go to "People of Williamsburg" and click on the person you want to read about.

To continue your journey into the lives of colonial Americans, go to "Experience Colonial Life" from the site's home page. This section concentrates on the social history of colonial America. For example, click on "Clothing" from the index that pops up and read descriptions and look at pictures of men's, women's, and children's clothing. You'll even find a glossary of terms, so you'll know why a *brunswick* was an essential part of every woman's wardrobe. You can go "Inside the Milliner's Shop" to learn who made colonial clothes and how they did it. Other topics in the "Experience Colonial Life" section include "Christmas," "Manners," "Religion," "Trades," and many more.

If architecture strikes your fancy, you'll want to explore "See the Places," which describes the historical buildings in Williamsburg. There you'll learn about the folks who used these buildings, as well as the connection of buildings to important events and people. And for those of you who want to put all this fun history into the context of events taking place, go to the "Colonial Dateline" section from the home page. You'll find three excellent time lines that help you with the political history of the period.

WOMEN'S HISTORY

Best Search Engine: http://www.google.com/
Key Search Terms: Women + U.S. history

Women's History in America
http://www.wic.org/misc/history.htm
high school and up

If you need a quick summary of women's history in the United States, this site is a good place to start. It discusses the history of suffrage, the evolving status of women, women at work, women in politics, and the role of women in reform movements. There is also a short section on feminist philosophies. This is not a fancy site. It's just an essay without links, but it will give you the overview you need to start your research.

WOMEN'S SUFFRAGE

Best Search Engine: http://www.google.com/
Key Search Terms: Women's suffrage + U.S.
                     Suffrage movement + U.S.

Votes for Women
http://www.huntington.org/vfw/addinfo.html
middle school and up

This should be the first stop for anyone interested in the history of women's suffrage. It's full of solid information on the people and events important in women winning the right to vote, and it's very easy to use. From the home page you can click on "Eras" for an overview of the status of women from the Civil War to the passage of the Nineteenth Amendment in 1920. You can use the "Chronology" for a more in-depth time line of events. The home page also leads you to information on key women's organizations and publications important in the suffrage movement as well as discussions of women's suffrage in national and state politics.

Finally, from the home page you can use "Important People" to access biographies of 29 leaders of the fight for equal rights. The entries include women such as Mary McLeod Bethune and Emma Willard who fought for the education of women as well as for their right to vote, Sojourner Truth and Lucy Stone who advocated the abolition of slavery and women's rights, and President Woodrow Wilson who pushed the Senate to ratify the Nineteenth Amendment. For some reason, the list of important people includes the Supreme Court case *Minor v. Happersett* in which the Court ruled that a women's right to vote was not protected by the Fourteenth Amendment. The decision prompted the national campaign for the Nineteenth Amendment. The biographies in the site provide only a quick identification of the person, so you will have to look elsewhere for in-depth information on these people's lives. Nevertheless the biographies do introduce you to the key players and enable you to see the range of interests these reformers had.

Votes for Women
http://lcweb2.loc.gov/ammem/naw/nawshome.html
high school and up

This site, part of the Library of Congress's *American Memory Project*, is perfect if you want to know what people were writing about aspects of women's suffrage. The site includes 167 books and pamphlets in the Library's National American Women's Suffrage Association (NAWSA) collection. You can read the text of Elizabeth Cady Stanton's "Bible and Church Degrade Women" or Isabella Hooker's 1888 address on the constitutional rights of women. The site allows you to access the documents through keyword searching or by browsing the subject and author. Unless you are very familiar with the subject, it's easier to find the document you want by subject or author than by keyword.

The site also contains a very detailed time line of the women's suffrage movement, which you can access from the bottom of the home page, and a good bibliography of print resources, also accessible from the home page.

Woman Suffrage and the Nineteenth Amendment
http://www.nara.gov/education/teaching/woman/home.html
high school and up

If you need a quick source for key documents in the suffrage campaign, go to this site developed by the National Archives and Records Administration for the 150th anniversary of the Seneca Falls Convention. Here you'll find nine documents that trace major steps on the road to women's suffrage. Each document contains a short introduction that puts it in historical perspective. A review of the introductions gives you a quick summary of the suffrage crusade. You can also get an overview of suffrage history by reading a script entitled "Failure Is Impossible" that the National Archives produced on the 75th anniversary of the Nineteenth Amendment.

Oral Histories: Suffragists
http://www.lib.berkeley.edu/BANC/ROHO/ohonline.suffragists.html
high school and up

If you want to learn about women's suffrage from the perspective of those who led the fight, go to this site that contains interviews of 11 leaders and participants in the struggle. These include Alice Paul, founder and leader of the National Women's Party that brought suffrage into the political mainstream, and Jeannette Rankin, a Montana suffrage campaigner and the first women elected to Congress. Beware, these histories are very detailed. They cover not only the subject's activities in winning the vote, but also their formative years and subsequent careers. So be prepared to spend some time here.

Women's Rights: 1848 to the Present
http://usinfo.state.gov/usa/womrts/
high school and up

See **Seneca Falls Convention** for full description.

WORK PROJECTS ADMINISTRATION

Best Search Engine: http://www.google.com/
Key Search Terms: Work Projects Administration

By the People, For the People: Posters from the WPA
http://memory.loc.gov/ammem/wpaposters/wpahome.html
middle school and up

The Work Projects Administration (WPA), originally the Work Progress Administration, was the centerpiece of President Roosevelt's New Deal effort to get millions of unemployed Americans back to work. The WPA wasn't just about building dams and houses, though. An integral part of the WPA was the Federal Art Project (FAP). The FAP was created to give work to unemployed artists, but it also had a broader purpose. Roosevelt believed that art was a public good and that the FAP could bring art to everyday men and women—not just to America's elite.

This amazing site from the Library of Congress's *American Memory Project* showcases the posters the FAP made between 1936 and 1943. What's especially helpful about this site is that you'll learn about the WPA as you look at these cool posters made by some of the country's cutting-edge artists and designers. The FAP made these posters to advertise the services offered by other branches of the WPA, such as the Civilian Conservation Corps. As you view the exhibit, you'll get a quick lesson on the different federal agencies involved in the WPA.

This exhibit is huge. You might want to start research here by reading "About the Collection," an essay that gives some background information on the FAP. You'll see the link to this essay from the middle of the home page. Near it, there's a link that takes you to an interview with a FAP artist. If you just want to get a sense of this exhibit, click on "Collection Highlights" from the middle of the home page. For those of you who want to find specific posters or to browse the collection to get an idea of all the different WPA programs, you can search the site by "Keyword," "Subject," or "Creator." Look for these links at the top of the page.

WORLD WAR I

Best Search Engine: http://www.google.com/
Key Search Terms: World War I + history
                                    World War I + U.S. + history
                                    World War I + battles
                                    World War I + documents

Encyclopedia of the First World War
http://www.spartacus.schoolnet.co.uk/FWW.htm
middle school and up

Turn to this excellent Web site for its exhaustive coverage of World War I. The site, which is a gigantic collection of interconnected essays on every imaginable topic related to the war, is *the* place to start your online research! In addition to being packed with useful information, *Encyclopedia of the First World War* is also incredibly easy to use. All the essays are housed in the site's handy index/table of contents and arranged into subject categories. But while you'll find almost every fact you'll need, some of the essays are a bit colorless. The tone and style sometimes feel more like a print encyclopedia than an interactive experience. The site could also use some photographs, maps, and primary documents. But these shortcomings are nothing compared to the site's positive features.

Encyclopedia of the First World War is divided into about 20 subject categories listed in the index on the home page. These topics range from a straightforward chronology of the war and an overview of important battles to more specific collections on "Trench War" and "Women at War." When you select a heading that interests you, you are taken to an even longer index of the individual essays on that topic. The essays are identified by subject, so it's simple to browse the lists. For instance, if you select "Trench War" from the home page, you can scan a long list of topics on life in the trenches including such things as "Boy Soldiers," "Body Lice," "Gas Attacks," "Western Front," and "Tank Attacks."

Other main headings on the site are "Outbreak of the War," "Important Battles," "The Soldiers," "War Literature," "Strategies and Tactics," "War in the Air," "Major Offenses," and "War Statistics." There are at least 20 essays in each of these broad headings. But don't worry about finding the "right" essay, since all material on this site is linked together like a spider web. Just click on the hypertext as you read an essay, and up pops another essay on that topic.

Trenches on the Web
www.worldwar1.com/
middle school and up

This site is another big one that provides a range of material about World War I. Why do you need another comprehensive Web site about the war? Because this site fills in some of the gaps found in *Encyclopedia of the First World War*. Plus, *Trenches* has some great features, like zoomable maps of the Western front and exhibits of primary source material, that make it worth checking out. Its tone is also totally different from that of the *Encyclopedia. Trenches* is more light-hearted and allows more user participation. This is not to say that it doesn't have as impressive a collection of material as the *Encyclopedia*, because it does.

Navigating this site is definitely a little harder than at the *Encyclopedia*. Most of the information is in the "Library." You'll see the "Reference Library" link about halfway down the home page. The "Library" is divided into pretty straightforward sections. The one titled "When" provides an interactive chronology of World War I. Click wherever there is hypertext to learn more. Click on "Who" from the "Library" main page for an index of biographies.

The best part of this site is in the "What" section of the "Library." Here, you'll find the site's special features on a lot of different subjects. These features combine historical documents and interpretive material. There's one on "German Postcards from the Front" and another on the "Tragedy on the Somme." If you just want to get a sense of these features and don't want to bother scrolling through the long index of titles, click on "Selected Titles" from the top of the list. For an interactive "War Atlas," go to the "Where" section of the "Library" and click on the country of your choice. The "Library" also has a massive collection of maps. (Select "Maps" to access it). Those of you with questions or comments can enter an online bulletin board from the home page (not the "Library" page).

Documents of World War I
http://www.mtholyoke.edu/acad/intrel/ww1.htm
high school and up

Stop by this no-frills Web site for a good collection of links that take you to documents related to World War I. You'll find hundreds of mostly primary documents, all loosely organized by year: "Pre-1914"; "1914"; "1915"; "1916"; "1917"; and "1918." Although the "World War I Documents Archive" on the *Wilfred Owen Multimedia* site (discussed below) has more texts available, this site is more manageable and gives you an interesting cross-section of primary sources. It contains all kinds of documents, ranging from the Triple Entente on No Separate Peace (1914), to the Zimmerman Note, Balfour Declaration, Treaty of Versailles, speeches by U.S. Congressmen opposing American entry into the war, and the Covenant of the League of Nations. Unfortunately, there's no clear arrangement pattern for the documents within each year, so you'll have to scroll though the index to find what you're looking for.

Wilfred Owen Multimedia Digital Archive (WOMDA)
http://www.hcu.ox.ac.uk/jtap/
high school and up

This Web site, named after poet Wilfred Owen, is another terrific place to conduct your World War I research, especially if you're looking for primary sources. The site has huge archives of World War I material. You'll find all kinds of cool stuff—war publications and propaganda, interviews with war veterans, video footage of battle sites, hundreds of full-text copies of war documents from around the world, and much more.

If you want to search for a specific document, select "Search the Archives" from the home page. But if you're new to the site or just want to get a sense of its holdings, click instead on "Browse the Archives." You'll then be able to choose which of the site's four archives you want to explore. Use the pull-down menu to view the different materials in the "Owen Archive," which includes Wilfred Owen's poems and letters, interviews with war veterans, and video footage. The second archive, "Owen's War Poems," contains the full-text version of all of Wilfred Owen's war poetry. Be sure to take at least a quick look at what is probably Owen's best-known work: "Dolce et Decorum Est." Don't let the Latin title scare you off—the poem is in English and well worth a read through. You'll find the link to it about two-thirds of the way down the left-hand column on this archive's main page. "Publications of the War" is devoted entirely to World War I publications—particularly propaganda papers and material intended for the soldiers at the front. Lastly, the "World War I Documents Archive" draws on two of the biggest electronic libraries of World War I sources to offer you a mind-boggling assortment of official documents.

WORLD WAR II

Best Search Engine: http://www.google.com/

Key Search Terms: World War II + History

World War II + United States + History

World War II Commemoration
http://gi.grolier.com/wwii/wwii_mainpage.html
middle school and up

World War II was a huge war, which means that there's an overwhelming amount of material on it out there. So where do you start your research? This site, produced by *Grolier Encyclopedia*, is a good bet. It gives you access to a lot of information, but it doesn't inundate you with it all at once. Instead, it breaks things up into digestible segments, allowing you to control the pace of your research.

The friendly looking site is divided up into six main sections: "The Story of World War II"; "Biographies and Articles"; "Air Combat Films"; "Photographs"; "World War II History Test"; and "World War II Links." As these user-friendly headings indicate, this site tries to make things manageable for you. If you're trying to get a sense of what happened during World War II, you probably want to start with "The Story of World War II." Click on that heading from the home page to find a one-paragraph summary of the war and links to 18 different essays about the war. But don't get overwhelmed—the first essay gives you a thumbnail sketch of the events of the war, while the remaining essays allow you to get more detailed information on an array of broad topics related to how the war was fought. "Biographies and Articles" allows you to focus your research more closely with essays on many of the major (and some not-so-major) players of World War II as well as on key battles, the development of the atomic bomb, and war crimes.

"Air Combat Films" and "Photographs" will probably be less directly relevant to your research, but they are worth checking out if you have time. "World War II Links" can help you take you research farther afield when you've exhausted this site (which could take a while), and the "World War II History Test" is a great way to find out how well you've been paying attention.

Documents Related to World War II
http://www.mtholyoke.edu/acad/intrel/ww2.htm
high school and up

Do you need World War II primary source documents? This site has them coming out of its ears. This drab looking Web page has links to pretty much every official document relating to World War II that you could possibly image. Unfortunately, it can be difficult to find any specific one unless you know *exactly* when it was made—the site runs in strict chronological order with no groupings by topic. (It desperately needs a search feature!) But *Documents Related to World War II* does provide a phenomenally comprehensive look at the materials generated during the war. You can find everything ranging from telegrams sent between diplomatic personnel to speeches by the major political leaders of the period to the Japanese surrender documents. There's also a link to a stunningly detailed time line at the top of the page, but that's about all you'll find to help you put this massive collection in context.

World War II
http://school.discovery.com/homeworkhelp/worldbook/atozhistory/w/
    610460.html
middle school and up

This basic site makes a great overview, but don't expect much detailed material. For an easy-to-read overview about the Allies, click on "The Allies Attack in Europe and North Africa" under "World War II: Article Outline" on the home page. You'll find an essay that covers the overall strategy of the Big Three (Franklin Roosevelt, Josef Stalin, and Winston Churchill), a discussion of the Soviet front, the war in North Africa, the air war, the invasion of Italy, and D-Day. The site has some photographs as well as helpful links that allow you to put events in context. Click on "Important Dates in Europe and North Africa: 1943–1945" (which you'll see at the start of "The Allies Attack" section) for a time line of key events.

What Did You Do in the War, Grandma? Women and World War II
http://www.stg.brown.edu/projects/WWII_Women/tocCS.html
high school and up

One frequently overlooked aspect of World War II is the contribution women made to the war effort. If you want to see how American women fought the war at home, this is a great place to start. The site contains an excellent essay on the contribution of American women to the war, a time line of key events, a glossary, and a bibliography.

The central part of this site is interviews with 26 women who tell of their experiences during the war. You can read about a psychiatric nurse in the Philippines, a member of the All-American Girl's Professional Baseball League, and a journalist. But these interviews are not just about careers. They tell you a lot about life in the United States during the war. There is an interview with a woman who had to raise six children by herself while her husband served in the Pacific and one with a Jewish woman whose family escaped the Nazis and who faced prejudice in America. Because these interviews are so wide-ranging, you get a real feeling for the domestic front during the war.

This site has one downside: The links to other Internet sites are dead.

XYZ AFFAIR

Best Search Engine: http://www.google.com/
Key Search Terms: XYZ affair

The American Presidency: John Adams
http://gi.grolier.com/presidents/ea/bios/02pjohn.html
middle school and up

In 1797 French agents suggested that the United States pay bribes to high French officials before discussions on a treaty between the nations could begin. The incident, known as the XYZ affair, nearly brought the two nations to war. You can learn all about the affair in *The American Presidency*, an excellent Web site by *Grolier Encyclopedia*. The site focuses on presidential biographies, but it has an entire section on the affair, President John Adams's part in it, and the mark it left on his presidency. You'll find this section by selecting "EA Contents" from the menu at the top of the page. Scroll down the page to the "Presidential Scandals" heading. Click on that and then on "XYZ Correspondence." Some names and events are linked to pages with more detailed material.

One of this site's strengths is that it presents information clearly and concisely. You'll find the facts you need to make sense of the XYZ affair, but you won't get bogged down with over analysis. It's also handy to be able to jump to a biography of Adams. Links to articles on the Federalists and on Elbridge Gerry, one of the American emissaries to France, help put the affair in a broader perspective.

The XYZ Affair
http://history1700s.about.com/homework/history1700s/library/mresource/
    metexts/politics/blxyzaffair.htm?terms = %22XYZ + Affair%22
high school and up

This page, on the *about.com* site, contains the full text of the speech
that President John Adams delivered to Congress in 1797 after the XYZ
affair became public. To read Adams's speech simply scroll down the
page.

3

———⊲⊳———

Materials and Resources for
U.S. History Teachers

Each of the sites reviewed here reflects the unique needs of U.S. history teachers. Without a doubt some of these sites are ones you will want to bookmark on your computer. We've arranged the sites in this section into two broad categories: "Web Resources" and "Hands-on Opportunities." Keep in mind, however, that sites earmarked for teachers are by no means off-limits to other audiences. Parents who are home-schooling their kids, for instance, can use these sites to develop excellent at-home activities, lessons, and field trips. See also the general sites listed in "The Basics" section in Volume I of this set.

WEB RESOURCES

American Memory: The Learning Page
http://memory.loc.gov/ammem/ndlpedu/

The *American Memory* site, created by the Library of Congress, provides access to over five million historical items, such as unique and rare documents, photographs, films, and audio recordings.

The "Learning Page" section was created to help educators use the American Memory site to teach about the history and culture of the United States. Here, you'll find tips and tricks for using the collections as well as frameworks, activities, and lessons arranged by grade level that provide context for their use. Lesson plans, created by *American Memory* fellows, include such topics as "Brother, Can You Spare a Dime?" that uses *American Memory* resources to explore, in this case, the Great Depression and the New Deal programs it spawned.

"Resources" can help you answer your students' sticky questions on copyright and citing electronic resources (they do ask those questions, don't they?). Go to "Activities" for gamelike exercises that will introduce your students to the collection. In one such activity, students become historical detectives, searching for clues in the death of Billy the Kid.

To delve in further, consider one of the professional development programs offered by the Library of Congress. These include workshops, video conferences, and the *American Memory* Fellows Program, all of which offer teachers the opportunity to interact with one another while learning to integrate *American Memory* resources into their classrooms.

Crossroads: A K–16 American History Curriculum
http://ericir.syr.edu/Virtual/Lessons/crossroads/

Click on the "High School Curriculum" button to find detailed lesson plans, complete with activities and recommended reading, on such topics as "The Ambiguous Democracy, 1800–1848" and "A Nation in Quandary, 1975–."

A joint project of a school district and a local college in Syracuse, New York, this site stands out for its excellence. And though you won't find lots of bells and whistles, the site covers lots of ground with a complete curriculum for the elementary, middle school, high school, and postsecondary history classroom.

Discovery School's Lesson Plans Library: U.S. History/Government
http://school.discovery.com/lessonplans/ushis.html

This site places the many multimedia resources of the Discovery Channel at your fingertips. The lesson plans—for elementary, middle, and high school—provide reading assignments, discussion questions, related activities, vocabulary from the lesson, comments about evaluating the work, and specific guidelines on how the lesson addresses learning standards in the curriculum. Web links related to the topic can also be found. If you'd like to design your own worksheets, puzzles, and quizzes, just go to "Teacher Tools."

Historic Audio Archives
http://www.webcorp.com/sounds/index.htm

Remember the sound of Richard Nixon saying, "I'm not a crook."? Well, maybe not. But you and your students can hear it for yourselves at this site. Audio files of many of America's most famous and infamous personalities can be played in your classroom. You'll also find Joe McCarthy in a scene from a witch hunt, Mayor Daley defending the

Chicago police after the 1968 riots, and even George (Senior) Bush's comments on broccoli.

History Matters
http://historymatters.gmu.edu/

The folks at *History Matters* designed their site specifically for U. S. history teachers at the high school and college levels. You'll find primary documents in text, video, and audio that emphasize the experiences of ordinary Americans, guides for analyzing these primary sources with interactive activities, articles and resources that link the past with current events, an annotated list of hundreds of Internet sites, annotated syllabi, teaching assignments that use Internet resources, a reference desk, examples of student work on the Internet, and comments from distinguished teachers who share their strategies and techniques. If you could access only one site, this just might be it.

History/Social Studies for K–12 Teachers
http://www.execpc.com/~dboals/boals.html

This site received a *Britannica* Internet Guide award, and it's easy to see why. An intriguing menu with buttons to many different social studies topics opens the site. Click on "American History" for a list of standard topics such as "Imperialism," "Vietnam," and "Civil Rights." However, when you click on any one of these topics, you find much more than just a standard resource. For example under "Civil Rights," 67 links, each one annotated, take you to such sites as "The Malcolm X Home Page" and a page devoted to historic sites connected to civil rights that can help you plan your next class field trip.

Popular Songs in American History
http://www.contemplator.com/america/index.html

No lesson plans or clever activities here, just a stellar collection of music files, lyrics, and historical information on songs that supports the history curriculum. Arranged chronologically, beginning with the seventeenth century, and including songs that are associated specifically with certain wars, this site will get your students singing the stories of America's past.

Smithsonian National Museum of American History: Virtual Exhibitions
http://americanhistory.si.edu/ve/

The Smithsonian is a gargantuan museum, and this little web site is much easier to navigate than the actual concrete structures in Washington, D.C. Click on "Timeline" to explore our American heritage using pieces from the Museum's collection or go to "Virtual Exhibitions" for some intriguing ways to study American history. Exhibit titles include "Paint by Number: Accounting for Taste in the 1950s" and "Between a Rock and a Hard Place: A History of American Sweatshops, 1820–Present." These exhibits will help you and your students view specific periods in history through a cultural lens.

Social Studies School Service
http://www.socialstudies.com/

This commercial site will entice you to research (and purchase) new teaching materials and texts and to explore professional development programs; but its list of activities, broken down by discipline, is the best reason to visit. Go to the "Online Activities" page and click on "U.S. History." Here are 260 links to concise, curriculum-specific activities to teach your students about everything from immigration to the Scientific Revolution. A sampling of activity titles includes "The Pilgrim Life Adventure," The Trial of Susan B. Anthony," and "The U.S. Recognition of the State of Israel."

Each activity includes an introduction, description of the activity, list of resources to use, directions, an explanation of how to evaluate student work, and the complete lesson plan from which the activity is drawn. Thorough and varied, this site is easy to use and fully searchable.

United States History
http://www.usahistory.com

Need a quick reference on the dates of a war, the statistics from a presidential election, or a copy of the Constitution? This is a handy, easy-to-use reference tool with some fun history trivia to enliven your classroom, too.

HANDS-ON OPPORTUNITIES

NEH Projects
http://www.neh.fed.us/projects/si-school.html

Summer institutes abound for history teachers, but the ones offered by the National Endowment for the Humanities are among the best. The topics are intriguing, the locales diverse, and the stipends generous. Eligible applicants must teach full time in an American K–12 school, or if they teach abroad, a majority of their students must be American.

Topics for past Seminars and Institutes include "Boundary Lines: Women Rewriting the American South," "Beginnings: Four First Novels of Native America," and "Four Centuries of Struggle: The History of the Southern Civil Rights Movement." Take a look at the complete current list, and start planning now. Applications are due by March 1 each year.

Lewis and Clark Workshops, The University of Montana
http://www.lewisandclarkeducationcenter.com/

This one might be of interest if you're a history teacher with a hankering to hike. The two Institutes offered each summer are " . . . for K–12 teachers who have a broad range of interests and backgrounds in teaching about the "Corps of Discovery" and/or a desire to expand their abilities through innovative technologies, interdisciplinary learning, and field-based experiences of the Lewis and Clark Trail."

Old Northwest Frontier Tours
http://www.onwfrontiertours.com/liability_forms.htm

If going to summer camp sounds like fun to you, check out these Summer Teacher Institutes and History Camps. Situated in Wisconsin, these programs offer, according to the organizers, a "working vacation," where you can enjoy a multidisciplinary, hands-on approach to learning about the world of early people in Wisconsin. Suitable for teachers of grades 4–12 as well as for college professors, school administrators, history buffs, and those interested in Native American history.

Teacher Training in Folk Arts, Folklife, and Oral History
http://www.tapnet.org/sum01b.htm

Interested in oral history? Or maybe in teaching history through local culture? If so, don't miss this one. The National Network for Folk Arts in Education, funded by the National Endowment for the Arts, advocates the full inclusion of folk and traditional arts and culture in the nation's education. Look here for a list of festivals, seminars, and institutes around the country that offer special programs for educators. "Place as Text: Creating Exciting Curriculum from Where You Are" and "Jazz across the Curriculum" are just two of many intriguing options offered previously.

4

⟨⟨⟨⟩⟩⟩

Museums and Summer Programs for U.S. History Students

In this chapter, we've scouted out the best Web sites for museums, organizations, and summer programs for U.S. history students. This part of the book is designed to help you learn about U.S. history in a more hands-on manner. We'll describe Web sites where you can take a virtual tour of Salem Witch trial sites, interpret the stories from a buffalo hide painting, or write the president of the United State a personal e-mail.

We've also found amazing sites that'll convince you to log off your computer—to attend a Governor's Scholars Program in your state or to volunteer for the summer in Colonial Williamsburg, where Internet connections are few and far between.

See also the general sites listed in "The Basics" section in Volume 1 of this set.

MUSEUMS

Colonial Williamsburg
http://www.history.org/

If you can't get there in person, this Web site is the next best thing. It's especially good for younger students who may be studying colonial history for the first time and for teachers looking for resources that are easily used in the classroom. From the home page, click on "History" for the following choices: "Resources for Teachers and Students"; "Electronic Field Trips"; "The History Explorer"; "The Libraries of Colonial Williamsburg"; "Research"; "The Museums of Colonial Williamsburg"; and "The Williamsburg Institute."

There's so much here that it's hard to decide where to start, but we recommend "The History Explorer." "Meet the People," See the Places," "Colonial Dateline," "Experience Colonial Life," and "Additional Resources" are the five sections from which you can choose. Opt for "People," and you'll be presented with the following: "African Americans"; "Colonial Children"; Families" (and there are several specific families to choose from); "Founders"; and "People of Williamsburg." You can read biographies and descriptions of these varied folks until you're thoroughly acquainted and want to experience colonial life for yourself. Just click on the section of the same name, where you can explore gardening, animals, religion, and Christmas, for example.

You'll probably be drawn to "Electronic Field Trips" back on the home page; but be aware that while these offer more live and multimedia resources, they do take place on a specific date and time and require that you register in advance.

Exploring the West from Monticello: Home
http://www.lib.virginia.edu/exhibits/lewis_clark/home.html

If you're interested in cartography and early navigation or even if you're just a Lewis and Clark buff, you'll love this site. An online companion to a 1995 exhibit held at the University of Virginia and subtitled "A Perspective in Maps from Columbus to Lewis and Clark," this site exhibits artifacts that demonstrate the evolution of cartographic knowledge of North America up through the time that Lewis and Clark set out on their journey. You'll find all kinds of maps, dating back to the early 1500s, navigational tools, and a section on the planning of Lewis and Clark's expedition.

Jamestown Rediscovery
http://www.apva.org/jr.html

Actually the Web site of an archaeological project investigating the remains of 1607 Jamestown, this site offers two online exhibits that are companions to actual physical exhibits at Jamestown as well as an excellent brief history of Virginia's first English settlement. Click on "History of Jamestown" on the home page to read about the English settlers and the life of Jamestown from 1607 up to the present. You'll find hyperlinks within the article to in-depth discussions and images of specific places and people from Jamestown such as Captain John Smith, the Virginia Company, and the 1639 church tower.

If you'd like to take an online tour, head back to the home page and click on "Our Exhibits." The "National Geographic Exhibit" link will take you to "Jamestown Fort: Rediscovered," which includes the following sections: "The Story"; "The People"; and "The Things." In each of these sections, you'll find links to artifacts, maps, and excerpts from primary source material and to biographical information on some of Jamestown's most notable residents.

"The Dale House Exhibit" is of particular interest to archaeologists. It allows you to view some of the most recent finds in the Jamestown Rediscovery Project and to observe the workings of its archaeological laboratory.

Library Exhibits on the Web
http://www.sil.si.edu/SILPublications/Online-Exhibitions/online-exhibitions-frames.htm

Here's a fun place to browse if you haven't narrowed down the topic of your research yet and are looking for inspiration and ideas. The Special Collections Department at the University of Houston maintains this list of links to online exhibits curated by libraries. The majority of the exhibits have a historical theme, and all of them contain digital images and descriptions of text. Recent exhibits included in the list were "1492: An Ongoing Voyage" at Cornell University; "A 1940 Tour of the Oregon Coast" at the Oregon State Archives; and "1981 Hunger Strikes: America Reacts" at New York University. You can be sure that the exhibits listed here are worth the time it takes to visit.

National Museum of American History
http://americanhistory.si.edu/

One of the most popular museums in the country, the National Museum of American History is part of the Smithsonian Institution, the largest museum in the world. The "Virtual Exhibitions" are excellent and explore topics like the disability rights movement, American sweatshops, and the Star Spangled Banner. "Not Just For Kids" has a "Hands-On History Room" where, among other activities, you can send a telegraph or interpret the stories from a buffalo hide painting. Perhaps you'd just like to use the "Timeline" to explore, for example, the Revolutionary War using the Museum's collections. Click on the image of George Washington and find yourself in his tent, searching through his mess chest and examining his swords. If you move on up the time line, you can click on a picture of a Model 37 Oldsmobile to learn a bit about the history of the automobile in America. A picture of Barbara Bush in an evening gown takes you to a brief display on First Ladies and their fashions.

Plimoth Plantation
http://www.plimoth.org/Museum/museum.htm

Plimoth Plantation is the living history museum of seventeenth-century Plymouth, Massachusetts. Step inside the year 1627 and experience how history repeats itself in the "Living History," "First Person," and "Interpretive Artisan" programs. Sections include "The 1627 Pilgrim Village," "Hobbamock's Homesite," "Mayflower II," "Irreconcilable Differences, 1620–1692," "The Carriage House Crafts Center," "Special Events," and "Historical Theme Dining." There are also special pages (see the links at the bottom of the home page) on "Thanksgiving," "Pilgrim Myths and Realities," and "The Wampanoag Indians," to name just a few.

For a really interesting read, click on "Mayflower II" and then choose "Mayflower Passenger List." More than just a list of names, this document details the relationships between passengers (who married whom, etc.) as well as describing when and how they died, which many of them did the first winter.

Many sections are available in Dutch, German, Italian, French, and Spanish as well as English. This is a stellar site for all ages.

Salem Witch Museum
http://www.salemwitchmuseum.com/learn2.html

Maps and photographs of important sites relevant to the Salem Witch Trials of 1692 take you on a virtual tour of this gruesome period in early American life. Eleven locations are listed as links. Click on "Peabody" and find yourself at the John Proctor House, the residence of Mary Warren, a maidservant, and John Proctor who were both hanged during the witch trials hysteria. The brief text provided tells the sad story of John and his wife, Elizabeth, who tried to save their servant, Mary, from hanging only to be accused themselves. John was tried and hanged. Elizabeth escaped only because she was pregnant at the time of the trials.

A concise but thorough history of the witch trials and a FAQs section round out the offerings here. Although quite specialized, this little museum is worth the visit if witchcraft and the Massachusetts Bay Colony interest you.

Schomburg Center for Research in Black Culture
http://www.nypl.org/research/sc/sc.html

This is a national research library with several excellent online exhibits including "Harlem 1900–1940: An African-American Community" and "The African Presence in the Americas, 1492–1992." The Harlem exhibit offers the following sections: "Activism"; "Arts"; "Business"; "Community"; "Sports"; and "Writers and Intellectuals." Each section contains articles on numerous people, events, and organizations such as "Marcus Moziah Garvey" and "The Silent Protest" under "Activism" and "Harlem Hospital" and "The Wedding Party" under "Community."

There's also an excellent digital collection of texts at this site—"African-American Women Writers of the 19th Century," that contains works by Sojourner Truth and Phillis Wheatley as well as by many lesser-known writers. Other offerings include a "Timeline," "Database," and "For Teachers" that offers lesson plan ideas. "Additional Resources" is packed with a well-organized list of other Web sites on Harlem, broken down into specific topics.

Smithsonian National Museum of American History
http://americanhistory.so.edu/

Don't overlook this Web site just because you think museums are boring. This excellent resource, which was created as a companion to the Smithsonian National Museum of American History in Washington, D.C., is full of interesting exhibits, useful information, and quirky factoids . . . all offered without the crowds.

If you are hunting for a good research topic or just want to take a walk back in time, view the site's extensive "Virtual Exhibitions" that you can access from the home page. These comprehensive exhibitions, which include written history, photographs, sound recordings, and interactive features, cover a range of topics. Interested in the history of time itself in the United States? Then select "On Time," a multimedia exploration of the changing ways Americans have measured, used, and conceived of time for the past 300 years. Or maybe you're curious about American labor issues. If so, check out "Between a Rock and a Hard Place" that examines the history of American sweatshops from 1820 to the present.

For those of you looking for information about the presidency, you'll appreciate this site's huge exhibit "The American Presidency: A Glorious Burden." The link for this is on the home page. You can start with a general overview of the election process by reading "On the Campaign Trail." "The Foundations" explains how the Founding Fathers thought about the office and how they shaped it and examines the responsibilities and limitations of the position. "Life and Death in the White House" provides anecdotes of everyday life in the world's most famous residence. The exhibit also contains a section pertinent to those of you interested in the image-making process. In "Communicating the Presidency," you can dive into an essay on the roles of the media and advertising in our perception of a president. Possibly the coolest aspect of this exhibit is its moving time line at the top of the page. Click on the picture of one of the presidents to read a brief biography as well as an essay on the era in which he led. You can also view objects from his term in office.

Although this Web site is not ideal for finding specific information (after all, would you expect your town's museum to keep data on every possible topic you might want to research?), you can search through the archives of past exhibits. Simply click on "Search" from the home page, and then enter key terms. Be sure to place any names in quotations because the search function is Boolean.

National Museum of the American Indian
http://www.nmai.si.edu/

Click on "Education and Programs" at the Smithsonian's National Museum of the American Indian and then go to "Virtual Exhibitions" to tour exhibits such as "Who stole the teepee?" that explores what happened to Native American traditions as missionaries, soldiers, government officials, and others impacted Native culture. Contemporary artwork by Native Americans are intermingled with photographs and artifacts from the museum's collection in this thought-provoking work. Other exhibits include "Woven by the Grandmothers," which presents traditional nineteenth-century Navajo textiles, and "Agayuliyaraput— Our Way of Making Prayer," on the living tradition of Yup'ik masks.

If you want to learn more about Native American art and culture, this is a great place to start. "Information for Teachers" provides guidelines for teaching about Native Americans and teaching materials, including a couple of downloadable guides that accompany some of the online exhibits.

National Civil Rights Museum
http://216.157.9.6/civilrights/main.htm

If you're studying African American history and the Civil Rights movement, you won't want to miss the interactive tour at this museum. Click on "Interactive Tour" on the home page to begin a journey, called "Voices of Struggle," that introduces you to some of the many African Americans who fought for civil rights and gives you an overview of civil rights history. The tour covers slavery, the Civil War, the Emancipation Proclamation, the many Civil Rights Acts passed between 1866 and 1875, the migration of Blacks away from the South, Jim Crow laws, education, Booker T. Washington, philanthropies, the vote, Ida B. Wells, W. E. B. DuBois, race riots, and many other topics. Click on the names at the bottom of the page when you first begin the "Interactive Tour" if you'd like to read brief biographies of key individuals.

In addition to the tour, this site offers plenty of information about the museum and its activities. It also provides directions for visiting the museum, which is located in Memphis, Tennessee.

National Women's History Museum
http://www.nmwh.org/

The online exhibit, "Motherhood, Social Service, and Political Reform" walks you through the history of women's suffrage and shows you more than 50 historical images associated with the suffrage movement.

Click on "Featured Exhibit" on the home page, and you'll enter the exhibit with a page that offers you the option of taking an "in-depth journey through the history of women's suffrage" or a "walking tour through the image gallery." There's also a time line, a quiz, a list of additional resources, and dozens of interesting articles to support lesson plans in this subject.

Choose the in-depth journey, and you won't be disappointed. The historical overviews are well illustrated with photographs of suffragists and other significant images and contain primary source material such as the 1848 Report on the Seneca Falls Women's Rights Convention. The in-depth journey begins with the Seneca Falls convention and covers much terrain including the involvement of women in the Civil War, the various organizations founded to campaign for women's right to vote, the impact of the Progressive Era on the Suffrage movement (don't miss the "Suffrage Songs" link on this page), the creation of a female political culture and imagery, and mainstream use of domestic images and motherhood to name some of the topics.

The White House
http://www.whitehouse.gov/history/

If you've always wanted to enter the White House, here's your chance. At the "History and Tours" page of *The White House* Web site, you'll find an online historical tour that leads you through 11 rooms in the presidential residence. You'll see the famous Blue Room, the State Dining Room, the China Room, and others, all with full-color photographs accompanied by intriguing histories. No tour guide needed.

This site also boasts a trivia quiz, "Presidential Hall," that contains biographies of all the presidents as well as trivia questions, a "First Ladies" section, and a "Facts" page, among other offerings. The site is fully searchable, available in Spanish, and contains a "Contacts" page with e-mail addresses for the president and vice president, just in case you've been meaning to write.

SUMMER PROGRAMS

Education World's Countdown to Summer: Free Summer Programs for Teens
http://www.education-world.com/a_curr/curr074.shtml

Interested in an academically enriching summer program in U.S. history even though you may not have the funds? Here you'll find a list of freebies, including Governor's Honors Programs. Although most states offer such programs, not all of them are free.

Each state's Governor's Honors Program differs a little from the next, but most are month-long, residential programs for academically motivated students who have just completed junior year. Apply online to the free programs listed here, or contact your state's Governor's Honors Program for more information.

Peterson's Summer Opportunities
http://www.petersons.com/summerop/select/a068se.html

Here you'll find 168 sponsors who offer summer history programs. Most are traditional academic programs, so use this list if you're looking to beef up your transcript for college. Prestigious programs at places like Phillips Andover, Harvard University, the University of Chicago, and many other excellent schools are listed alongside a few untraditional offerings such as Cottonwood Gulch Expeditions that integrates the study of regional history into its outdoor adventure programs.

Landmark Volunteers
http://www.volunteers.com

Travel to one of 55 nationally renowned historic landmarks to work for two weeks. Opportunities have included working in Acadia National Park in Maine, with the Boston Symphony in their summer residency at Tanglewood, in Colonial Williamsburg, or on the Cumberland Trail in Tennessee. This nonprofit community service organization for high school students houses and feeds you while you're on the job, but you pay your own way to your volunteer site. Check out the Web site for a complete listing of summer volunteer opportunities and a free brochure. You can even apply online if you decide this one's for you.

Historic Preservation Internship Training Program
http://www2.cr.nps.gov/tps/hpit_p.htm

Are you one of those history buffs who never tires of visiting America's battlefields and historic landmarks? If so, this might just be your dream summer job. Open to undergraduate and graduate students, this program lets you undertake research and administrative projects within the National Park Service during the summer or school year. Its purpose is to help train America's future historians, archeologists, architects, curators, planners, and archivists by fostering an awareness of the cultural resource management activities of the Park Service.

Check the Web site for internships available next summer. Such internships are in museum management, cultural landscaping, architecture, archeology, and many other history-related disciplines with the National Park Service, the Department of the Interior, or the General Services Administration.

Summer Program in Historic Preservation
http://www.usc.edu/dept/architecture/special/specialprogla.
    html#preservation

This University of Southern California program offers two full weeks of classes designed to introduce you to the field of preservation. If you're a college student, you may find that you can get credit for the work done here. However, the classes are open to anyone with an interest in the subject.

In addition to classroom work, you visit such historic sites in Los Angeles as the Gamble and Freeman houses, Rancho Los Alamitos, the Workman and Temple Family Homestead Museum, and the Getty Conservation Institute. These field trips serve as a context for examining a broad range of legal, economic, aesthetic, and technical issues associated with the documentation, conservation, and interpretation of historic structures, landscapes, and communities.

5

—❀—

Careers

Whether you're simply gathering information to help you turn your passion for U.S. history into a livelihood or actively searching for your first job in the field, the Internet can play an integral role in the development of your career.

Your idea of a perfect job that uses your background in U.S. history may involve, for example, teaching in a secondary or postsecondary school, working as a museum curator, or working in government, law, or journalism—the choices are remarkably varied. Regardless of the specific field you're interested in, you'll discover numerous Web sites with tools to help you determine your career aptitudes, match your academic interests with a university program, locate funding for a research project, find online peers, register for professional conferences or student workshops. Of course, you'll encounter dozens of job database sites including those specific to history-related careers.

We've selected what we consider the best career-building history Web sites with the needs of upper-level high school and college students firmly in mind. These sites, which include professional organizations and societies, federal and state agencies, and nonprofit groups, should give you a good jump start on your career.

See also the general sites listed in "The Basics" section in Volume I of this set.

PROFESSIONAL ORGANIZATIONS AND SOCIETIES

American Association of Museums
http://www.aam-us.org/

Scroll down the page and click on "Museum Careers" to read about what museums do and what types of work museum professionals perform. A handy list of common duties and positions lets you test your own interests against those of museum workers. This site also contains specific information on education and training for jobs in the museum world as well as a section called "How to Find Internships and Employment." Nothing fancy about this professional association's site, but it answers some basic questions for you if you're considering pursuing a career in museums.

The American Historical Association
http://www.theaha.org/

The Web site for the largest professional association for historians in the United States provides general information on the Association, conferences, job lists, and the *American Historical Review*.

If you're interested in working in education, *The American Historical Association* Web site should be one of your first stops when exploring career options in history. The site offers a "Job Service" where you can peruse current job offerings in the field, most of them teaching positions. You'll also want to take a look at the primer on teaching history that includes information for both secondary and postsecondary educators.

Go to the bottom of the page to find a databank of information aimed at historians pursuing a teaching career at the university level. Information and statistical reports on Ph.D. production, hiring, salary data, enrollment trends, and part-time employment can help you decide if this is a path you'd like to pursue. If you're already advancing along a career path in postsecondary history education, you may want to browse the AHA's extensive list of dissertations in progress, too.

Why Become a Historian?
http://www.theaha.org/pubs/why/blackeyintro.htm

Ten historians of varying backgrounds share insights on their chosen profession in this collection of essays written by historians for students. The pamphlet provides good food for thought if you're considering a career in history.

The easiest way to access it is to type in the address. The links from the AHA home page are too difficult to follow.

The Association for Living History, Farm, and Agricultural Museums
http://www.alhfam.org/welcome.html

Like to play dress-up and make-believe? If so, living history might just be for you. Living history museums attempt to breathe life into static exhibits by recreating the work and the daily lives of the people who populated particular historic environs.

ALFAM is the professional association serving those who work in living history museums. In addition to the standard offerings of such associations—newsletters, conferences, regional meetings, etc.—you'll find links to more than 80 living history Web sites, including many international ones, and "Living History HELP," a glossary and bibliography that helps you understand more about careers in living history museums. If you already know that you want to work in this field, use the site's extensive job listings to locate employment opportunities in places like Colonial Williamsburg in Virginia, Mystic Seaport in Connecticut, and the Betsy Ross House in Philadelphia.

The Organization of American Historians
http://www.oah.org/

According to their site, this group is the largest society devoted to the study of American history. Founded in 1907 as the Mississippi Valley Historical Association, the OAH promotes the study and teaching of America's past through a wide variety of activities. Again, this site is for those of you interested in an academic career. The organization publishes *The Journal of American History,* one of the most esteemed publications in the field. Membership gets you a subscription to the journal as well as access to an online database of scholarships, fellowships, and grants. It might be worth your while if you're a college student who wants to pursue graduate studies in history. There's also an "Online Jobs" page to peruse if you're a member.

The Society of American Archivists
http://www.archivists.org/

North America's oldest and largest national association for professional archivists might be of interest to you if you enjoy identifying and preserving historical records. Check out this site to learn more about the variety of employment opportunities in the field and the education requirements needed to become an archivist.

FEDERAL AND STATE GOVERNMENT ORGANIZATIONS

Bureau of Land Management: Student Career Experience Program
http://www.nc.blm.gov/jobs/SCEP/SCEP.htm#

In case you think BLM stands for some kind of sandwich, it's time for a proper introduction. The Bureau of Land Management (BLM) is an agency within the Department of the Interior that administers 264 million acres of America's public lands, located primarily in 12 western states. If you happen to live in one of those 12 states—or wish you did—read on. Like many other government agencies, the BLM offers employment programs—two of them—to help students build their careers while still enrolled in school.

The Student Temporary Employment Program (STEP) places students in temporary (up to one year) jobs that are not necessarily related to their academic fields. The Student Career Experience Program (SCEP) hires students—often those with STEP experience—to work in their academic field. SCEP students generally attend college on a regular semester or academic quarter schedule, and work for the BLM during summer vacation and holiday periods. You'll find specific and current info about openings in both programs at BLM's Web site.

The Society for History in the Federal Government
http://www.shfg.org/index.htm

Founded in 1979 as a nonprofit professional organization, the Society promotes the study and broad understanding of the history of the United States government and serves as the voice of the federal historical community. Historians, archivists, archaeologists, curators, librarians, editors, preservationists, and others interested in government history belong to this informal professional group. It publishes a newsletter, an academic journal, and the *Directory of Federal Historical Programs and Activities*. If you're interested in a job with the federal government that would allow you to express your interest in history, these folks just might have a tip or two for you.

State Historic Preservation Officers
http://www.achp.gov/shpo.html

These folks administer the national historic preservation program at the state level, review National Register of Historic Places nominations, maintain data on historic properties that have been identified but not yet nominated, and consult with federal agencies. They are designated by the governor of their respective state or territory.

This page is part of a larger Web site that belongs to the Advisory Council on Historic Preservation. In addition to the information about working in historic preservation, you'll find intriguing articles on current issues in historic preservation around the country as well as a section on training and education.

NONPROFIT ORGANIZATIONS AND SPECIALIZED WEB SITES

High School Journalism
http://www.highschooljournalism.org

Because they often enjoy research and writing, many historians become journalists. At this cool site, you can chat with a pro about the ins and outs of working as a journalist or newspaper editor or bone up on the basics you'll need for pursuing a career. There's a list of awards for high school journalism students, links to hundreds of journalism schools, and a plethora of scholarship info.

Test your journalism skills with the site's quick quiz. Questions like "According to the Associated Press Stylebook, what is the abbreviation for Minnesota?" give you clues to the type of knowledge you'll need to succeed in this field. The quiz changes every day; so if you don't like the results today, study and try again tomorrow.

History as a Career
http://www.ub-careers.buffalo.edu/cdo/chistory.htm

Part of a larger State University of New York Web site on careers, this page has solid information on 12 different career options for historians. Everything from government archivist, which we've covered a bit here, to advertising representative, which we haven't covered, is discussed. This is a good source if you need to brainstorm about possibilities.

History Departments around the World
http://chnm.gmu.edu/history/depts/

Are you applying to college and interested in majoring in U.S. history? This searchable database from George Mason University lets you explore the offerings in U.S. history at more than 1,214 locations around the world. Just follow the links for the college or university of your choice, and you'll be taken directly to its history department.

Index

Page numbers in bold indicate main discussion of a topic.

About the Authors

ELIZABETH H. OAKES is the author of more than 15 books, including *Career Exploration on the Internet* and *International Encyclopedia of Women Scientists*.

MICHAEL S. MAYER is Professor of History at the University of Montana, where he specializes in post-World War II American culture.